Assimilation and Acculturation in Seventeenth-Century Europe

Recent Titles in
Contributions to the Study of World History

Assimilation and Acculturation in Seventeenth-Century Europe

Roussillon and France, 1659–1715

David Stewart

Foreword by John C. Rule

Contributions to the Study of World History, Number 57

Greenwood Press
Westport, Connecticut • London

Library of Congress Cataloging-in-Publication Data

Stewart, David, 1965–
    Assimilation and acculturation in seventeenth-century Europe :
Roussillon and France, 1659–1715 / David Stewart ; foreword by John
C. Rule.
        p.   cm.—(Contributions to the study of world history, ISSN
0885–9159 ; no. 57)
    Includes bibliographical references and index.
    ISBN 0–313–30045–3 (alk. paper)
    1. Roussillon (France : Province)—Politics and government.
2. Allegiance—France—Roussillon (Province)—History—17th century.
3. Legitimacy of governments—France—Roussillon (Province)—
History—17th century.   4. Acculturation—France—Roussillon
(Province)—History—17th century.   5. France—Politics and
government—1643–1715.   I. Title.   II. Series.
JS4845.R68S73   1997
320.944′89—DC20   96–18221

British Library Cataloguing in Publication Data is available.

Library of Congress Catalog Card Number: 96–18221
ISBN: 0–313–30045–3
ISSN: 0885–9159

First published in 1997

Greenwood Press, 88 Post Road West, Westport, CT 06881
An imprint of Greenwood Publishing Group, Inc.

Printed in the United States of America

The paper used in this book complies with the
Permanent Paper Standard issued by the National
Information Standards Organization (Z39.48–1984).

10 9 8 7 6 5 4 3 2 1

For Alison Jelayne and Arianna Jessica

Las Mevas Nenas

Contents

Illustrations

Foreword

It is a cliché but nonetheless true that the Western European State emerged from its feudal chrysalis in the fifteenth and sixteenth centuries. This early-modern State took many political guises. It was sometimes a monarchy, as in Spain, Portugal, France, England, or the Northern Crowns of Denmark and Sweden; sometimes an aristocratic-oligarchic republic, as in Venice, Genoa, or the United Provinces of the Netherlands; sometimes a confederation, as in Switzerland; sometimes an elective monarchical commonwealth, as in Poland; sometimes an elective feudal empire, as the greater Austria of the Hapsburgs; sometimes an elective ecclesiastical principality, as in the Papacy or three of the electorates in Germany; and sometimes city-states, as in the Germanies and northern Italy. The complex and often confusing pattern of sovereignty did not disguise the fact that authority was increasingly being placed in the hands of a prince or principality.

The State, however, was not only a political entity but a socio-cultural religious polity, often shaped by its territorial-geographic limits. Geography played an important, indeed, at times decisive role in the emergence of the early-modern State. England, for example, confined and sheltered in its island kingdom, inevitably clashed, then came to terms with its less powerful insular neighbors, Wales and Scotland. Yet another island, Ireland, found little protection in its insular location. The three crowns of Aragon, Castile, and Portugal, crowded into a peninsula, fought a common enemy, the Moors, and then one another. The Swiss in their mountain fortress and the Danes in their remoteness used geographic location as a defense. A Frenchman, son of a French foreign minister and himself a future minister, described the Norwegian coast where craggy headlands and the rocks below the surface of the water "protect Danish territory better than any fortress would."[1] But other countries were not so blessed. The broad expanses of the great Northern Plain, stretching from the Germanies into Russia, invited invasion and continual conflict.

Similarly, the Low Countries of Belgium and the Dutch Netherlands merged into the no less fertile plains of northern France; armed clashes were so common here that the area became known as the cock pit, the dueling field, the *pré carré* of the West.

Thus as the early-modern State emerged and was transformed into what the eighteenth century would call a Nation, boundaries became important. They were variously called borderlands, boundaries, frontiers, both natural and man-made, marches, neutral zones. The French State, which seemed especially vulnerable to invasion, developed a specialized vocabulary to describe its borders: *limites, cordon défensiv, régions frontières, frontières fortifiées, les côtes de France, portes,* even *frontières naturelles.* One such frontier or borderland was the Catalan province or *Comtat* of Rosselló and the mountainous region of the Cerdanya near Andorra. These areas spanning the Franco-Spanish frontier frame the location of David Stewart's study of the assimilation and acculturation of Roussillon.

In an incisive and insightful study of the Franco-Spanish borderlands, Stewart analyzes the gradual process of "francisation" by which the Catalan *Comtat* of Rosselló and the adjacent mountainous Cerdanya were transformed from a Spanish into a French province.

By the terms of the Peace of the Pyrenees, signed by France and Spain in 1659, Spanish Rosselló and the Cerdanya became the French Roussillon and Cerdagne. As a contemporary commented, "these mountains which had divided the Gauls from the Spains shall henceforth separate the two kingdoms formally."[2] The French crown had claims to Roussillon stretching back to the Gauls and Charlemagne. Indeed, in the mid-fifteenth century, Louis XI had annexed the area, only to have it returned to Spain by his successor.

What was to be the final cession of Roussillon coincided with the beginning of Louis XIV's personal reign in the early 1660s. The young and ambitious king was eager to impress his new father-in-law, Philip IV of Spain, with French administrative efficiency and military might. Through his secretary of state, the Marquis de Louvois, Louis XIV inaugurated a program that became known as francisation, which as defined by Stewart embraced the double goal of political assimilation and social acculturation. The Marquis de Louvois was blunt about the intention of political assimilation: It was to inculcate in the populace "the fear of God, obedience to their prince, submission to the laws, respect for the magistrates, [and] love for their country."[3]

There can hardly be a more concise definition of what historians oft mistakenly call absolutism. Clearly what both Louis XIV and his ministers had in mind was a centralized monarchy under the rule of law, administered by the magistrates and the prince, not a personal despotism.

Stewart treats the theme of political assimilation with clarity and cogency. The French, following the dictum of obedience to the laws, magistrates, and prince, established a sovereign court in the capital of Perpignan and subsidiary courts in the lesser towns. The magistrates were drawn largely from the local judges and notables loyal to France. From Perpignan commissioners, engineers, surveyors, and cartographers ventured into the maze of borderland valleys, not only to define the borders but also to map strategic sites where frontier fortresses could be built. In their wake came the great French military engineer, Vauban, who initiated the building of the fortress-town of Mount-Louis and other strategically placed strongholds. In addition to the system of courts and the corps of inspectors and engineers, the king was represented by a military governor chosen from one of the premier noble families of France, and by a civil intendant representing the magisterial power of the king's councils.

As Stewart asserts, French political assimilation did not go without challenge. The Roussillonnais were tenacious of their inheritance, what Stewart calls their string of rights: dignities, honors, privileges, franchises, exemptions, and liberties, extending back into the Middle Ages, if not before. And though the population was scattered, the Catalan resistance in the early years of the French governance could be fierce, filled with "sporadic and spontaneous acts," such as assassinations, conspiracies, betrayals, and open revolt. Slowly, however—certainly by 1680—opposition subsided and francisation took hold. Success was credited, *inter alia*, to the weakness of the Spanish armies, to the employment and rewarding of Catalans loyal to France, to French investment in the local economy, to a program of public works, the establishment of a mint, and to favorable trade regulations. A barometer of resistance to the French could be read in the number of Roussillonnais in the service of Louis XIV. The figures drawn from archival sources indicate that between 20 percent and 30 percent of the military-aged population of the province was in the service of France in 1690. By the end of Louis XIV's reign, Stewart notes, "one of every 214 residents in Perpignan was serving in the armies of France. This proportion was far higher than in towns such as Nantes, Pau, Marseilles, or Bordeaux, all of which had been assimilated long before Roussillon."

Acculturation was far more difficult to achieve than political assimilation because it rested in large part on the inculcation of values through the education of the social and political elites and their children. The basic curriculum was quite simple: The French language must be taught, along with Christian doctrines of obedience to the laws and the prince, the practical arts of readings, writing, and arithmetic, and the principles of Latin. Beyond these basic requirements there followed changes in the laws, festivals, religious practices, and even clothing. Xenophobia was unleashed by the French innovations. Foreigners, especially the French newcomers, were scorned as *gavatxos*, contemptible foreigners. Many of the deeply religious Roussillonnais feared the invasion of heresy carried on the coattails of French soldiers and merchants. As one Catalan exclaimed, "[Satan] opened the gates of

Hell, dispatching his emissaries Luther, Zwingli, and Calvin."[4] The Catholic clergy, playing on the inherent fears and latent conservatism of the populace, opposed francisation long after the notables, officialdom, and men of commerce had accepted French rule. Church services remained in Catalan, children were seldom baptized with French names, and as late as the nineteenth century a school inspector wrote "that the French language is as foreign to our young students as English, German, or Italian." Stewart is thus justified in concluding that by "1680, French political control of the province was assured. [A]t the same time, French efforts to acculturate the province were largely unsuccessful."

Through his meticulous study of the documents and his tightly focused and balanced narrative, David Stewart has produced a significant contribution to the study of State-making and the mystery of "border people."

John C. Rule
Ohio State University

Preface

In this work, "political assimilation" and "acculturation" are defined as two distinct processes. Political assimilation occurs when some group or community accepts an individual or institution as the legitimate source of political authority. This acceptance may be the result of conscious attempts at assimilation or may simply evolve without encouragement. The key to political assimilation is that acceptance be given by the group or community. If political authority is imposed against the will of the people, assimilation has not occurred. If, however, that imposed authority is eventually accepted as legitimate, then assimilation has occurred. The evidence by which the success of assimilation may be judged includes such criteria as the absence of insurrection, compliance with governmental directives, the payment of taxes, and a variety of similar measures. Thus, in the context of seventeenth century Roussillon, the French desired the Roussillonnais to accept Louis XIV as the legitimate source of political authority in the province. The French initially imposed political authority upon a hostile population but eventually won acceptance for the governance of Louis XIV.

Acculturation is the adoption of a new cultural identity by a group. Acculturation is evidenced by changes in language, religious practices, festivals, clothing, and similar measures among the study group. The word "acculturation" dates only from the late nineteenth century, and it is therefore somewhat anachronistic to apply it to the goals of Louis XIV. But the idea of consciously subsuming other cultures dates to the ancient world, and it was the goal of the French in Roussillon to substitute French culture for Catalan. Therefore, the word "acculturation" does accurately describe the goals of Louis XIV, even if it was never employed by the French.

This study offers a departure from the existing historical literature in explaining French actions in terms of two interconnected goals, rather than in terms of a single goal. Most scholars who have studied Roussillon in the reign of Louis XIV discuss the French attempts to control the province without explicitly defining the nature of that control. Political assimilation and acculturation are referred to collectively as "francisation." The fact that they are referred to collectively should not, however, obscure the fact that two distinct, although complementary, goals existed.

Acknowledgments

I would like to thank many individuals for their help in bringing this project to completion. First, I would like to thank Dr. John Rule. It was he who suggested that I investigate·Roussillon, a suggestion I never regretted. In addition, he has offered me much useful advice, guiding me toward the most useful archives in Paris, suggesting strategies for research, and reading components of this evolving work.

There have, of course, been many other individuals who have contributed in some way to my project. Dr. Richard Rothaus of Oklahoma State University spent several days with me examining the classical history of Iberia and the Roman writings on Gaul. Professor John Guilmartin of Ohio State University and Professor John Lynn of the University of Illinois at Urbana-Champaign were kind enough to listen to some of my ideas and to offer thoughtful advice on those ideas.

I should like to commend the staff of the Archives Departementales des Pyrénées-Orientales in Perpignan, the Arxiu de la Corona d'Aragó in Barcelona, the Arxiu Històric de la Citutat de Girona, and the Service Historique du Armée de Terre at Vincennes, who were all unfailing helpful and pleasant.

Finally, I owe a debt of gratitude to my friends and family, who have provided me with support throughout my efforts. In Barcelona, the Bassols and McKeithen families provided me with asssistance, diversion, and moral support. My deepest thanks are for my wife and children, who endured much and always did so with graciousness. Despite the wealth of help I have received, I retain all responsibility for the errors, misjudgments, and mistakes that remain.

Abbreviations

ACA	Arxiu de la Corona d'Aragó, Barcelona, Spain
ADPO	Archives Départementales des Pyrénées-Orientales, Perpignan, France
AHCG	Arxiu Històric de la Ciutat de Girona, Girona, Spain
AN	Archives Nationales, Paris, France
BN	Bibliothèque Nationale, Paris, France
SHAT	Service Historique du Armée de Terre, Vincennes, France

Introduction

In 1659, at the Peace of the Pyrenees, the centralizing monarchy of Louis XIV acquired the province of Roussillon, which was inhabited by a distinct ethnic group, the Catalans. The French government was immediately and persistently confronted with significant questions that still resonate in the contemporary world. Can a culturally heterogeneous population share a single political allegiance? Can an ethnic minority survive within a vast population that possesses a set of cultural values hostile to that minority? Can adherence to a political or cultural standard be effectively compelled by economic, religious, military, or legal incentives? In short, the questions focus on one central issue: What is the relationship between cultural identity and political identity?

The answer at which the government of Louis XIV arrived for the latter question has been accepted in various forms by many governments since: There can be no shared political allegiance without shared cultural values. Thus a government, if it is to exercise its political authority in an area, must first make the region culturally homogeneous with the ruling nation. Louis XIV undertook to replace the Catalan ethnic identity with the French one, mandating the foods, clothing, legal sytem, language, educational institutions, and religious traditions that should be used in the province. The native Catalans, for their part, rejected the premise that political allegiance is predicated upon a common cultural identity, and resisted the efforts of the French to transform the culture of the province. That resistance ranged from relatively passive non-intercourse and smuggling to more active denunciations and legal battles to conspiracies, assasinations, and open rebellion.

Contemporary Europe is witness to a plethora of similar struggles between national governments and local groups. Central governments, for a variety of reasons, often demand increasing conformity to national standards in education, law, or even social traditions that ensure a uniformity of practice throughout their respective countries. Local interests, by contrast, frequently wish to obtain greater autonomy, usually to protect a distinct cultural heritage. Spain and France today continue to wrestle with the same fundamental issues raised over three centuries ago. The place of cultural minorities and regional autonomy in France is still debated among the Corsicans, Catalans, Bretons, and Algerians, and Spain still struggles with the role of the Basques, Catalans, and Gallegos in its polity. The Welsh, Irish, Scots, Croats, Flemish, Germans, Italians, and others make these questions current throughout contemporary Europe. Just as the Catalans resisted French hegemony with a variety of methods, so today ethnic leaders advocate non-violent resistance, armed insurrection, and a plethora of options between the extremes.

The issues centering on the relationship of the central government and ethnic minorities have been debated and fought over in Iberia for at least five centuries. The Catalans are a people inhabiting eastern Iberia and speaking a Romance language distinct from Spanish or French. By the seventeenth century, they possessed a strong tradition of self-government, a well-developed constitution and legal system, and a fervent devotion to the Catholic Church and the Pope's authority in it. Joined to Castile by a common monarch, titled the Count of Barcelona in Catalonia and King of Castile in Madrid, the Catalans had been permitted a free exercise of their political, religious, and cultural traditions into the middle of the seventeenth century. Gasper de Guzmán, the Count-Duke of Olivares, was the pre-eminent minister of Philip IV of Spain who sought to rationalize and centralize the adminsitration of the monarch's various territories.

In 1640, the Catalans, resisting the centralizing policies of the Count-Duke of Olivares, rebelled against the government in Madrid, launching the War of the Reapers. The leaders of the rebellion invited the French to aid the Catalan cause, and Louis XIII agreed to send an army to fight the Spanish, a traditional enemy of France. In 1641, he assumed the title of Count of Barcelona and became the ruler of Catalonia. He signed the Accords of Péronne as a guarantee that he would respect the traditional rights and privileges of the Catalans. French treaties were followed by French armies, and a general conflict between France and Spain was fought over the course of the next two decades. Very early in this conflict the French occupied the two counties of Rosselló and the Cerdanya in northern Catalonia, which they considered to be the "rampart of Languedoc."[5] When the Peace of the Pyrenees was concluded in 1659, France retained Rosselló and part of the Cerdanya valley as spoils of war, joining the two counties into a single administrative unit—the province of Roussillon. Roussillon, ethnically Catalan and traditionally Iberian, was thus incorporated into the absolute monarchy of France.

Louis XIV and his ministers were faced with the problem of incorporating into their political system an ethnic group that possessed a strong tradition of self-government, an extensive list of liberties and franchises, and a deeply ingrained national identity with distinctive language, customs, and mores. Throughout the reign of Louis XIV, the primary goal of the government in Paris was to foster an acceptance of French rule in the province among the population of Roussillon. Ramon de Trobat, a leading pro-French Catalan, stated that the goal of the government was to "imprint in our [Roussillonnais] hearts a love for the king."[6] When France gained legal control of Roussillon in 1659, many inhabitants of the province were not favorably disposed to the French presence. The Catalans had revolted in 1640 to defend their liberties against Castilian centralization. Now Roussillon was to be merged into an even more restrictive French system. The processes by which the the inhabitants were persuaded to accept French political authority as legitimate were varied, and spanned the period from 1659 to 1680. To encourage political assimilation, Louis XIV and his ministers pursued a second goal in the province, that of acculturating the Roussillonnais. The logic was clear: The residents demanded traditional Catalan rights and privileges because they viewed themselves as Catalans. Create a French cultural identity in the province, and the inhabitants would be willing to accept French rule. These two goals of assimilation and acculturation, collectively defined as francisation, shaped French policy in Roussillon throughout the second half of the seventeenth century. During the reign of Louis XIV, the primary goal of political acceptance was achieved, but the cultural identity of the Roussillonnais was not redefined.

The Catalan *Comtat de Rosselló* was composed of four distinct regions that varied in their resistance to or acceptance of French rule. The eastern plain of Rosselló, which contains the city of Perpignan and the Roussillonnais coast, gave its name to the entire county. This region was the most receptive to the dual goals of creating new political and cultural identities. The very mountainous valley of the river Tech, which includes the city of Ceret and much of the Spanish border, is known as the Vallespir. The Conflent, the equally mountainous basin of the river Tet, runs through central Roussillon. This valley contains the cities of Villefranche, Prades, and Ille-sur-Tet. The fourth region, the Capcir, is also quite mountainous, and marks the western extremity of Roussillon along the upper basin of the Aude. The Cerdanya, the small mountainous region lying between Rosselló and Andorra, was not properly considered part of the *Comtat de Rosselló* in Spanish Catalonia. Under French rule, however, the French Cerdagne was incorporated into the province of Roussillon, thus adding a fifth region to the province. The mountainous regions proved to be greater challenges to the French in forging new identities, with very little acculturation taking place, and political acceptance won only after a long struggle.

To bring Roussillon into obedience and loyalty to the crown, and to generate a new cultural identity, the French employed a wide variety of tactics and policies. These methods included administrative reforms, utilizing the local elites, controlling the local church, educational and cultural policy innovations, economic stimuli, and the use of military power.

Among the many political innovations the French introduced was the office of governor, a position given to Anne, Duke of Noailles and his heirs. Paris consciously chose to award this position to a non-native of the province, a decision that strained local sympathies. An even more dramatic change was the suppression of the provincial estates in 1659 and the suppression of most other local institutions by the Edict of Saint Jean de Luz the following year. The Royal Council of Perpignan, the most prestigious of the suppressed institutions, was replaced by the Sovereign Council of Roussillon. This new body of fifteen men served as a court of last resort for the province. Other administrative innovations included creating an intendant of Roussillon, establishing an admiralty court, beginning instruction in French law, and restructuring local government. One particularly disruptive change was the introduction of the *gabelle*, a tax on salt, in 1661. The Catalans had been exempt from such taxes for centuries, and this new levy created a great deal of hostility and even open rebellion. In most cases, however, the French did not flagrantly violate the traditional rights of the Roussillonnais. The government, both in Paris and in Perpignan, took great pains to work within existing traditions and institutions whenever possible. Thus the Sovereign Council could be seen as simply a new form of the traditional Royal Council, Catalan law was used in the courts of the province throughout the reign of Louis XIV, and the admiralty court was similar to an existing Catalan institution. One of the important reasons the French ultimately met with success in creating a new political identity was their apparent willingness to work within existing structures, even when introducing innovations.

Another way in which Louis XIV and his ministers eased the transition to French rule was to employ the local elites in positions of leadership, and curry favor with them. Many of the important positions in the provincial administration were filled by Catalans. Don Vincenç de Margarit, Josep de Fontanella, Francesc de Sagarra, Don Felip de Copons, Francesc de Marti, Isidore Prat, and Ramon de Trobat were all Catalans who were named to positions of real importance in the province, and both an intendant and a bishop were drawn from their number. Louis XIV also sought to curry local favor and loyalty through the distribution of cash and properties to loyal subjects. The property of those who fled from Roussillon was seized and used to reward dozens of faithful servants of the monarch. In the same manner, ennoblement was granted to a few Roussillonnais. The Comte d'Ille, the Marquis de Montferrer, the Marquis d'Aguilar, and the Seigneur de Planés et du Vilar d'Ovança were all Catalans who received their titles for faithful service to the French crown.

The Catalans in the Roman Catholic Church were among the most strident opponents of the French presence in Roussillon, and the government worked especially diligently to curb their influence and hostility. One important decision made by the government was the prohibition of all forms of contact between the clerics of Spanish Catalonia and Roussillon. To this end, seminaries were established so that religious training could be carried out in France, rather than in Barcelona. The regular clergy of the province were attached to the heads of religious orders in France. Only subjects of the king could become priests in the province, effectively excluding most hostile Catalans from Spain. In addition to trying to sever contact with Catalonia, the French reduced the influence of the papacy in the province, encouraged native Frenchmen to serve in Roussillon, and enjoined the bishop to watch constantly and to supervise closely the parishes in his diocese. These various efforts met with limited success in the reign of Louis XIV, but the clergy remained the group most hostile toward the French into the eighteenth century.

The French directed much of their energies in Roussillon toward their goal of acculturation, in the belief that political acceptance must flow from a common culture. A main thrust of the acculturation program was establishing schools to instruct children in French and thus gradually eliminate Catalan as the dominant language. In 1662 the Jesuits opened a college in Perpignan that taught the French language. The following year the Benedictine Enseignantes de Béziers were charged with instructing the girls of Perpignan in French. In an effort to expand the reach of the language program, the intendant Étienne Carlier in 1672 proposed opening several small schools to teach French to all children. The Marquis de Louvois, Secretary of State for War and the minister responsible for Roussillon, supported Carlier's idea, but the consuls of Perpignan opposed it, and little came of it. In 1682 the Sovereign Council returned to the idea of creating primary schools, mandating their establishment. Although the edict was generally ignored throughout much of the province, Perpignan did create a school. A number of other cultural policies were implemented, with mixed success. All laws discriminating against the French were repealed, French was officially recognized as the only language permissible in legal proceedings, and the king demanded that the Perpignannais forsake Catalan fashion. Cultural policies that complemented the French political goals, such as permitting Frenchmen to do business in the province, were successful and met with relatively few complaints. The attempt to turn Catalans into Frenchmen was, however, utterly unsuccessful throughout Roussillonnais society, from the cultural elite to the peasants of the mountains. The intendant Étienne de Ponte d'Albaret addressed the resistance to acculturation when he wrote "the people of Roussillon call themselves and regard themselves as Catalan and regard as a debasement and injury the name of French or of French-Catalan."[7]

Another method of winning local favor was to implement policies designed to integrate the province into the nation economically. In 1690, the intendant created a fair to be held every Tuesday and Saturday in the villages of Bellegarde, Mont-Louis, and Fort-les-Bains. This was done to generate greater traffic in the goods and foodstuffs necessary to supply the garrisons in those cities. Thus, by stimulating merchant fairs, the intendant sought to entice the residents into helping supply the French national army, thus contributing to national goals. The moving of the mint (*monnaie*) from Narbonne to Perpignan in 1710 drew Roussillon further into the French economic system, since the province became a center of currency production and circulation. The government spent huge sums of money in the province establishing and supporting various enterprises. Foundries, forges, munitions factories, and agricultural endeavors were among the many recipients of French spending. Spending money on local industry both stimulated the economy and tied the recipients more closely to France economically, if not emotionally.

The famous military engineer, Sébastien Le Prestre de Vauban, constructed extensive fortifications at Perpignan, Mont-Louis, Villefranche, Bellegarde, Collioure, and Salces to defend the province from attack by land or sea. These massive works, designed by one of the leading engineers of the time, served several purposes. The construction of these defensive positions caused the Sovereign Council to spend large sums of money in the province. Moreover, Vauban's fortresses were military masterpieces, making significant Spanish penetration of the province impossible. These fortresses are huge and dominate the landscape, and served as visual tokens both of French military power and Spanish impotence in Roussillon. Vauban's creations therefore dispelled hope of foreign intervention for the dissident inhabitants.

Despite the lack of external military support, there were numerous incidents of resistance and rebellion in the first two decades of French rule in Roussillon, and the military was active in suppressing these activities. French military activity ranged from simply garrisoning many towns as a preventive measure to taking the field against rebels. Overwhelming and convincing military superiority, and the willingness to employ it, was a prerequisite for French successes in the province. Once the inhabitants were convinced that the French could not be dislodged, the plethora of other inducements for political and cultural acceptance had, of necessity, to be considered by the Roussillon-nais. It is not coincidental that the widespread acceptance of French rule in Roussillon occurred just after a major rebellion ended, the Spanish were decisively defeated in the field, and a conspiracy against the government was foiled.

There had existed some tensions between the citizens of Perpignan and those of Barcelona throughout much of the seventeenth century, a fact that worked to France's advantage. In 1628, for example, Perpignan had launched a punitive expedition against Barcelona. The following year the city instituted an economic boycott of Barcelona, which then began to raise an army of 10,000 to march on Perpignan. The balance of the seventeenth century was marked by requests from Perpignan that Madrid separate the *Comtats de Rosselló i Cerdanya* from the Principat of Catalonia; such requests were ignored. While this pre-existing enmity was not as intense as some authors have suggested, it might have made the separation of Roussillon from Catalonia a bit easier to accept by the residents of the province.

Many arguments for resistance to the French centered on cultural issues. The various attempts to acculturate the people of Roussillon, the introduction of Protestant soldiers into the devoutly Catholic region, the tensions between the Gallican and Ultramontane traditions in the church, and disruption of the traditional economic patterns of the residents—all contributed to feelings of hostility and encouraged resistance. Political arguments were also used to explain why resistance was offered to the French. It was believed by many Catalans that the French government had not kept faith with the people and was violating the rights of the inhabitants by imposing new taxes, creating political and administrative bodies, and redistributing land and goods within the province. Still other explanations for resistance stemmed from habit and convention. The people of Roussillon had a long tradition of resistance. Tradition argued for an attachment to Iberia, not Gaul. The Roussillonnais had economic, family, political, and cultural ties to Iberia, and a desire to be reunited with Spanish Catalonia motivated some individuals, even in the absence of any particular grievance.

Resistance to the French presence in Roussillon was widespread for the first two decades after annexation. This opposition to the French presence took both active, violent forms and passive, nonviolent forms. The first incident of active resistance after the annexation was the murder of Don Emanuel de Sant-Dionís in December of 1661. Sant-Dionís was a Catalan officer in the French army, and was widely believed to be spying on a group of anti-French conspirators. He was stabbed fifty-two times and his skull was crushed. The official explanation of the incident was that he was killed in a lover's quarrel, and the woman found responsible was executed. The investigation, however, led to the flight of a number of persons from the country, and several others were condemned to imprisonment or the galleys. Strong circumstantial evidence indicates that there probably indeed was a plot, and that Sant-Dionís had learned too much.

The most striking example of the use of violence to resist French rule was the revolt of the Angelets against the *gabelle*. The Angelet revolt began in 1663 and was centered in the valley of the Vallespir. This was a major insurrection that tied down thousands of troops in the province. In the course of this rebellion, which enjoyed widespread support among the Roussillonnais, many French military units were defeated, several important towns were captured by the rebels, and leading pro-French leaders were attacked and killed. It was not until after the Peace of Nijmegen in 1679 that the rebellion ended and its leaders fled to Spain.

In 1674 conspiracies were planned to turn Villefranche-de-Conflent and Perpignan over to an invading Spanish army. In Villefranche, Carles de Llar, Emanuel Descallar, and Carles de Banyuls were at the head of the conspiracy. Having been in correspondence with the Spanish viceroy of Catalonia, they had planned to throw open the city on Holy Thursday. The plot was revealed to a French officer by the daughter of one of the conspirators. Flights and executions soon followed her revelations in Villefranche, and investigations were undertaken in the leading cities of the province to uncover other conspiracies.

A third type of active resistance to the French, in addition to rebellion and conspiracy, was spying for the Spanish. Many persons in Roussillon were sentenced to the galleys or were garroted for passing intelligence to the enemy. Numbered conspicuously among this type of rebel were several priests of leading towns and villages of the province.

There were many other forms of resistance. Soon after annexation, over 2,000 people left the province for Spanish Catalonia rather than live under French domination. The French government also exiled people from the region for subversive activities. In addition, many leading French collaborators, such as Don Josep d'Ardena, Josep de Fontanella, Don Josep de Margarit, Ramon de Trobat, and Francesc de Sagarra, fled to Roussillon to escape Spanish vengeance. This exchange of elites helped the French consolidate their control in the conquered province. Many leading opponents of French policies were no longer in Roussillon to organize resistance to the government and the new leading citizens were favorably disposed toward the French.

The Catalan clergy in Roussillon also generally resisted French attempts to impose their rule and culture, though they rarely advocated open violence. From the moment the French entered the region in 1641, the clergy protested the presence of the soldiers in the parishes. More than the general lawless and dissolute behavior typically associated with soldiers, the clergy were alarmed by the number of Protestant soldiers in the region. Protestantism had never gained a hold in Roussillon, and the Roussillonnais viewed Protestants with great antipathy. Another common form of clerical resistance to the French presence was working against and refusing to recognize French appointees to clerical positions. Such disputes embroiled Jean-Louis de Brueil, Jeroni Lléopart, and Josep de Trobat, who were appointed by the French government and strongly opposed by the clergy. The clergy evidenced further resistance to French rule in their continued employment of the Catalan language for religious services. As late as 1738, the Sovereign Council ordered the church to begin using French in their services.

The lower orders also resisted French attempts to impose their rule on Roussillon. The registers of the Sovereign Council and every leading town in Roussillon recorded complaints that the residents refused to do business with French immigrants, wouldn't allow them full rights in local government, and generally ignored or ill-treated the northerners. The peasants were, like all peasants of the Old Regime, reluctant to pay taxes to the French government, and engaged in smuggling as a regular occupation. These peasants came, in time, to accept the French government, but were never acculturated in the Old Regime.

Even the firmly pro-French political leaders of Roussillon resisted French intrusions at times. The Sovereign Council protested several decisions of the central government, and on several occasions delayed registering edicts for ten years or more. The consuls of Perpignan, Ceret, Collioure, Thuir, and other towns of the province dispatched repeated complaints and requests to Paris in objection to policies or decisions that were considered unacceptable. Other local leaders, including the Sovereign Council, continued to use Catalan law and custom in judicial proceedings, even for cases in which the use of French law had been mandated.

Louis XIV and his government were ultimately successful in achieving his primary goal of political assimilation. By the 1680s, the Roussillonnais had accepted the French as their political masters. Indeed, by the War of the Spanish Succession, the inhabitants fought against the Archduke Charles and his Catalan supporters, and no significant sentiment in favor of that claimant was found in Roussillon. The French were, however, completely unsuccessful in achieving their goal of acculturation. The Roussillonnais continued to conduct their legal, commercial, judicial, and religious business in the Catalan language, continued to dress as Catalans, to give their children Catalan names, and to celebrate traditional feasts. They were quite firmly French in a political sense, and equally firmly Catalan in their culture.

There are a number of factors to which French political success may be ascribed. The role played by the immigrants from Spanish Catalonia was one of the most important factors in achieving a high level of political loyalty in Roussillon. These men were able to implement successfully the designs of the government with a knowledge of Catalan customs and local temperament. Thus they could often ensure that an innovation appeared to be a long-standing custom, especially since they were the leading scholars of the Catalan Constitutions. They also provided living, daily examples of the rewards a Catalan could expect for faithful service. Among these leaders were councillors of the Sovereign Council, noblemen, a bishop, an intendant, and high-ranking military officers. These local elites knew both the goals of the French government and local sentiment well enough to dispense with certain ordinances when they would be counterproductive. This knowledge thus explains the delay in registering certain ordinances and the Sovereign Council's continued use of Catalan in sessions and proclamations. The intimate knowledge these Catalan leaders possessed about the region was invaluable for the success of the French political agenda.

Another factor that contributed to French success in creating a new political identity was the military and political impotence of Spain. Any real hope of liberation for Roussillon would have to come from Spain, and the Spanish monarchy repeatedly demonstrated its inability to defeat the French. Thus most Roussillonnais came to accept the idea that independence or reunion were not viable options, and resigned themselves to French rule. In a similar vein, the continuing struggle of Spanish Catalonia against Madrid for political liberties imparted a vicarious distrust for Spain to the inhabitants of Roussillon, who were in constant contact with their fellow Catalans.

Still another reason the French were able to foster political loyalty in the region was the impressive amount of money spent on fortifications and supplies. Huge sums were disbursed to the local populace to help in the construction of Vauban's fortresses, hundreds of soldiers needed to be fed, and raw materials and transportation were required for war materiel. The expenditure by the French government, especially in a province that had always been very poor, was an incentive to the inhabitants to accept the French presence in order to gain the money it brought.

A final factor that contributed to France's success in creating political loyalty in Roussillon is the fact that most of the young men of the province who opposed France were eliminated. Long term rebellion and sustained dissent are typically activities of young men, and these were weeded out. The murderers of Sant-Dionís, the conspirators of 1674, the Angelet leaders, and most of the spies were under the age of thirty when they became involved in their activities. Whether through flight, imprisonment, or execution, a generation of young leaders hostile to France was eliminated. Without this leadership, hostility to France offered no real impediment to French rule.

A bibliographic survey of the history of French Roussillon uncovers only a short list of works on this province. Most of those are general regional histories that address the reign of Louis XIV as only one small part of the whole opus. Books on Catalan history also tend to present Roussillon as only a small part of the general history. The few works that do address the process of assimilating Roussillon into France differ from this study in two ways. Some look at the period of French occupation during wartime (1640–1660) but don't consider the province after it formally became French. That is, certain authors study the process by which the territory of the province was acquired, rather than the process of acquiring the loyalty of the inhabitants. Other books on Roussillonnais-French relations tend to be episodic. Certain incidents are presented with clear and finite temporal bounds extending for a few months or years, with no relation to longer, ongoing processes or to public opinion and dissent.

This study offers an investigation of the processes by which political identity was created, and the resistance that those processes engendered. And, running concurrently with questions of political identity are complex issues of cultural identity. It is in the separation of these two concepts that this study offers a departure from existing literature. Political and cultural identity were not synonymous in the Roussillon of Louis XIV. By exploring the creation of a new political identity that was coupled to a traditional cultural identity, a new perspective on broader issues of both the political organization and the cultural identity of France might be obtained.

Chapter 1
Prelude to French Roussillon

THE REGION OF ROUSSILLON

Catalonia in 1640 was not an independent state but a region defined by common culture. This region was composed of four administrative units in two countries. Andorra was a Catalan country that retained nominal independence due to the fact that both Spain and France possessed feudal rights of suzerainty in the land. Rosselló and the Cerdanya were two very mountainous counties of northern Catalonia and marked the northeast border of Spain. The remaining portion of Catalonia, the large tract south of the Pyrenees, was called the Principat. Under the Spanish monarchy, Rosselló, the Cerdanya, and the Principat were all governed by the viceroy of Catalonia.

The French acquired all of Rosselló and part of the Cerdanya at the Peace of the Pyrenees in 1659 and joined their acquisitions as the new province of Roussillon. This newly constituted French province was composed of four principal geographic regions, of which three were very similar topographically and demographically. Roussillon is the name of a broad plain lying along the Mediterranean coast. This plain constituted the entire eastern portion of the province and gave its name to both the Catalan county and the French province. Economically, politically, and demographically, the plain of Roussillon dominated the province of Roussillon throughout the Old Regime. Perpignan (population approximately 10,000), the only true city in Roussillon, is in the center of this plain and was the political center of the province and the seat of the diocese that encompassed Roussillon. Other important places in the plain of Roussillon included Collioure, Canet, and Port-Vendres, active ports along the coast, and Salces, a medieval fortress near the border with Languedoc. Most of the commerce of the province came through the ports of the plain, making the eastern quarter of the province the most prosperous region.

A second region of the province was the Vallespir. This region was the east-west valley, which served as the basin of the river Tech and formed most of the southern border of the province. The region was extremely mountainous and poor, and marginal agriculture and smuggling were the primary occupations of the inhabitants. The most important towns were Ceret, which lay at the intersection of the plain of Roussillon and the Vallespir; Arles-sur-Tech, which led opinions and possessed the most influence in the valley; and Prats-de-Mollo, which was at the uppermost end of the valley and was thus a natural refuge from French authority. Also in the Vallespir was the important border fortress of Bellegarde, which controlled access through several important Pyrenean passes.

The third constituent region that formed part of the province of Roussillon was the Conflent, which was topographically very similar to the Vallespir. The Conflent was the basin of the Tet River and formed a long east-west valley that defined much of the northern border of the province. The Conflent was certainly as rugged as the Vallespir and possessed the highest and most sacred mountain in all of Catalonia—Canigou. Like the Vallespir, the Conflent was not well suited to highly productive agriculture, and most inhabitants were subsistence farmers. There were also some highly productive iron smelters and loggers.[8] Two of the most important and influential monasteries of Roussillon, Saint Martin de Canigou and Saint Michel de Cuxa, were near one another in the center of the Conflent. The leading town of the valley was Prades, near the midpoint of the Conflent. Villefranche-de-Conflent and Mont-Louis were both extremely important as defensive fortress-towns, since the Conflent formed a natural corridor between Spain and the plain of Roussillon.

Roussillon was not a populous province. It contained at the most 110,000 persons[9] in the reign of Louis XIV, with 80,00 to 90,000 being a more reasonable estimate. The largest city was Perpignan, which was credited by various late seventeenth-century estimations as having between 9,000 and 13,000 residents. The next most populous towns were Ceret and Ille-sur-Tet, which were perhaps 20 percent the size of Perpignan, with estimates ranging from 1,700 to just over 2,000 residents in the years after annexation. The other important towns of the province, such as Collioure, Villefranche-de-Conflent, Prades, Mont-Louis, and Arles-sur-Tech, were smaller still. The distribution of population, not surprisingly, mirrored the distribution of economic and political power in Roussillon. The plain of Roussillon was the most heavily populated region, and the poorer, more mountainous areas were more thinly settled.

The new French province of Roussillon was, despite its past and present political overlords, completely Catalan linguistically and culturally. Roussillon was considered by the Catalans to have been the birthplace of their language and culture, and the inhabitants of the region were jealous guardians of their heritage. The border created at the Isle of Pheasants did not mirror a division of languages or even of dialects, for the type of Catalan spoken in Perpignan was identical to that used in Puigcerda or Roses, now in Spain. Moreover, the Roussillonnais had long resisted allowing the Castillian or French languages to penetrate their idiom. There had been very little influence on the language from neighboring Foix or Languedoc. Indeed, the Catalan language had begun to make slight inroads in the Fonollet region of Languedoc. Even in matters as mundane as measurement, there was little common ground between the French and Catalans. The ounce, for example, was 33 percent larger in France than in Roussillon. This strong sense of cultural identity by the Roussillonnais meant that the French goals of acculturation would be difficult to achieve. [10]

When the French formally took control of Roussillon in 1659, the province had in place numerous Catalan organs of government. Some were quickly replaced, but others were retained throughout the Old Regime, especially those of municipal organization. One such retention, for example, was the division of Roussillon into three *veguerias*. One *vegueria* encompassed the plain of Roussillon and the Vallespir, the second comprised the Conflent and Capcir, and the third was the Cerdagne. Aside from the translation of *vegueria* to *viguerie*, the French made no alterations to these judicial districts or to the manner in which they functioned. In addition, there were a total of twenty-two municipalities that were governed by a royal, seigneural, or ecclesiastical lord. In each case, the French retained the form of government that those municipalities possessed at the time of annexation, even if the lords were sometimes changed.

Nearly all of the province of Roussillon fell within the diocese of the bishop of Elne. This prelate, despite his title, had sat in Perpignan since the early seventeenth century. There were approximately 150 parishes throughout Roussillon over which the bishop exercised jurisdiction. In addition, two villages depended upon the French archbishop of Narbonne, even before the annexation, ten Capcinais villages upon Alet, and scventeen Cerdanyol villages upon the bishop of Urgel in Spanish Catalonia. The abbey of Saint Michel de Cuxa possessed the rights of ecclesiastical authority over fifteen Conflentan parishes, the abbey of Notre Dame d'Arles controlled seven Vallespinais parishes, and Saint Martin de Canigou exercised jurisdiction over two parishes in the Conflent. In addition to the secular parishes, the province of Roussillon possessed several old and influential monasteries. Saint Genis des Fontaines, supposedly founded by Charlemagne, depended upon Nostra Senyora de Montserrat and was an important Benedictine house. Saint Michel de Cuxa, Saint Martin de Canigou, and Notre Dame d'Arles were all non-reformed Benedictine houses that were not attached to any mother house. The clergy of all these parishes and establishments in Roussillon, both secular and regular, numbered between 800 and 1,000 individuals. [11]

There were three commanderies of the Order of Malta in Roussillon in 1659: Masdeu; Orla, Bonpas, and Collioure; and Bajoles and Cabestan. This crusading order had a few residual feudal privileges in the province. For example, its members enrolled selected citizens in the order as part of municipal grants of nobility. They also received rents on some ovens in Perpignan.[12]

THE CATALAN REVOLT OF 1640

On 31 March 1621, Philip IV became king of Castile, Aragon, the Two Sicilies, Navarre, Valencia, and Portugal, Count of Barcelona and Flanders, and Lord of Biscay. The word Spain referred not to any country, but to this amalgamation of states, which centered on Iberia and shared a single monarch. In each of his realms, Philip possessed certain privileges and was burdened by special limitations, making the centralized administration of the empire difficult and glacially slow. In some areas the nobles could check the actions of the king to a significant degree, in other territories assemblies held most of the power to raise and disburse funds, and in still other lands the king possessed nearly absolute power. Spain in the seventeenth century was faced by a series of related problems, all of which were exacerbated by the plethora of restrictions placed upon Philip IV.

The *Usatges* were a compilation of juridical precedents that defined both the rights of Catalans and the limitations of their rulers. They were, like most medieval law codes, the product of a long evolution and many influences. Among the sources for the precedents and regulations laid down in the *Usatges* were the *Exceptiones legum Romanorum*, the *Interpretationes* of Annià, decisions from the Council of Clermont, fragments from the book of Tübingen, the *Lex Baiuvariorum*, and sections from the Visigothic *Liber iudiciorum*. Among the more important elements of the Constitutions of Catalonia were the complete exemption of all Catalans from salt taxes such as the French *gabelle*, the right of the people to present their grievances in a *Corts* (a representative body), and the control of all financial decisions by the *Corts*.[13]

One of the most severe problems that confronted Spain was the perception that the country was in decline, that the glory of Spain lay in the past. The Spanish monarchs had, in the century before Philip's ascension, commanded a state that was the pre-eminent economic, military, and political power of Europe, if not the world. Spain possessed an empire that encompassed the globe, annual treasure fleets brought enormous wealth to the imperial coffers, and the Spanish army had universal renown as the finest in Europe. Furthermore, Spain's enemies were weak throughout much of the sixteenth century. France was torn by civil wars, England was struggling to find a religious settlement, Italy and Germany were too politically fragmented to resist Spanish power, and even the Turks seemed to be in retreat. Whether this view of the sixteenth century was accurate is irrelevant, since these perceptions drove policy decisions in Madrid. The idea that Spain was once the center of the world, combined with the perception that their former glory was now dissipating, caused the Spanish to devise plans by which the splendor of Spain might be restored.

Philip IV's ascension to his thrones was accompanied by the rise of a *valido*, or favorite, to a position of political pre-eminence within the imperial administration. Gaspar de Guzmán, Count of Olivares (1587–1645), became the dominant force behind Spanish decision-making until his fall from grace in January 1643, a tenure of more than twenty-two years. At the center of Olivares's thinking for his country were two interdependent ideas: empire and reform. He sought to reassert the dominant position of Iberia in world affairs by recapturing the military and economic strength it enjoyed in the reign of Philip II, the golden age of Spain. To achieve this rejuvenation, it was necessary to reform the administration of the empire. These policies of reform, pursued by Olivares, led to the revolt of the Catalans in 1640 and, ultimately, the French acquisition of Roussillon.

Olivares's goal was to create a single, effective administration for all the realms of Philip IV, with all the territories contributing to a single common budget, all participating in a single military force, all sharing a single global empire, and all coming to think of themselves as Spaniards first. Although sometimes naively optimistic, Olivares was realist enough to comprehend that his plans for a complete reorganization of the Spanish monarchies would not be accomplished by a single law and would in fact require decades of evolutionary change to induce the various assemblies and nobles to surrender their rights to a central monarchy.

The first step Olivares proposed in the creation of a truly national government came in 1624, when he issued his plan for the Union of Arms. This was to be a military reserve comprising individuals from all the king's lands. Its mission was to defend the territories from hostile attack. It was to be purely defensive in nature, and each territory would contribute money and soldiers based upon its wealth and population. Portugal, Valencia, Catalonia, and other Iberian territories were not usually under constant threat of attack, but Naples and the Low Countries were, and so this plan was widely understood to be an attempt to force the whole of the peninsula to pay for the king's adventures in Italy and Flanders. Olivares's ultimate goal, centralization, was well known and stridently opposed by most non-Castilians, and especially by the Catalans and Portuguese.

The Catalans were especially suspicious of any plans coming from Madrid due to events that had occurred in the last decade of the reign of Philip III. From 1611 to 1615, the Viceroy of Catalonia was so weak and ineffectual that order had broken down and the province had bordered on anarchy, with bandit gangs controlling most of the countryside. That Madrid would permit such a deplorable condition to develop and to endure persuaded the Catalans that the government had little concern for their well-being. The two subsequent viceroys, the Duke of Alburqurque and the Duke of Alcalá, set about restoring order, but their methods were as alienating as the original breakdown of order. Both of these men willfully ignored and violated the traditional rights and privileges of the region whenever it was necessary or convenient to do so, and Madrid did nothing to correct them. Alcalá was so extreme in his behavior that he alienated even the towns of Catalonia, the traditional bases of support for viceroys of Catalonia. Given this prelude to the Union of Arms, the Catalans were extremely distrustful of Olivares's plans for centralization. The Catalans perceived the Union of Arms as yet another assault on their rights and liberties.

Relations between Madrid and Catalonia remained very poor throughout the 1620s and 1630s. Throughout this period, Spain was at war with France, a conflict that was generally fought in the Low Countries rather than along the Pyrenean border. In 1637, however, the French invaded Catalonia, and the Catalan militias and local governments were very slow to respond to this incursion. A similar event occurred the following year, when the French laid siege to the Basque town of Fuenterrabía. With the single exception of Catalonia, all the provinces of Philip IV's dominion sent troops to help raise the siege. That the Catalans did not seem to be eager to defend themselves or their fellow countrymen from the enemies of Spain seemed to Madrid evidence of hostility toward Philip IV, if not tacit sympathy for the French. At the same time, these incidents provided the Catalans with still more evidence that they were to suffer for the ambitions of Castile and its empire, an empire from which Catalans were barred.

Olivares decided that the best way to compel Catalan participation in the war effort was to embroil the province in the fighting. Thus he decided to launch his offensive of 1639 from Catalonia, and thereby bring the reluctant subjects into full obedience. In the event, the French pre-empted his plans, capturing the important northern Catalan fortress of Salces in July 1639. Olivares immediately began levying Catalans to supplement his army besieging the fortress. He then ordered the Viceroy of Catalonia, the Count of Santa Coloma, to ignore the rights and privileges of the region if they interfered with the well-being of the army. Earlier viceroys had violated the *Usatges* when they deemed it necessary and received no reprimand from Madrid. Olivares himself had acted in much the same manner over the Union of Arms. Now, however, the government was explicitly commanding its representative to violate the Constitutions of Catalonia as a matter of policy, and resistance to Madrid reached a new level among the Catalans.

The resistance to Madrid and its policies of centralization was initially led by the clerics of Catalonia, especially the lower-ranking clergy. Pau Claris, a leading member of the *Diputació* (governing committee) of

Catalonia, was also a canon of the cathedral chapter of Urgel, which was among the most important dioceses in Catalonia. Under the leadership of Claris, the *Diputació*, which was wholly staffed by Catalans, became increasingly opposed to Spanish policies in Catalonia and increasingly reluctant to assist the Spanish cause. Olivares, realizing that Catalonia was becoming a serious problem, decided to billet a 9,000-man army on the Catalans during the winter of 1639-1640 to impress the people with the king's power and presence. As a result, there were repeated and violent confrontations between the Catalans and the soldiers whom they were forced to board, and dissatisfaction with Madrid increased constantly throughout the winter months.

In the spring of 1640, Olivares decided to check the discontent by removing its leaders. He had Francesc de Tamarit, another dominant figure in the *Diputació*, arrested and ordered a thorough investigation into the activities of Claris. These actions only exacerbated the situation, and in April a royal official was attacked and burned to death in the town of Santa Coloma de Farnés. In reprisal, Castilian soldiers sacked the town and razed it. The bishop of Girona then excommunicated the entire group of soldiers. A peasant army gathered and forced the royal army to retreat toward the coast. Emboldened by their successes, the peasants marched to Barcelona, stormed the royal prison, and freed Tamarit. These developments inspired Olivares to change his severe position toward the Catalans, and in May he ordered that conciliation and pacification be undertaken in the region. It was, however, too late to stem the nationalist sentiment that had been unleashed.

An example of the nationalism that fueled Catalan discontent can be seen in a passage from Fra Joan Gaspar Roig i Jalpí. During this period he wrote *Libre dels feyts d'armes de Catalunya*, a history of the region. He emphasized medieval Catalan heroes and rulers to inspire resistance. Jaume I was one monarch so used, and was described in the following manner: "and we have inherited from him excellent decrees which he made in Catalonia for the good government of the Catalans . . . and he spoke almost all the time in our Catalan tongue, for in those days it was the most elegant in the whole of Spain."[14] Roig emphasized good government, one of the grievances of the Catalans against Madrid. He also stressed the Catalan language, underscoring the importance the Catalans placed on their culture.

Each year on Corpus Day, *segadors* (day laborers) from around Catalonia converged on Barcelona in search of work. On that holiday, 7 June 1640, 400 or 500 men dressed as *segadors* entered the city. There were a number of true laborers among them, but many of the immigrants were rebels in disguise. Once inside Barcelona, the rebels incited rioting throughout the city. Several of the king's ministers were attacked, and many of their homes were sacked. The Viceroy of Catalonia, the Count of Santa Coloma, was murdered as he attempted to flee from the crowds down the beach. Based upon the actions of these laborers and rebels, the Catalan revolt of 1640 is sometimes called the *Guerra dels Segadors* (War of the Reapers), especially among nationalist Catalans. Even after this violent display, however, a definitive break had not been made with Philip IV, and indecision marked both Barcelona and Madrid throughout the summer.

Meanwhile, the inhabitants of Perpignan had rioted on 4 June 1640, because it was believed that soldiers were to be billeted on them. When a Spanish army from the Principat arrived at Perpignan on 11 June, the consuls of Perpignan refused to admit the soldiers, for fear that more rioting would occur. The troops remained outside the walls without food or supplies, becoming increasingly desperate. Finally, on 15 June, the Spanish governor began an artillery bombardment of the city, which destroyed 564 houses. Perpignan surrendered the following day. Once inside the city, ten to twelve soldiers were billeted on each house, justifying the initial fears of the residents.[15]

On 1 December 1640, the Portuguese also rebelled against Philip IV. This left Olivares facing war with France in Italy, Flanders, and Iberia, war with the Dutch, and major rebellions on both the east and west coasts of the peninsula. To the leading Catalans in Barcelona, this seemed like a propitious moment to obtain a favorable settlement from Madrid, and overtures were made to the central government. The peasant and laboring classes were, however, no longer disposed toward reconciliation with Castile. On 24 December a major riot occurred in Barcelona, and several of those who favored negotiations were murdered. The lower clergy were still an important force behind the break with Castile, encouraging open violence against the king's forces. Don Juan de Garay, the commander of Philip IV's forces in Roussillon, pointed out this fact in a letter to the king: "In the confessional and the pulpit they [clerics] spend their entire time rousing the people and offering the rebels encouragement and advice, inducing the ignorant to believe that rebellion will win them the kingdom of heaven."[16] Garay's observation is particularly ironic, as the Roussillonnais clergy spent the years from 1640 to 1659 encouraging resistance to Castile in favor of French intervention, and the following decades encouraging resistance to France with Spanish aid.

The pressure of the lower orders, together with an increasingly pro-French leadership, led to the proclamation of an independent Catalan republic under French protection on 16 January 1641. One week later, the republic was dissolved and the rebels declared Louis XIII of France to be the Count of Barcelona and hereditary ruler of the Catalan government. On 18 September 1641, Louis XIII signed the Accords of Péronne, by which he agreed to accept the title of Count of Barcelona, and to respect all the Catalan rights, privileges, and *Usatges*.

There were many Catalans who actively encouraged this French involvement in Catalonia, with different motivations and goals. Foremost among the native Catalan leaders who assisted the French in asserting their control in the region were members of the *Reial Audiència* such as Francesc de Sagarra, Don Felip de Copons i d'Ayguaviva-Tamarit, Josep de Quéralt, and Francesc de Marti i de Viladomar. Other leaders of the pro-French faction included Francesc de Tamarit, Josep Fontanella, Don Josep de Margarit i de Biure, Ramon de Trobat, Francesc de Vilaplana, and Don Josep d'Ardena. Most of these men were, for one reason or another, out of favor with Philip IV when the struggle began, and French domination offered the possibility of preferment. Fontanella's father, for example, had long been refused a coveted seat on the *Reial Audiència*, Margarit had been jailed for skirmishing with his neighbours and was later accused of murder, and Vilaplana had been sentenced to perpetual exile for the murder of a government official in 1620. In addition, many of these young men were, in some degree, idealists and believed that the *Usatges* were worth defending and that French aid might ensure their success. Despite their common goals, however, these leaders were divided into two distinct factions mirroring long-standing Catalan hostilities, and did not all like one another. Although divided among themselves, they had little to lose and much to gain from French domination of Catalonia, and so they worked to ensure that domination.[17]

In 1641, fighting began in earnest between the forces of Castile and those of the Catalans and French, but to little effect. In September 1642, the second most important city in Catalonia, Perpignan, fell to the armies of Louis XIII, marking the end of the Spanish presence in the county of Rosselló. Indecisive fighting continued for several years with no real advantage gained by either side. In 1648 the Spanish concluded the Peace of Münster with the Dutch, which allowed Philip IV to turn more of his attention to the French and Catalans. At the same time, the uprising of the Fronde preoccupied the French. Cardinal Jules Mazarin, having achieved pre-eminence in French political circles, was realigning French foreign policy to emphasize Italy over Catalonia. Thus events conspired to increase Spanish pressure on Catalonia even as the French were withdrawing from their commitments in the region. As a result, the Spanish were slowly able to restore their control over much of Catalonia. On 13 October 1652, Barcelona fell to Spanish troops, and Philip IV issued a general pardon to the rebels. Despite the pardon, most of those Catalans who had been actively pro-French fled to Perpignan, which the French still occupied. Inconclusive fighting made little difference over the next several years, and negotiations for peace were soon opened.

In 1656, Hughes de Lionne traveled to Madrid on behalf of the French king and opened preliminary discussions for a peace settlement with Don Luis de Haro, representative of Philip IV. Among the instructions given the French representative was the command to preserve for France all territories north of the Pyrenees. This directive points to one reason the French were interested in Roussillon: The province defined a natural frontier of France. One of the predominant French policies during the reigns of Louis XIII and Louis XIV was to achieve France's natural frontiers. The Rhine River, the Alps, and the Pyrenees were among those natural features the French considered to define the logical extent of the state. The French could therefore justify their interest in and eventual acquisition of northern Catalonia as part of a process of obtaining defensible borders defined by obvious geographical landmarks.[18]

Another reason the French sought to retain Roussillon was that the monarchs of France possessed some tenuous legal claims to the region. The Counts of Roussillon had offered fealty to Charlemagne, Louis IX had possessed some legal rights of suzerainty in the province, and Louis XI had been given the region as surety for a loan. The publicists of Louis XIV thus claimed that the region rightfully belonged to him by virtue of these rights, ignoring the several repudiations of those rights made by earlier French monarchs. Thus Louis XIV claimed Roussillon not only as a logical frontier of France, but as part of his legitimate patrimony.

As the negotiations for a treaty wore on, Spain agreed to cede Rosselló to France, but, since the term "Rosselló" possessed various definitions in different contexts, the two powers disagreed over exactly what constituted it. The Spanish argued for a narrow geographic description, offering to surrender only the coastal plain of the northernmost region of Catalonia. The French insisted that they receive the entire *Comtat de Rosselló*, which included the mountainous valleys of the Conflent and the Vallespir. The French arguments carried the day for two reasons. First, the French, despite some Spanish successes, clearly possessed superior military power. Second, the arguments developed for Mazarin by Ramon de Trobat, a Barcelonan legal scholar, proved to be more compelling than those of the Spanish. On 13 August 1659, the Peace of the Pyrenees was signed at the Isle of Pheasants. Among other terms, this treaty gave France possession of the *Comtat de Rosselló* and part of the *Comtat de Cerdanya*, which were combined to form the French province of Roussillon. The following year, in March and April, a Franco-Spanish commission met at Ceret to delineate formally the new border between the two monarchies. To commemorate the event, a fountain was erected in that town, and on it was inscribed: "The Lion has been made a Cock."[19]

FRENCH CLAIMS TO SOVEREIGNTY

Having acquired Roussillon through the Peace of the Pyrenees, the French were anxious to legitimate their possession of the territory, since they were aware that many Roussillonnais opposed their control. Throughout the reign of Louis XIV the French repeatedly asserted their legitimacy based upon legal, historical, and practical arguments in order to convince the inhabitants that they were indeed the rightful rulers of the region.

The French argued that their presence in Roussillon should be acceptable to the residents of the province for two legal reasons. First, in a line of reasoning that bordered dangerously on constitutionalism, the French explained that the Catalans had, acting of their own accord, invited the French in not only as allies, but as rulers. Since Louis XIII had accepted the Accords of Péronne, he and his heirs had been accepted as the legitimate rulers of the Catalans by that people. Therefore the French had been given permission to rule Roussillon by the Catalans themselves, since the Catalans had requested French rule. That Louis XIV did not rule the whole of Catalonia did not alter the fundamental fact that the Catalans owed homage to him. This line of argument, although occasionally offered by pro-French Catalans, was rarely emphasized, perhaps because it implicitly justified rebellion, self-determination, and consititutionalism.

The second legal argument used by the French to justify their rule was that Louis XIV had legally acquired Roussillon in the Peace of the Pyrenees. Some Roussillonnais claimed that they had not been party to the invitation extended to Louis XIII, and that the offer was a political machination carried out by a few conspirators against the will of the Catalan people. This point of view had become increasingly common in the Principat in the 1650s as Castilian troops occupied most of Catalonia and one-time rebels sought once again to reconcile themselves with Madrid. A growing party of loyalists and neo-loyalists thus repudiated the French assertion that an invitation had bestowed legal rights of governance upon Louis XIV. By this reasoning, Philip IV had always been the legitimate ruler of Catalonia, including Roussillon, and Louis XIII's claim on the province was void. The French could accept these arguments with equanimity. At the Isle of Pheasants, acting within his legitimate rights as sovereign, Philip IV had effectively ordered his subjects to adhere to France. The Roussillonnais therefore had to obey and embrace the French.

Another type of argument employed by the French to legitimize their claims to sovereignty over Roussillon was historical. The French recalled a selective history of Roussillon to prove that the province should not be Catalan, and that it was historically and legitimately French in origin and character. Often those histories of Roussillon written by or for the French would begin by citing Titus Livy, who claimed that Ruscino, the ancient capital of Rosselló, was founded by people from the tribes of Gaul, not Iberia. The works of Spanish and Catalan writers who disputed the claims of a Gallic foundation of Ruscino were casually dismissed: "Those [histories] which the Catalan authors report from before this epoch are nothing but fables."[20] Under Roman domination, the people who governed Ruscino were Gauls, and the Romans recognized the Col de Pertus, lying between Rosselló and the Principat, as the border between ancient Gaul and Hispania.

In the early medieval period, the role of Charlemagne, king of France, was always heavily emphasized in the French histories. He liberated Rosselló from the Moors. Charlemagne's victory served to demonstrate that the French were the historic defenders of Christianity in the region. The passage of a Carolingian army through a small valley at the western end of the Conflent gave his name to the valley—the Carol valley, a shortened form of *Valles Carolimagni*. Charlemagne was also given credit for founding one of the most ancient and important monasteries in Catalonia, Saint-Genis-des-Fontaines in Rosselló. Further, it was this storied French leader who was alleged to have created the *Comtat de Rosselló*, the *Comtat de Conflans*, and the *Comtat de Cerdanya* as part of his border marches. According to French accounts, the hereditary counts of these three estates always swore allegiance to Charlemagne and his successors. Catalan authors proposed a different reading of many of the details of early medieval Roussillon, but these differences were dismissed: "the history of the Counts of Roussillon made by Catalan authors is full of errors, and no credit should be attached to them."[21]

French writers usually made a point of claiming that even during those periods in which the region was governed by the Counts of Barcelona or the kings of Aragon, Rosselló had always remained under the suzerainty of France. When the last Count of Rosselló died without heirs in 1178, he left his estates to Alfonso, king of Aragon. But the Aragonese kings continued to recognize the suzerainty of the kings of France in Rosselló and the Cerdanya. It was only in 1258 that King Louis IX exchanged his rights in Rosselló with those of King Peter of Aragon in Carcasonne. Seven years before this exchange the king of Aragon had substituted the *Usatges* for French law in Rosselló. Thus, the Constitutions of Catalonia had been illegally introduced without the consent of the rightful monarch, the king of France. Moreover, it was thus claimed that French law was more ancient, and thus more legitimate, than the *Usatges*. The *Usatges* had in fact been introduced to Catalonia during the reign of Ramón Berenguer I the Old (1058–1076). Even then, they were not an innovation, but rather a codification of various laws already in use.

The Aragonese offered Rosselló to the French in 1462 as surety for a payment. Charles VIII returned the land to Aragon once again in 1493, but without receiving the price of engagement. These historical arguments were used to demonstrate that the French were the natural masters of the region. Rosselló had been settled by the French, the Romans had defined it as part of Gaul, and the region had been nominally governed by the French for all but 361 years of recorded history. By attempting to demonstrate the historical validity of their claims to Roussillon, the French sought to gain acceptance from the inhabitants of the province. These historical justifications for French control of Roussillon were written by native Frenchmen rather than Catalans. Even those Roussillonnais who embraced the rule of Louis XIV usually rejected most of these arguments as fraudulent.[22]

The third justification for the French presence in Roussillon was the right of conquest. As the French repeatedly noted, "Louis XIII carried his victorious arms into this province, and reduced it to obedience."[23] The armies of France had conquered the major places of the province, seizing Perpignan itself after a protracted siege. By allowing France to retain what it had seized, the Peace of the Pyrenees confirmed Roussillon's status as a conquered province, a spoil of war. Indeed, in the instructions to their agents negotiating the Peace of Pyrenees, the French government emphasized in equal measure its legal and military claims to Roussillon. *"His Majesty is well aware that he would be universally condemned if he allowed himself to be dispossessed of a place so important, which belongs to him by right, and to renounce the grace which God has given him to recover it by force."*[24] Since the French arms had taken the province, and Spain had neither the will nor the means to dislodge the new rulers, the only practical course of action for the inhabitants was to accept French rule.

FRENCH GOALS IN ROUSSILLON

Throughout the reign of Louis XIV, the French pursued two fundamental goals in their new province of Roussillon, political assimilation and acculturation. The first goal was to compel or persuade the Roussillonnais to accept the French as the legitimate rulers of the province. At the time of annexation there were a number of inhabitants who disliked the French and wished to see them withdraw from Roussillon. These dissidents saw their new masters as a threat to the traditional liberties of the province and believed them to have no legitimate claims for ruling the region. An even greater number of the inhabitants were not particularly hostile but did not embrace the French with enthusiasm. Thus the majority of the province did not conceive of themselves as supporters of Louis XIV, but were instead attached to the traditional Catalan political forms. The new regime sought to change the way in which these neutral or hostile residents viewed themselves, to convert their political self-identity from Catalans into French.

To speed the achievement of this goal, and to maintain it once achieved, Paris decided that a policy of acculturation would be profitable. So long as the Roussillonnais celebrated Catalan holidays, worshipped in Catalan, learned in Catalan, and conducted business in Catalan, they would inevitably continue to focus on their connections to the Principat and continue to view France as a separate country. Therefore, to make the inhabitants participate in the French state, it was decided to make them part of the French nation. A policy was pursued in which education in French was mandated, commerce with Languedoc and the ports of southern France was encouraged, all languages except French were proscribed, and clerics were commanded to use the French tongue. If the Roussillonnais could be made to consider themselves part of the French cultural nation, it was believed that they would accept their role in the political state.

Chapter 2
French Efforts to Achieve Their Goals

Having secured full legal possession of Roussillon in the Peace of the Pyrenees, the French government turned its attentions to incorporating the province into France. To achieve their two goals of political assimilation and acculturation, Paris pursued a wide variety of policies designed to bring the Roussillonnais closer to the French. In the administration of the province, the French replaced Catalan governing bodies with institutions developed in France. The pro-French Catalans, however, generally took great pains to make these new introductions appear to be only cosmetic alterations of the bodies they replaced. Thus the Sovereign Council, the governor, and the *Amirauté de Collioure* were introduced as the continuation of Catalan traditions within a slightly different administrative structure. Not all innovations could be so easily obscured, and some of the French introductions were made without any pretence of reference to traditional Catalan forms. The office of intendant, the most important agent of the French government in the province, was one such creation. The introduction of new forms of taxes was also hard to disguise, and the *capitation* and *gabelle* were both simply imposed upon the Roussillonnais.

In addition to the administrative reforms undertaken by the French, other methods were used with varying effectiveness in the effort to assimilate the province. The French made extensive use of Catalan leaders, both Roussillonnais and refugees from Spain, in controlling and shaping opinions in the region. With the exception of the governors and intendants, most administrators of the French crown in Roussillon during the reign of Louis XIV were native Catalans. The lower clergy was one group that offered great resistance to the French presence, and so great efforts were made to control the church in the province. Appointing loyal Catalans and Frenchmen to leadership positions, deporting troublesome priests, and reorganizing church structures were all employed in Roussillon in an attempt to create a more loyal and submissive institution.

The French employed several policies explicitly designed to foster acculturation. Various attempts were made to create schools to teach children the French language. The Catalan language was gradually excluded from public life in the hope that the public use of French would gradually translate into a personal acceptance of French nationality. The French were encouraged to move to Roussillon and to participate in the religious, economic, and political life of the province; again, it was believed that such immigration would encourage the development of a French cultural and political identity in the region.

The French also fostered ties with their country by encouraging the development of trade and commerce within Roussillon. By spending hundreds of thousands of livres and stimulating the development of local industry, the French created more prosperity in Roussillon than the province had seen in at least thirty years. The French, for example, created arms production centers in Ille and Perpignan for their armies in Spain, established a mint in Perpignan, offered special tax exemptions to certain mercantile activities, and repaired roads and harbors to foster commerce. It was hoped that these economic stimuli, and the knowledge that continued prosperity depended upon the trade and favour of France, would encourage the Roussillonnais to accept French rule in the province as the price of economic success.

Finally, although preferring persuasion, the French could, when necessary, resort to the use of military force to impose their will on the province. This use of force could be relatively benign, as in the construction of Vauban's fortifications throughout the province or the garrisoning of towns. In certain situations, however, the French employed their armies against the Roussillonnais. A rebellion against the salt tax lasted over fifteen years and finally required nearly 10,000 troops to crush, and at least one town was completely razed for a separate act of resistance to France. All of these administrative, personnel, religious, cultural, economic, and military policies were designed to achieve the two French goals in Roussillon of political and cultural assimilation.

To administer successfully their newly acquired province, the French had to find it a place within the existing administrative framework in Paris. It was therefore decided by the king and his ministers that administrative supervision of the province would fall to the Secretary of State for War, Michel Le Tellier and his successors, who reported to the Council of Dispatches. The result of this decision was that the Secretary of State for War had far more influence in the province than any other French minister of state, and both his policies and his clients were given preference in Roussillon. Thus the important leaders of the provincial government throughout the Old Regime were, with few exceptions, were closely allied with the Le Tellier family. For example, Ramon de Trobat, an intendant of Roussillon, named Louis-François Le Tellier, Marquis de Barbezieux, as the executor of his will in 1698. Hierosme Lléopart, although disliked by both pro-French administrators and anti-French clerics, retained his position as head of the church in Roussillon until his death due to his connections to the Le Telliers. Francesc de Sagarra, *president à mortier* of the Sovereign Council, obtained his position through the influence of Le Tellier. The Dukes of Noailles, governors of Roussillon, were related by marriage to the Le Telliers. The most important French administrator who was not a client of the Le Telliers was Josep de Fontanella, another *president à mortier*, who had Jean-Baptiste Colbert as his protector until the former's death in 1680.[25]

POLITICAL AND ADMINISTRATIVE REFORMS

The Sovereign Council

Among the most important of the French actions in the province was the creation of the Sovereign Council of Roussillon. With the Edict of Saint Jean de Luz of 18 June 1660, Louis XIV formed this new administrative body to control the judicial, legal, and administrative activity of the province. The new Sovereign Council replaced several different institutions that had been created in the days of the kings of Aragon—the Consistory of the Deputation, the Tribunal of the Royal Patrimony, and the Royal Council of Perpignan. The Sovereign Council was more powerful than its predecessors because it combined their respective jurisdictions. It was also a court of last resort, while decisions of the older institutions had been subject to appeal to Barcelona. This new body was solemnly installed on 16 July 1660 by the bishop of Orange, Hyacinthe Serroni, since the See of Perpignan was vacant at that time. The Sovereign Council was to be, from its inception, the primary agent of centralization and integration in Roussillon.[26]

As initially created, the Sovereign Council was composed of a First President, two *presidents à mortier* (salaried at 2000 livres apiece per year), six councillors (1000 livres each), an *avocat généraux* (500 livres), a *greffier en chef* (500 livres), a *procureur général*, two *commis*, a *hussier audiencier* (300 livres), two *hussiers à verge*, four *alguazils*, one *chancellerie-garde des sceaux*, and a single *chancellerie-secrétaire et garde-minutes*. To this number were later added several *conseillers d'honneur* and *conseillers honoraires*, and a *commis adjoint*. In addition to the formal composition of the council, the governor of Roussillon was the *de jure* presiding officer of all meetings of the Sovereign Council, with the intendant and lieutenant-general of the province permitted at all sessions. In fact, one of the latter two men usually presided over the Sovereign Council, since the governors were rather infrequently to be found in Perpignan.[27]

According to the Edict of Saint Jean de Luz, there was to be a first president of the Sovereign Council at its creation. In practice, no one was appointed to this position until 18 April 1691, when Ramon de Trobat was finally named first president. Poor relations between the first two *presidents à mortier*, Josep de Fontanella and Francesc de Sagarra, were largely responsible for the delay in the filling of the position. There were strong jealousies and competition between these two men and their respective supporters. These tensions stemmed in part from centuries-old divisions among Catalans in the Principat. The hostility between the two men also in part reflected the tense relationship between their protectors in Paris, Le Tellier for Sagarra and Colbert for Fontanella. One example of the tensions between the two *presidents à mortier* is the series of anonymous attempts made to discredit Sagarra in the eyes of the king, efforts that were dismissed as stemming from envy and jealousy on the part of his fellow councillors. These tensions made it impossible for either of the principals, or anyone else, to be granted the position of first president until 1691, by which time they had both died. In finally filling the position, Louis discreetly noted that "certain considerations" had kept the position vacant until then.[28]

The intendant sat on the Sovereign Council by right from that body's inception, but it wasn't until 1718, after the death of Louis XIV, that he became the first president by right. Indeed, of the seven intendants of Roussillon during the reign of Louis XIV, only two ever served as first president. Ramon de Trobat, who became first president on 18 April 1691, and Étienne de Ponte d'Albaret, who held the position from 4 May 1698 until 1718, were the only men to fulfill both roles. No first presidents were appointed during the administrations of the first three intendants due to the Fontanella-Sagarra rivalries, and d'Albaret held the position until his death, even after he had been removed from the intendency in 1709.[29]

Conseillers d'honneur held salaried positions on the Sovereign Council based on birth or benefice, while *conseillers honoraires* were officials whom the king permitted to sit on the council without pay. The former were considered to be far more prestigious than the latter by the elite members of Perpignannais society. Among the *conseillers d'honneur* were two of the bishops of Perpignan, and several of the leading abbots of Roussillonnais religious establishments, including Saint-Michel de Cuxa, Nôtre-Dame de la Real, and Sainte-Marie d'Arles-sur-Tech. These men were typically well-born and well-connected individuals, men such as Pere Pont, Josep de Trobat, Jean-Baptiste Chiaveri, and Francesc de Montpalau.

The *conseillers honoraires* were generally from positions and families that were less important, both socially and politically, than those of the *conseillers d'honneur*. Despite their lower social standing, the advice of these men was sometimes needed on specific issues. Thus a *juge des gabelles* was a *conseiller honoraire* due to the Angelet revolt against the *gabelle*. A *grand-*

archidiacre d'Elne and a *vicaire général* were both appointed as *conseillers honoraires* to help in the pacification of the clergy. All of these councillors, both *d'honneur* and *honoraires*, were rarely found at meetings of the Sovereign Council and played very little role in the daily functioning of the council except when their special competencies might be required.[30]

In creating the Sovereign Council, the government of Louis XIV wished to ensure that the body remained loyal to the king and his ministers, especially since this institution was the primary mechanism for wedding Roussillon to France. To ensure the requisite loyalty and obedience of the council, several measures were taken to regulate its membership. All members of the Sovereign Council sat at the king's pleasure. No one was permitted an automatic seat by virtue of his position within the province, his birth, or influence. In practice, however, certain officials, such as the bishop, were almost always granted a seat on the council if they requested one. The intendant, lieutenant-general, and governor of the province were the only exceptions to this rule, being the only three persons in Roussillon permitted an automatic seat by virtue of their position within the province. Claims from leading abbots that they were entitled to a seat in the Sovereign Council by right, as they had been allowed one in old Royal Council of Perpignan, were frequently put forward. Such claims were invariably rejected by both the Sovereign Council and the ministers in Paris.

Another mechanism for ensuring the fidelity of the Council was the absolute denial that any councillor personally possessed his position. No one was allowed to purchase or sell a seat on the council, and seats could not be passed on to children as an inheritance. Six of the twenty-eight councillors in the reign of Louis XIV did succeed to their father's seats, but only after an explicit appeal was made to Paris, and a specific dispensation was granted, permission that Paris always carefully noted did not establish a general precedent.

Louis was quite successful in creating an institution that faithfully served the needs of the French government throughout his reign. It is, however, an exaggeration to describe the Sovereign Council as "only the docile and respectful agent of royal power,"[31] as one historian has. The loyalty of the council was never really in doubt, and its members firmly supported French interests in Roussillon. The council did, however, also seek local advantages, and was at times recalcitrant in fulfilling the wishes of Paris. As shall be seen in Chapter 6, the Sovereign Council refused to register certain edicts of the king, continued to use the Catalan language and *Usatges*, and protested royal policies in the province. The Sovereign Council was certainly a respectful agent of royal power, but most assuredly not a docile one.

The Sovereign Council of Roussillon was either the court of first instance or appeal for nearly all judicial proceedings in the province. The only exceptions to this universal competence were the *tribunal de la Monnaie de*

Perpignan (tribunal of the Mint of Perpignan), which was created in 1711 and could appeal to the court at Lyon, and military tribunals, which had their own appellate system. While the Sovereign Council could make itself the court of first instance in any matter, it rarely did so, limiting the exercise of this right to the most serious cases of murder and treason. Thus the Sovereign Council more often functioned judicially in the role of an appellate court, much like the provincial *parlements* throughout France. Roussillonnais jurisdictions that were appealed to the Sovereign Council fell into four broad categories: ordinary jurisdictions, extraordinary royal jurisdictions, extraordinary municipal jurisdictions, and ecclesiastical jurisdictions.

When the Sovereign Council was created in 1660, existing Catalan judicial apparatus was used to administer justice at the local levels. All of the courts of ordinary jurisdiction in post-annexation Roussillon were Catalan institutions whose names had simply been translated into French. *Clavaris* became *clavaires*, *batlles* became *bayles*, and *veguers* became *viguiers*, to cite but three examples. The men holding those positions did not always retain them, but the positions themselves were transferred with relative ease. The Sovereign Council did not even bother to translate *Sobreposats de la Horta* in French, but simply referred to it in the Catalan. In addition to retaining many traditional Catalan juridical institutions, the French introduced five French courts into the province. The *Capitainerie Générale, Amirauté de Collioure, Juge des Gabelles, Juge des Traites,* and *Juge des Tabacs* were innovations to the Roussillonnais.

There were four sources of appeals in the ordinary jurisdiction: the *cours des viguiers,* the *cours des bayles royaux, justice seigneuriale,* and the *corps de ville.* The province of Roussillon was divided into three *viguieries,* that of Roussillon and the Vallespir, the Conflent and Capcir, and the Cerdagne. The *cours des viguiers* were the courts of first instance in civil and criminal cases that involved the consuls or *bayles* of villages, those to which ecclesiastical communities were party, all cases judging crimes committed within the *viguerie,* and cases arising from actions committed on any of the roads of the *viguerie.* In addition, any cases involving a noble, the rights of a noble, or a dispute between a seigneur and his vassals were judged by the *cours des viguiers.* Finally, all other cases not specifically assigned to the competence of another court were heard in the *cours des viguiers.* In the *cours des viguiers,* justice was rendered by the judge of the *viguerie,* and not by the *viguier* himself. It was after a judgment was rendered by the judge of the *viguerie* that a dissatisfied party to a case might appeal to the Sovereign Council.[32]

There were eight royal bailliages in Roussillon: Perpignan, Thuir, Collioure, Prats-de-Mollo, Vinça, Prades, Villefranche, and Mont-Louis. In addition, there were three royal villages that had been ceded to seigneurs: Argeles, Le Boulou, and Salces. The *cours des bayles royaux* judged the same type of cases as the *cours des viguiers*, but decided cases arising in the eleven named municipalities.

In addition to the *cours des bayles royaux* and the *cours des viguiers*, there existed two *cours des tiers*. These courts were elective in jurisdiction. The phrase *sous peine et écriture de tiers* could be inserted into a contract by mutual consent. When a dispute arose out of any such contract, the *cours des tiers* was automatically the court of first instance in the case. From these courts, appeal could be made to the *cour de bayle royaux de Perpignan* or the *cour de viguier du Roussillon*, and then, ultimately, to the Sovereign Council itself.

Seigneurial justice was rendered in Roussillon in those areas in which the lord had obtained from the monarch the right to administer justice in a *cour de justice seigneurial*. Such permission typically predated the French annexation by a hundred years or more. The French usually respected the established rights of seigneural justice, even when seizing seigneuries from disloyal Roussillonnais and transferring them to new lords. The noble was required to appoint a *bayle* for his lands, who then acted as judge in all matters in the lord's demesne. Spanish nobles who held rights of seigneural justice in Roussillon were usually permitted to continue in the exercise of those rights, on the condition that the *bayle* appointed be a faithful subject of Louis XIV. The *cours de justice seigneuriales*, like the preceding judicial bodies, could be appealed to the Sovereign Council if a disputant was dissatisfied with the conclusion of the *bayle*.

The final source of ordinary justice in Roussillon were the *cours des corps de ville*. The *corps de ville*, or citizens of village, annually elected consuls to govern their village, and these consuls in turn appointed men known as *clavaires* to judge legal disputes within the village. If a party in the lawsuit was unhappy, the decision of the *clavaire* could then be appealed to the full body of consuls. Their decision could, in turn, be appealed to the Sovereign Council.

In addition to these ordinary jurisdictions within the province, there were several extraordinary royal jurisdictions, and their associated judicial apparatus. The *Chambre du Domaine* or *Consistoire du Domaine* was created at the same time as the Sovereign Council, in the Edict of Saint Jean de Luz of 1660. The *Consistoire du Domaine* was formed to replace the traditional Catalan institutions of the *Cour du Procureur Royal* and the *Cour du Domaine*, which predated the French occupation of Roussillon. This new court had competence in all matters concerning the regalian rights, *causes domaniales*, and all matters pertaining to the *amirauté*. Since there was no Master of Water and Forests in Roussillon, disputes regarding the rights to and usage of watercourses in the province were also judged by the *Consistoire du Domaine*. The *Consistoire du Domaine* existed as a completely independent institution until 1688, when it was joined to the Sovereign Council, and each councillor served a year as *Councillor Commissaire*, judging cases with the *avocat général* and *procureur* of the Sovereign Council.[33]

The *Capitainerie Générale* was established to judge all cases involving the governor's fifty mounted personal guards, artillerymen, and those to whom the governor had granted letters of safeguard, such as doctors, agents, the spouses of soldiers, or artisans serving the needs of garrisons. Enrollment in the *Capitainerie* exempted an individual only from the ordinary jurisdiction of justice; it did not provide exemption from the *gabelle*, extraordinary jurisdictions, or other royal rights. The judge of the *Capitainerie Générale* was known as the assessor, and had complete jurisdiction over all criminal and civil matters involving those on his rolls. Appeals from the *Capitainerie* were heard by two members of the Sovereign Council, who were called commissioners and chosen biannually. To these two men fell the task of resolving the inevitable jurisdictional disputes between the *Capitainerie* and other courts.[34]

The *Amirauté de Collioure* was an institution created in April 1691 and given competence in all cases involving death at sea, all crimes committed at sea, and any grievances involving shipping. Disputes arising from cases judged by this group were, like most judicial decisions, appealed to the Sovereign Council in Perpignan.

The position of *Juge des Gabelles* was created in 1661 to hear cases involving disputes with the officers and policies of the *gabelle*. The *Juge des Traites* was established in May 1691 to resolve disputes over the payment of *douanes* and other matters regarding commercial entrance and egress from Roussillon. The *Juge des Tabacs* was created on 16 June 1699 to judge grievances with the tobacco monopoly. The latter two institutions, while in principle separate organizations, were in practice usually combined into a single functioning unit.[35]

There were several extraordinary municipal jurisdictions in Roussillon that were also appealed to the Sovereign Council. The *Consulat de la Llotja de Mar de Perpinyà* was a tribunal created by King Jean I of Aragon on 22 December 1388 to try cases arising from mercantile activity in Perpignan, both maritime and terrestrial, even those cases involving non-residents. The *Consulat* was headed by two consuls who were elected annually, one of whom was chosen from the nobility, and the other from the merchant class, and both men were typically residents of Perpignan. The *Consulat* also was responsible for levying the *pariatge*, an old Catalan *ad valorum* tariff of approximately 0.2 percent on all goods in transit that came through the province. The *Consulat de la Llotja de Mar*, which the French viewed as the equivalent of their *bourses*, also served as a merchants' organization, striving to promote commerce within the region.[36]

The *Tribunal de la Pieuse Aumône* was an institution that had once possessed judicial powers, but by the seventeenth century was strictly an administrative unit. It was responsible for administering poor relief, operating the home for orphans, and managing the hospitals in the province. Since it was no longer a judicial body, the Sovereign Council exercised authority over this tribunal by allocating funds to it and overseeing its operations.

The *Juridiction des Fours Banaux de Perpignan* had jurisdiction over the Knights of Malta, to whom the last Count of Roussillon, Guinard II, had given control of the five common ovens of Perpignan in 1172. Although the Knights of Malta were still present and active in Roussillon in the seventeenth century, with three commanderies and considerable property, most cases that came before the *Juridiction des Fours Banaux* dealt with issues involving the baking of bread and other problems concerning bakeries.[37]

Problems arising from the administration of the revenue of the university and issues concerning its discipline were taken before the *Tribunal de l'Université de Perpignan*. The university, which had been founded in 1379, was the intellectual center of the province, and the center of several controversies during the reign of Louis XIV, forcing the Sovereign Council to intervene more than once in its affairs.

The *Sobreposats de la Horta* were local bodies that judged the damage done by animals to private property. These bodies did not establish guilt, but were empowered solely to act as estimators, determining the amount of damage done to a piece of property so that compensation could be awarded. Typically, a *Sobreposat* would be composed of three individuals, of whom two were always gardeners, since animals most often damaged fields or other agricultural improvements and the expertise of gardeners permitted fair estimates to be made of damages. The only *Sobreposat de la Horta* that did not appeal directly to the Sovereign Council was that of Perpignan, which appealed to the *bayle* of that city, and thence to the Council.[38]

In addition to these three general categories of competence, the Sovereign Council had jurisdiction in certain ecclesiastical matters, particularly those arising from clerical abuses. The exact nature and limitations of this ecclesiastical jurisdiction were never clearly defined, which led to many conflicts between various elements of the church in Roussillon and the Sovereign Council throughout the reign of Louis XIV.

One additional competence assigned to the Sovereign Council was that of representative of the king in matters concerning the principality of Andorra. The king of France was, through a complicated medieval arrangement, co-seigneur of the small Catalan country of Andorra, sharing that responsibility with the bishop of Urgel. Any appeals of justice directed to the king from that country were to be heard by the Sovereign Council.[39]

In creating the Sovereign Council and in giving it such comprehensive powers, the French government fashioned an instrument by which its will could be effectively introduced into the province. All justice, laws, and administrative tasks were in the hands of men loyal to the king. These men could therefore introduce loyalty and French values into the lives of the

Roussillonnais. By demanding conformity with French practices, promoting French culture, propagating the French language, and co-operating with the French, the Sovereign Council could cultivate a habit of respect and obedience among its subjects. This is the task the council undertook during the reign of Louis XIV, with varying degrees of success.

Intendant

Another important institution for the imposition of French will in the province was the office of intendant. The *Intendant de la Justice, Police, et Finances* was the most important single French administrative official in the province. He was far more important than the governor, who was usually absent, and the lieutenant-general, who was usually preoccupied with military affairs. The *généralité*, or jurisdiction, of the intendant was coincident with the province of Roussillon throughout the reign of Louis XIV, allowing the intendant to focus solely on the problems of control and assimilation in Roussillon. The intendant of Roussillon reported to and was selected by the Secretary of State for War in Paris, and earned over 20,000 livres per year.[40]

The powers of the intendants were great. These men were charged with the collection of taxes; the promotion of agriculture, commerce, and industry; the maintenance of roads and bridges; the imposition of order, the recruitment and supply of troops in the province and in Catalonia; and the supervision of the church in Roussillon. To accomplish these goals, the intendants were given a great deal of power. The intendant sat on the Sovereign Council by right, supervised that body in the absence of the governor, and was often responsible for the conclusions reached by that group. He also audited the financial records of the province and could dispense some limited amount of patronage in the form of municipal offices, militia commissions, and low-ranking positions in the provincial administration. Moreover, being a client of the Le Tellier family gave the intendant considerable influence in Paris and respect among the provincial elites.[41]

During the reign of Louis XIV, the position of intendant was held by seven men in succession. The first intendant, Charles Macqueron, had been a secretary of Michel Le Tellier. This close association with the Secretary of State for War gained him the position of intendant in Roussillon in 1660, a post he held until 1669. Étienne Carlier, Vicomte d'Ully et de Pargnan, was a native of Picardy. Before coming to Roussillon, he had served as an intendant in Franche-Comté. He came to Roussillon in 1670 and served as intendant until 1676, when he was transferred to Hainaut. Germain Michel Camus de Beaulieu was the intendant from 1676 until 1681, when he was sent to Franche-Comté. Ramon de Trobat, a native of Barcelona, was the only Catalan intendant of Roussillon, serving from 1681 to 1698. Of all seven intendants who served in Roussillon during the reign of Louis XIV, he was the most popular with the Le Tellier family. He was described in the minister's correspondence as "a celebrated Intendant of the frontier, instructed in the maxims of the previous wars and sound in all details."[42] He was succeeded by Félix Marie Étienne de Ponte d'Albaret, who was intendant from 1698 to 1709. D'Albaret was a noble from Piedmont and had previously been first president of the Sovereign Council of Pignerol, and *president à mortier* in the *Parlement* at Rouen. When he was replaced as intendant in 1709, he remained in Perpignan to serve as first president of the Sovereign Council. Antoine de Barrillon d'Amoncourt, Marquis de Branges, held the office of intendant for a brief period during the years 1710 and 1711. He was a Parisian and had become a councillor of the *Parlement* of Paris in 1692, and master of requests in 1700. The Duke of Noailles was openly hostile toward Barrillon, considering him to be "the biggest petty quibbler there has been in France"[43] and believing him to lack the ability to be a good intendant. Due to Noailles's dislike, Barrillon was appointed to the intendancy of Pau in February 1711. Charles Deschiens de la Neuville was the last intendant during the reign of Louis XIV, serving from 1711 to 1715. He had previously served as intendant and in the *Parlement* at Pau, and went on to become the intendant of Franche-Comté after his service in Roussillon.[44]

Governor

Another important position created by the French in Roussillon was that of governor. An office that had existed in France since at least the time of Francis I, the governor was in many ways an honorific title. The governor was, in theory, responsible for governing the province. He sat as the presiding member of the Sovereign Council and was empowered to render justice in the province. In practice, however, Louis XIV was wary of allowing his governors much real power, and thus shifted the burden of governing to the intendants.

The office of governor, valued at 38,000 livres of rent in 1698, was held exclusively by the Noailles family throughout the Old Regime. The first governor of Roussillon was Anne, Duc de Noailles, who was succeeded in turn by his son Anne Jules (served 1678–1698) and grandson Adrien-Maurice (1698–1718). The dukes of Noailles, although governors of Roussillon, were very rarely in the province. They were military leaders, and both Anne Jules and Adrien-Maurice were created marshals of France. Their military obligations were one reason they were so rarely in the province, since they were often on campaign in the Low Countries or Catalonia. Being important peers of France, the Noailles also spent a great deal of time at court, forging alliances and giving council to the monarch and his ministers. The family, like so many others associated with Roussillon, was also allied with the Le Tellier family. The daughter of Anne-Jules, for example, married the grandson of Louvois. The many wars against the Hapsburgs and political maneuvering at court kept the Noailles away from Roussillon, and help explain why the governor was such an unimportant figure in the province.[45]

Amirauté de Collioure

The *Amirauté de Collioure* was introduced in Roussillon in April 1691 to eliminate the effective power of the *Consulat de la Llotja de Mar*. The latter was a Catalan institution in Perpignan that claimed the same jurisdiction as the *amirautés* of France, but rendered judgment according to the Constitutions of Catalonia. In granting maritime jurisdiction to the *Amirauté de Collioure*, French law was introduced into the ports of Roussillon, and Catalan customs and privileges were excluded.

The creation of the *Amirauté de Collioure* is an example of a French attempt to suppress ancient Catalan institutions. *Amirautés*, created throughout much of France in 1681, were courts having jurisdiction over all criminal and civil grievances regarding maritime activities. In addition, *amirautés* were administrative institutions responsible for registering ship masters and watching the coast. Murders, piracy, fraud, and any other crime committed at sea, in a port, or on a river would be brought before an *amirauté*, as would cases involving fishing rights or the rights of the admiral of France. Justice in the *amirautés* was administered in the name of the Grand Admiral of France, the Count of Toulouse (1683–1737), and was ultimately appealed to the *Table de marbre* in Paris.

One significant problem associated with the *Amirauté de Collioure*, as with all Old Regime legal institutions, was the frequent overlapping of competencies. For instance, jurisdiction over cases involving fishing on the large lakes along the coast of Roussillon was claimed by the *amirauté*, the *Chambre du Domaine*, certain seigneurs, and the *Consulat de la Llotja de Mar*, among others. These frequent conflicts could work to the advantage of the French by allowing the Sovereign Council to assign jurisdictions and resolve cases in a manner that best suited French needs and goals in Roussillon. The seigneural rights of a noble who was not an enthusiastic supporter of France could, for example, be slowly eroded by awarding jurisdiction over his domains to other bodies. As his judicial power waned, so too would his influence in his area diminish. Thus, as his influence decreased, his hostility toward France would have less of an impact on the inhabitants of the region. At the same time, such an example might encourage other notables to adhere to the French cause more closely and exert a pro-French influence in their local regions. Thus, competing jurisdictions could be made to serve the goals of the French in Roussillon.[46]

The Administration of Taxes

The French not only created new institutions to aid in the control and assimilation of the Roussillonnais, but also introduced new taxes and levies into the province. The taxes were primarily fiscal devices, but also served secondary roles as vehicles of assimilation. The most significant was the tax on salt, the *gabelle*. The kings of France had, since 1343, possessed a monopoly on the sale of salt in their realms. They used this monopoly to impose a tax on salt purchased or brought into the realm, thus realizing a large income. The *Usatges* of the Catalans had, since the *Corts* of Montçó in 1283, prohibited any tax or restriction on the transport and sale of salt.[47] In November 1661, Louis XIV revoked almost 400 years of Catalan law by imposing the *gabelle* in Roussillon, joining the province to the *petite gabelle* of southern France. The goal was not only to raise revenue, but also to incorporate the Roussillonnais into the French political and economic system. Old Catalan law was being explicitly and consciously rejected in Paris, and French law was being introduced to replace it. Colbert, like many French officials, repeatedly remarked that the inhabitants must pay the tax not only because it would raise additional funds, but also because paying the levy was "the obedience which is due His Majesty."[48] Indeed, in Roussillon the *gabelle* was lower than in most of the rest of France, underscoring the political nature of the levy. The inhabitants also saw the new imposition as more than a mere fiscal device, for the rebellion provoked by the *gabelle* was justified not in economic terms, but in political and legal ones. Everyone in the province of Roussillon recognized that the introduction of the *gabelle* was an attempt to further the process of political assimilation in the region.

The *capitation* was first introduced in Roussillon and the rest of France in 1695 as a response to fiscal crises between 1692 and 1694, and to help cover the enormous costs of the War of the League of Augsburg. The *capitation* was a personal tax on subjects of the king of France. This tax, like the *gabelle*, also contributed to the process of political assimilation in Roussillon, although unlike the *gabelle*, the *capitation* was not explicitly linked to that purpose. The *capitation* was important because it, like the *gabelle*, helped create a distinction between Spanish Catalans and French Catalans. This tax, although not a clear violation of the *Usatges*, was still quite unpopular. The Roussillonnais thus struggled to protest the tax, and in so doing presented themselves as loyal subjects of Louis XIV. Further, the displeasure of the province with the new tax was shared by the entire country, thus helping the Roussillonnais find common ground with the rest of their new countrymen. Repeatedly depicting themselves as good subjects sharing a common bond suffering with all of France helped, however slightly, to reinforce that commonality in the minds of the Roussillonnais, thus distancing them from their Catalan kinsmen in Spain.[49]

Another fiscal innovation introduced by the French into Roussillon were customs duties, or *douanes*. The Roussillonnais had been accustomed to paying duties on goods being shipped between the province and France before 1640. The French, however, imposed an additional custom tax. In addition to maintaining the earlier customs, a tariff was established on all goods traveling to or from Spain, Thus, the Roussillonnais were expected to pay customs on their traditional trade with the Principat, suddenly turning what had been internal commerce into international traffic.

Other Administrative Innovations

Another tactic used to reinforce a sense of common identity with France was the adaptation by the provincial government of Catalan institutions to French innovations. One such incident occurred on 23 January 1683, when the Sovereign Council gave the intendant control of the *pariatge* of the *Consulat de la Llotja de Mar*. The *pariatge*, or *droit d'empereage*, was a tax the *Consulat* had levied since 1394 on all commerce and goods passing through the ports of Roussillon. The *Consulat* was an ancient body in Perpignan, held in high esteem by all the citizens, and its membership was determined by all the citizens of Perpignan in an annual election. Since it was so popular, the Sovereign Council did not move against it directly, but stripped it of real power by taking control of the *pariatge*. By giving the intendant the power to spend the revenue of the *Consulat*, the Sovereign Council linked the fortunes of a prestigious Catalan institution with the key administrative representative of the new French government, thus drawing the two together.[50]

Another example of this tactic was the 1671 assumption by the intendant Étienne Carlier of the right to name the *burgès honrats* of Perpignan, a special grant of nobility. Since the days of the Muslim conquests, the city of Perpignan had possessed the right to ennoble by annual election any number of its citizens. Louis XIV himself reconfirmed this right in 1660, and the Council of State did so as well on 1 December 1702. The class of urban nobles created by this process was called the *mà major*, and they were the leading class of citizens in the city of Perpignan. The *mà major* posed considerable difficulties for the French, however. There was no exact equivalent for these urban nobles in France, and many debates were conducted by French legal scholars as to the status and privileges of these aristocrats. It was not until 13 September 1703 that the Council of State finally provided the definitive explanation of the nature of the *mà major*, defining them as the fourth class of nobility of Catalonia and Roussillon. Since ennoblement carried with it certain economic and political privileges, including exemption from taxation, it was a highly coveted prize in the city. The French government decided that, due to the status of these nobles, they could be valuable tools in the process of political assimilation. The urban bourgeoisie had been, under Spanish rule, a center of resistance to Castillian acculturation, and was, under the French, likewise resistant to French influence. The French decided that by controling the coveted honors of this class, they would thereby increase its loyalty.

To control this process, on 22 November 1671 the Sovereign Council effectively took control of the process by placing several significant limitations upon it; these limitations were confirmed on 26 May 1714. All persons nominated for the election had to earn at least 100 pistoles per year, a sizeable sum that precluded many of the lesser bourgeoisie from consideration. Further, a candidate was not permitted to work, again barring most citizens from candidacy. Only two persons could be granted ennoblement each year, thus preventing a flood of nobles in the city. And, most important, the intendant had the right to veto any nomination he found unfavorable, ensuring that only pro-French candidates would achieve this honor. In January 1702, the Sovereign Council further modified the procedure, requiring the patents of nobility to be written in French, and specifically defining French patents to be fully equal to those in any other language. By assuming control of this traditional Catalan institution, the French managed to build their basis of support and work toward assimilation, since anyone who wished this honor had to be actively pro-French.[51]

Another traditional institution that was modified by the Sovereign Council was the annual election of consuls in the communities of Roussillon. Traditionally, communities had the right of self-government, selecting their own consuls. The Sovereign Council modified this procedure, still allowing the residents to select a list of nominees, and to elect their own consuls. Between these two steps, however, was interposed the intendant. He reviewed the list of potential consuls, selecting individuals who were "the best disposed for the King's service,"[52] and only those men were allowed to stand for election. By thus controling the candidates, the intendant ensured that only pro-French citizens served as consuls, and those men would then work to further assimilation in their town or city.[53]

Yet another action taken by the French to promote loyalty, or, more accurately, discourage disloyalty, was the prohibition of unauthorized assemblies. On 30 October 1662 the king decreed that no residents of Roussillon were "to convoke and form any general assembly in the absence and without the participation of the *viguiers* or *bailles* on pain of disobedience."[54] By dictating that royally selected officials were to be present at all meetings, the French hoped to prevent open discussion of grievances and plans for resistance or protest. Two major problems immediately presented themselves. First, ignoring this edict would hardly trouble those residents who were already planning resistance to other French ordinances, such as the *gabelle*. More important, the primary assembly of most villages, the Sunday Mass, did not fall under this directive. Thus, if a priest opposed French policies, he might use the Sunday meeting as a political platform and condone action against the French. Such clerical resistance did in fact occur frequently throughout the Vallespir during the revolt against the *gabelle*. This prohibition against unauthorized assemblies may have reduced the number of gatherings called to protest minor injustices, but it certainly had no impact on defusing the tensions resulting from major grievances against the government.

Another administrative tactic undertaken by the French to foster loyalty to and acceptance of their rule was the maintenance of traditional forms whenever possible. Old Catalan institutions were often maintained, although quite often severely modified, and new institutions were frequently modeled on previous organizations. Even when an innovation was so radical that there was no traditional structure that could be copied, some attempt was generally made to explain and disguise it, even if thinly, behind some Catalan custom, law, or institution. Thus the administrative subdivision of Roussillon into three *viguieries* was maintained under both Castillian and French domination, rights of seigneural justice were upheld under the French administration, the *Tribunal de la Pieuse Aumône* was used by the French as it had been by the Spanish, as were the *Juridiction des Fours Banaux de Perpignan* and the *Sobreposats de la Horta*. In a similar manner, the *Consulat de la Llotja de Mar* was retained, although only nominally, as was its associated levy, the *pariatge*. The University of Perpignan was also maintained by the French, although it too underwent some significant alterations during the French administration. In the same way, the *Burgès Honrats* of Perpignan still existed and were regularly created, but under modified circumstances, and consuls still controlled the communities, but only with French approval. The Sovereign Council, the administrative body of the province, was compared with the Royal Council of Perpignan which had existed since the days of Catalan independence, and the *Chambre du Domaine* was explicitly described as a replacement for the former *Cour du Procureur Royal* and *Cour du Domaine* of Roussillon. By creating new institutions with old models, and retaining traditional forms and institutions, even with new purposes, the French sought to create a government in Perpignan that would be accepted by most citizens as representing an acceptable continuity with the old Catalan forms.[55]

One other, more radical, plan for francisation was proposed, but quickly aborted. In July 1661, it was proposed to suppress the newly created Sovereign Council and replace it with a presidial court. The civil and criminal jurisdiction that had been the competence of the Sovereign Council was to be given to the Court of Aids and Accounts in Montpellier. This was part of a grand scheme to integrate all of the newly annexed territories of Louis XIV into the French legal, political, and cultural systems. It was believed that this plan would rapidly increase francisation, since a purely French body would be judging and imposing law on the provinces. The Sovereign Council of Roussillon, together with other bodies, protested this proposal vigorously, and the plan was dropped.[56]

In summary, the French employed a variety of administrative methods to ensure the loyalty, or at least acquiescence, of the inhabitants of Roussillon to the rule of Louis XIV. These methods included the creation of new institutions, such as the Sovereign Council, intendant, governor, and *Amirauté de Collioure*. Such institutions provided a mechanism for the French to exert their control in those areas they considered to be most important, and these new creations were therefore among the most important institutions in French Roussillon. The French also introduced new taxes, such as the *gabelle*, *douanes*, and *capitation*, which did nothing to increase loyalty to or affection for the French. They did perhaps, in a small way, contribute to the formation of a French identity in Roussillon, as opposition to these imposts were addressed to the king of France, and thus France would be emphasized in protests. Finally, the French used existing institutions whenever possible, attempting to cloak innovation in traditional Catalan practice. The moderate nature of these administrative innovations contributed to the ultimate success of the French in convincing the Roussillonnais to accept French rule. There were no mass executions, wholesale persecutions, or other forms of harsh treatment meted out; this made the French administrative presence perfectly tolerable, and thus it came to be accepted, if not embraced.

THE ROLE OF THE LOCAL ELITES

In addition to utilizing their administration to help foster loyalty in the province, the French also worked with the local elites to build a favorable public opinion. The French believed that if the leaders of the region could be convinced to accept the French presence, the rest of the people, conditioned to follow their betters, would likewise accept French rule in Roussillon.

One method of building a favorable opinion among the local notables was to encourage immigration from Spanish Catalonia. Immigration increased the number of nobles favorable to France and diluted the influence of malcontents. When the Peace of the Pyrenees was signed, many nobles who had fought against Spain during the rebellion fled to Roussillon. Anyone who had fled from Spain was probably unwelcome there, thus ruling out a return to that country. With no place to go, immigrants from Spain would be on their best behavior for fear of expulsion. A more important advantage of the immigrants from the French point of view was that they were generally without local ties in Roussillon. This meant the new arrivals were dependent upon the French administration for lands, favors, and even economic support. The native nobility might, and often did, use its local bases of support to resist French policies in the region. Immigrants had no such local support and thus were forced to be loyal to the French.

The king encouraged immigration to Roussillon by dispensing favors to the refugee Catalans, offering full citizenship to them, giving them land and money, and granting them positions of importance in the religious and political structures of the region. Among those who immigrated into Roussillon and were prominent in the pro-French cause were Pere Pont, abbot of Arles; his brother Rafel, governor of Bellegarde; Josep d'Ardena, a general in the French army; Josep de Fontanella and Francesc de Sagarra, *presidents à mortier* of the Sovereign Council; Ramon de Trobat, intendant of Roussillon;

and Vincenç de Margarit, Bishop of Perpignan. The French encouraged these men to immigrate in order to build a solid base of pro-French opinion among the region's elites. Encouraging immigration was, in general terms, far easier and more successful than trying to convert the neutral or hostile native nobility. These immigrant men, being themselves Catalan by birth and pro-French in outlook, served as effective intermediaries between Paris and the people of Roussillon.[57]

Another way in which the immigrant local elites were used by the French was in staffing positions in the local administration. To ensure the Sovereign Council's loyalty to Louis XIV, for example, the council was filled with immigrants from Spanish Catalonia who had fled to France in 1659. When the Sovereign Council was created in 1660, there was only one councillor from Roussillon. Both *presidents à mortier*, five of six councillors, the *greffier en chef*, both *commis*, and at least one of four *alguazils* were refugees from Spain. The first bishop under French rule, Vicenç de Margarit, was an immigrant from Barcelona, as was Ramon de Trobat, who served as intendant from 1681 to 1698. There were, in addition to these major figures, many immigrants who served lesser roles in the provincial administration, serving as *viguiers*, abbots, canons, rectors, vicar-generals, governors of fortified villages, army officers, university professors, and *juges de bayle*, among other offices. The selection of immigrants to staff these positions ensured that the loyalties of the office holders would be to France, as those men were entirely dependant upon the good favor of Paris. Thus, interposed between Paris and the inhabitants of Roussillon were administrators who had some understanding of and sympathy for the inhabitants of the province, as well as a compulsion to serve the interests of the state. The result was that French edicts were tempered to suit the mood of the people when necessary, and the Roussillonnais came to view government, as represented by the immigrants, as a bureaucracy that responded to local concerns.

Not only did the French provide positions in the local government to the immigrant elites to ensure their loyalty, but other rewards were also generously provided to individuals, whether immigrant or native, who demonstrated their faithfulness to the crown. For example, during the massive rebellion against the *gabelle*, men who remained loyal to France when their neighbors were in rebellion were indemnified by the government. The sums involved ranged from modest awards of about 100 livres for residents of small villages to thousands of livres for leading figures on the Sovereign Council. Money was not the only reward for loyalty, and faithful servants of the crown were often provided with estates, privileges, or, in rare cases, grants of nobility. Josep de Quéralt, Miquel Tamarit, Galceran Cahors, the Baron of Monclar, Josep de Fontanella, Josep Ricart, Francesc de Calvo, Felip de Copons, and Francesc de Sagarra were among the hundreds of individuals, men and women, who received lands, money, and confiscated goods as rewards for their faithful service to Louis XIV. Don Josep d'Ardena i Çabastida, for example, was created the Comte d'Ille by Louis XIV and Don Josep de Margarit i de Biure was created Marquis d'Aguilar. Lesser grants were more common, and the seigneuries of Cuxous, Pollestres, Garrius, Alenya, and Vilar d'Ovança were among those given to reward the faithful followers of France.[58]

ECONOMIC POLICIES

The French understood that commerce was vitally important to the province of Roussillon, and sought to use that fact to their own advantage. If the government could redirect the commercial and productive capacities of Roussillon to make the province dependent upon France, that would be one of the best guarantors of fidelity and acceptance the French could have. To achieve this end, the French undertook a series of economic reforms in the province to draw the attention of the Roussillonnais away from Catalonia, the traditional economic partner of the province, and focus their efforts on the French economy. These reforms included prohibiting commercial contact with Catalonia, fostering the development of various industries in Roussillon, and encouraging French penetration into the province.

The first step in the French program to assimilate Roussillon economically was to break the old commercial ties that bound the province to the rest of Catalonia. The bulk of commercial activity, especially outside Perpignan, involved Roussillonnais taking their lumber, ore, grain, or livestock to a large town in the Principat for sale. This traditional pattern of commerce dated back centuries and was a major irritant to the French. Not only did these journeys continue to orient Roussillon southward economically, but by these trips the residents remained culturally and politically linked to their kinsmen in Spain. The Sovereign Council therefore repeatedly ordered all commerce with Catalonia to end, hoping similar patterns would develop between the Roussillonnais and Languedoc or Foix. Had the French stopped with a simple prohibition, very little would have been accomplished, even with vigorous enforcement. Indeed, the reign of Louis XIV was dotted with many persons being arrested and fined for smuggling goods out of Roussillon, that is, following traditional trade practices. However, the French were eventually successful in reorienting the economy of Roussillon toward France for two reasons, one planned and one coincidental. First, the Sovereign Council complemented its prohibitions with positive actions to encourage and compel commerce with France, such as tax incentives, requisitions for the armies, and encouragement of local industry. The second reason the French were successful in shifting the focus of the Roussillonnais away from Catalonia is that the Principat became devastated by the decades of war between France and Spain, wars often waged in Catalonia. As the economy of Catalonia worsened, the Roussillonnais were compelled to find other outlets for their goods, and thus turned to southern France. As the French plan succeeded, the province became increasingly dependent upon France for its economic prosperity, and the Roussillonnais merchants were also influenced in some small way by increased contact with the French mercantile community.[59]

Among the French economic undertakings in Roussillon was creation of a cannon foundry in Perpignan and a munitions and small arms production center in Ille-sur-Tet in the 1690s. These workshops directly employed a number of Roussillonnais, such as craftsmen, overseers, and laborers, and indirectly employed still more, such as those providing raw materials, transporting goods, and constructing the new physical plants. These various establishments served to infuse a great deal of money into the local economies of Roussillon. In less than one year, for example, over 10,627 livres were spent on Roussillonnais iron at one foundry in Perpignan, and almost 900 livres were spent in a single month at Ille. An even wider circle of people than simply employees enjoyed the benefits of the money that these establishments injected into the local economies, as the employees spent their salaries on food, lodging, and finished goods from throughout their regions. By involving a range of people in these new factories, these enterprises served not only to provide war materiel for Louis XIV's frequent wars with Spain, but also helped in several ways to bring the Roussillonnais into the French political and social world. First, the money injected into the local economies by these workshops increased economic interaction with and dependence upon the French. As people came to realize that their economic well-being was tied to France and French interests, the inhabitants of Roussillon slowly accepted the French political system and its goals as their own. Moreover, the nature of the work encouraged the development of an identity in Roussillon counter to the traditional Catalan self-image. By producing small arms with which the French fought Catalans in Spain, the Roussillonnais distanced themselves from the Principat, which was seen as the enemy. [60]

Another economic innovation undertaken by the French government was the creation of a *Hôtel de Monnaie* (mint) in June 1710. Louis XIV was worried because a great amount of Spanish money was circulating in Roussillon. Since every point of contact between Roussillon and the Principat could work to retard the assimilation desired by the French, the government decided to work aggressively to introduce French currency into the province. This was accomplished by moving the university out of its quarters and installing the mint in that building. This mint, which replaced one which had been in Narbonne, struck coins of gold, silver, and copper, and served to strengthen further the ties between Roussillon and France. The first year of its existence, for example, the mint produced more than 400,000 livres in copper coins alone. By providing coins for the entire southeast of the country, the Roussillonnais were forced into greater contact with the country as they became integrated into the monetary system of France.[61]

Still another method used by the government to encourage increased economic integration was to provide incentives for French merchants to immigrate to Roussillon. Both Louvois and the Sovereign Council used loans, grants, and special tax advantages to encourage native Frenchmen "to establish themselves in the city of Perpignan and other towns of Roussillon."[62] Among the benefits offered French immigrants were complete exemptions from all taxes for four years, including customs duties and guild dues. The benefits of immigration for the government were two-fold. First, natives from other parts of France would maintain contacts with the regions from which they came, and introduce those contacts into Perpignan, thus linking the province more closely to France. Further, as these native French became successful in business, they would become increasingly influential in the province and would thereby help transmit French culture throughout the region. There are no concrete data concerning the number of French merchants who became active in Roussillon, but in 1678 Port Vendres docked over 200 French ships, a number that rose throughout the reign of Louis XIV.[63]

A special attempt was made by the intendants Ramon de Trobat and Étienne de Ponte d'Albaret to bring the Roussillonnais into closer co-operation with the French soldiers garrisoning the province. In 1690, Trobat issued an ordinance that twice each week exempted residents of the towns of Bellegarde, Mont Louis, and Fort-des-Bains from taxes at special markets. Any provisions that the inhabitants brought to market on the specified days would be free from most of the levies that the government normally imposed upon commerce. Similarly, the animals used to bring those goods to market were to be similarly relieved of all taxes, duties, and tolls. Trobat's plan lasted only for his lifetime, ending in 1698. The plan met with some success, and so d'Albaret reinstituted it in 1700. The intendants had several goals for their markets. Foremost among these was ensuring adequate supplies for the French troops in the Vallespir and upper Conflent valleys. A secondary purpose was, however, to have the soldiers and inhabitants interact with one another under pleasant conditions twice a week. By allowing the Roussillonnais to see the soldiers in a non-confrontational situation, it was hoped to make their presence more tolerable. Finally, the more the residents took advantage of these special proposals, the more the economy would be oriented toward France and its needs, and the less commerce would be conducted with Catalonia. In this manner, the intendants sought to discharge their duties of military supply and assimilation simultaneously.[64]

In summary, in their efforts to assimilate Roussillon, the French engaged in a series of economic endeavors designed to strengthen ties between the province and the rest of France. By encouraging commerce and interaction with France, the government increased the prosperity of Roussillon. For the mercantile classes, this increasing wealth and productivity was a very strong tie binding the region to France. Even the lower classes, who had little direct economic contact with France, enjoyed the benefits of French control. The leading citizens, who were profiting from direct contact, had more money to spend and thus indirectly spread French wealth among the common citizens. The French themselves, through massive constructions, army requisitioning, and favorable tax decisions, distributed a substantial amount of money throughout all classes of society. As the inhabitants of Roussillon came to associate the French with a substantially improved economy, their willingness to accept the French was expected to increase correspondingly. Increased prosperity did not, however, serve as an immediate prelude to acculturation. The Roussillonnais of all classes accepted French money without incorporating much of French culture in the process. Thus, the economic plans followed by the French in Roussillon, like many of their plans, led to increased acceptance of their political domination of the province but changed little of the local culture.

MILITARY POLICIES

In addition to the administrative, religious, cultural, and economic policies pursued by the French in their efforts to assimilate Roussillon, the military was used in the province in a variety of ways to promote the goal of assimilation. The military was first of all a mechanism by which French money was injected into Roussillon. Through supplying troops, the construction of fortresses, and other incidental expenses relating to the care of soldiers, the French spent a great deal of money in Roussillon. Another way in which the military was employed was in garrisoning the province against invasion or rebellion. A third use for the army was suppressing rebellious subjects. A final military policy used by the French in Roussillon was that to create favorable local sentiment by incorporating residents into the French army.

The single greatest military expense in the province was the massive fortifications built by the brilliant military engineer, Sébastien le Prestre de Vauban, to defend southeastern France against Spanish armies. The fortresses at Mont-Louis, Bellegarde, Perpignan, Villefranche, and Collioure were among the more important and extensive of the engineer's designs in Roussillon. Each of these edifices required many hundreds of thousands of livres and employed hundreds of men in their construction. For example, indemnifying residents of Perpignan for their lands cost the Sovereign Council more than 90,000 livres in 1683 alone. Other sums were also spent on military ends in the province, although generally far less grand in the quantity of money disbursed and number of men employed. These expenses ranged from creating a school to train officers of artillery, with the attendant ongoing expenses of food, lodging, and incidentals, to mundane cartage and miscellaneous expenses for infantry garrisons. Even the minor expenses provided a generous influx of money into the region. In July 1694, for example, over 127 livres were paid to several Roussillonnais just to bury the dead horses of the cavalry. The total of such miscellaneous expenses amounted to large sums of money for the local population.[65]

In addition to increasing the amount of money in circulation, Vauban's forts in particular also served as a symbol of French power in the province. These monumental fortresses dominated the landscape of Roussillon. The Cerdagne was overlooked by Mont-Louis, Villefranche controlled the Conflent, Bellegarde defended the approaches to the Vallespir, and Perpignan dominated the plain of Roussillon. These fortresses were more than mere symbols; they were exceedingly well-designed defenses against Spain. Due in part to these fortifications, the Spanish never succeeded in penetrating Roussillon in force, despite repeated attempts throughout the seventeenth century to do so. Thus, Vauban's works discouraged rebellion not only by their imposing appearance, but also by effectively precluding Spain from rendering any substantial assistance to rebels in the province.[66]

The French employed their military forces in Roussillon to discourage local rebellion by garrisoning the soldiers in towns and villages throughout the province under the command of the lieutenant-general. The number of troops in the region could be overwhelming, especially during wars with Spain and during times of discontent in Roussillon. In January 1672, for example, when France was at war with Spain and the Vallespir was in rebellion, well over 2,000 troops garrisoned the province. Arles, a town of less than 1,000 residents was required to house 100 troops, and Villefranche, an even smaller town, had to find beds for 300 troops. Perpignan, as the largest town in the province, was forced to accommodate almost 1,500 troops, over 10 percent of its size. Two years later, the total number of soldiers in Roussillon had increased to over 2,500, and the troops were redistributed to garrison potentially disloyal towns more effectively. The peak of garrisoning in Roussillon had come a few years earlier, however, when more than 6,000 troops were employed in the Vallespir alone to ensure its faithfulness after years of open rebellion. The presence of so many soldiers dramatically lessened the possibility of revolt and conspiracy. The troops could respond quickly to any situation that developed, and their presence made an early detection of treason in the towns likely.[67]

At times the French employed their forces against the Roussillonnais to restore obedience to the crown. The largest operation undertaken against the inhabitants was the military response to the Angelet revolt that occurred in the Vallespir and Conflent. Begun in 1663, this rebellion lasted two decades and forced the French to employ their troops to drive the rebels out of the province. The initial French response to the rebellion was negotiation, coupled with gradually escalating military operations. At the height of the actions against the rebels, the army in the Vallespir numbered over 6,000 troops. Despite the costs of waging war on the Roussillonnais and the long duration of the rebellion, the French army continued to hunt down the rebels, and ultimately triumphed. The Vallespir was not the only scene of open defiance to the French, although it is the most memorable. The town of Aiguatèbia, in the Carol valley, chafed under French rule. The citizens and soldiers were constantly at odds, and acts of violence were undertaken by both sides. Tensions mounted until "on 5 February 1675, Saint Agatha's Day, the French incinerated all of Aiguatèbia, even the rectory."[68] The Sovereign Council considered this just punishment for the town's violence against the troops, and the razing served to demonstrate that continued hostility toward the French and their soldiers would not be tolerated. There was no real alternative to French rule for the residents of Roussillon. The universally successful use of force in response to armed acts of defiance demonstrated to the Roussillonnais that the French would not be dislodged from their possession. Combined with the apparent impotence of the Spanish in the face of French power, the inhabitants of the province finally resigned themselves to French control of Roussillon.

Yet another military policy designed to assimilate the province was the incorporation of the Roussillonnais into the army. From the lowest ranks of the infantry through the lieutenant-generals of France, the inhabitants of Roussillon were represented at every level of the French army. The French raised both line units and militia units in the province, as well as incorporating Roussillonnais into other regiments of the French army. The Royal-Roussillon Infantry Regiment, raised primarily from among Catalan immigrants and the Roussillonnais, had existed since 1657, when it was created as the Catalan-Mazarin. In addition to serving as a unit that incorporated Roussillonnais soldiers, the regiment was commanded by at least two Catalans during the reign of Louis XIV, thus providing both officer and enlisted career possibilities to interested subjects. The Royal-Roussillon Cavalry Regiment was formed in 1665, and the Duke of Noailles's Cavalry Regiment in 1688. Both of these units also enrolled many Roussillonnais as enlisted men and officers. Don Josep d'Ardena, Don Francesc de Banyuls, Don Francesc de Blanes, Don Josep de Ximenés, and Don Narcis de Camprodon were among the many Catalan and Roussillonnais nobles who served as officers in the French infantry and cavalry during the reign of Louis XIV. The most famous of all Catalan officers in the reign of Louis XIV was Don Francesc de Calvo. He served in the king's armies in Franche-Comté, Hungary, Catalonia, and the Low Countries. So great was his reputation that Louis XIV once commented, "I have four men that the enemy respects: Montal, Chamilly, Calvo, and Dufay."[69] Calvo, and the many other Roussillonnais who served in the armies of Louis XIV, demonstrated to the Roussillonnais that material and honorific rewards were available to the Catalans.[70]

In addition to the creation of permanent line units in the regular army, militia units were also created in Roussillon. The first attempt at the creation of such units was begun in March 1689, when the intendant Ramon de Trobat offered to create a militia in the province, which he did the following year. The militia was composed of eleven companies of fifty men each, two from the artisans of Perpignan, four from the rest of the plain, two from the Vallespir, two from the Conflent, and one from the Cerdagne. The militia offered the local notables opportunities for service and honor, while incorporating the Roussillonnais into pro-French activities. This militia did help to assimilate politically the Roussillonnais, but offered little support to the process of acculturation. The militia were, for example, clothed in the Catalan style, "retaining a cap instead of a hat, espandrilles instead of shoes, and having bare legs."[71] The militia system was reorganized in 1691, when the Duke of Noailles ordered the city of Perpignan to form a thousand-man bourgeois militia, commanded by the first consul of the city. Among the leading citizens who served as officers in the various provincial militias were Josep d'Albert, Don Esteve de Blanes i de Planque, and Tomàs de Bordas i d'Amich.[72]

In addition to these regular militias, the Catalans possessed a tradition, in common with many lands, whereby a levy could be called out in times of danger. This levy, known as *somatens*, was also employed by the French when it suited their needs. In July 1697, for example, Trobat called 900 *somatens* for offensive operations against the Spanish in Catalonia. Despite protests that such a use of the force was illegal, the intendant raised the entire complement and had them at Barcelona by 29 July. Thus in military matters, as in other political matters, the French redesigned existing institutions to serve their purposes while retaining a traditional color.[73]

Military service, whether regular army or militia, served two important roles in the assimilation of Roussillon into the French political system. First, the army afforded opportunities for common men and the notables to achieve an increase in status, and perhaps even material gain. The intendant Ramon de Trobat recognized that men crave glory, and that the military was the best opportunity most had of achieving it. In a speech to the Sovereign Council of Roussillon, he stated, "I know, Sirs, that all the peoples of the earth, whatever different temperaments and dispositions they may possess, are perhaps in agreement on this point—that they attach the first degree of glory to the profession of arms."[74] Thus, by providing a means by which the Roussillonnais might obtain honor, the French bound those soldiers to the fountain of honors—the king of France.

Encouraging enrollment in the army provided another, perhaps more important, reinforcement for assimilation. Whether he fought willingly or not, a soldier hoped that his army was quickly victorious so that he might return to Roussillon. In hoping for the success of his army, he would be sharing the aspirations of the French nation and was thereby assimilated in some degree. Moreover, the enemies the Roussillonnais most frequently fought were the Spanish and Catalans. Thus the soldier from Roussillon would find himself working for the defeat of the Spanish Catalans. By so doing, he would forge a distinct self-identity for himself, one that coincided with the goals and values of the French government. Finally, for every soldier that marched off, an extended network of family and friends remained in the province. To speak, plot, or work against the French state in such a situation would be far worse than treason; it would implicitly undermine the safety of loved ones enrolled in the French army. To conspire with the Spanish would be associating with those devoted to killing one's relatives. In this manner, for every soldier conscripted for war, an uneasy allegiance to the king would be created among dozens of people. These new sympathies, however unwillingly developed, were not completely discarded upon the return of the soldiers, and so a basis of allegiance was evolved in Roussillon through military service.[75]

Through variously employing, garrisoning, repressing, and enrolling the province, the French succeeded in achieving some degree of political assimilation in Roussillon. At the same time, however, those same efforts created little, if any, acculturation among the inhabitants of the province. This pattern describes all of the French efforts in Roussillon in the reign of Louis XIV.

Chapter 3
Religious and Cultural Efforts

In addition to the administrative, economic, and military policies followed by the French in the francisation of Roussillon, efforts were also made to alter the religious and cultural traditions of the province. Unlike the former policies, which were designed primarily to ensure the political assimilation of the province, the religious and cultural innovations introduced by the French were generally created to effect acculturation among the Roussillonnais.

RELIGIOUS POLICIES

At the national and provincial levels, the French government recognized religion as of primary importance in the quest to incorporate Roussillon fully into the French political, economic, and social systems. Not only was the Roman Catholic church the strongest organization in the region in 1659, but it also tended to be the most anti-French in sentiment, especially at the level of the common priests, both regular and secular. In an effort to gain favor from and control over the church, the French attempted several different types of reforms. They sought to eliminate the foreign influences from Roussillon. Reorganization was also employed, with new superiors directing and controlling their subordinates in an effort to promote French policies. Fundamental changes were introduced into the administration of the church in the province, to better enable the French to exert their control.

Interdiction of Contact with Catalonia

The clergy of Roussillon at the annexation were, coming from the Iberian tradition, firm Tridentines, believing in the supremacy of the Pope in all matters, secular and ecclesiastical, international and intra-national. The French government was a proponent of Gallicanism, the idea that the king is pre-eminent in secular affairs and that the French church should be autonomous. The French viewed the Iberian ultramontane tenets with deep mistrust and wanted to eliminate them from the church in Roussillon. Since these were Iberian ideas, it was obvious that no further clergy should be introduced into Roussillon from the seminary in Barcelona, where Tridentine theology was taught and Catalan culture thrived. To this end, the Sovereign Council and the intendant repeatedly issued ordinances prohibiting priests who had studied in Barcelona or were natives of Spanish Catalonia from taking benefices in Roussillon. The advocate general, Ramon de Trobat, remarked on just such a prohibition in a letter to the king, commenting that "the laws of the land prohibit all persons from giving to foreigners or permitting them to hold pensions in the benefices of the region," and the king responded with complete agreement. The ban took some time to become completely effective, but eventually the Roussillonnais clergy were composed solely of French subjects.[76]

To combat reliance upon Catalonia, and thus reduce the power of Iberian ideas, the intendants and Louis XIV repeatedly prohibited clerical trips to Catalonia, whether the journeys were to attend seminary, to seek advice, or to obtain bulls. Before the annexation, most of the clergy of Roussillon had gone to Catalonia to be officially installed in their offices, seek advice from their colleagues, or request assistance from their fellow clerics. Every trip a cleric took to Catalonia served further to entrench the ideas that the French sought to eliminate. Thus, as early as December 1660, the French began restricting such travel. The Sovereign Council, in the name of the king, issued the following declaration:

[We] prohibit all beadle rectors, curates, priests, clerks and all other ecclesiastical persons from this time forward from daring or presuming to present, or to be presented with, or to allow to be published so much as one word, whether written in letters, placards, or any other form which are dispatched from any ecclesiastical court or by any official or ecclesiastical minister which does not have its ordinary residence in our obedience.[77]

This declaration was met with protests and resistance on the part of the Roussillonnais clergy, who recognized such directives as efforts to undermine the theological and cultural identity of the province. That the legislation of the Sovereign Council was unsuccessful is evident in the repeated injunctions that were made to the clergy to stop going to Spain. Louvois wrote the intendant Germain Michel Camus de Beaulieu in 1681, for example, ordering the latter to stop the clergy from going to Catalonia to take orders. In response, the intendant seized the revenue of the abbot of Arles, who was arrested for encouraging several priests to take their orders in Gerona. None of these efforts to ban contact were completely successful, and throughout the reign of Louis XIV the clergy continued to go to Catalonia to take orders, although in reduced numbers.[78]

Another related problem facing the French in attempting to assimilate the clergy of Roussillon was the fact that there were several religious institutions that were attached to houses or superiors in Spanish Catalonia. There was not, of course, anything unusual in the Old Regime about parishes and religious houses being attached to foreign dioceses. Several parishes in the Low Countries, for example, were supervised by Cambrai, Comminges-Mirepoix oversaw some Spanish parishes, the parishes of Tautavel and Vingrau in Roussillon itself had long been attached to Narbonne, and most of the Capcir had always been under Alet. Attachments to Spanish Catalonia were a problem in Roussillon, however, because they served as conduits for Tridentine theology and traditional Catalan political theory. Worried about the "dangerous consequences that the diversity of mores and sentiments could cause,"[79] Louis XIV sought to separate the religious institutions of Roussillon from Catalonia. In October 1660, for example, he ordered all the heads of the religious orders in France to assume authority over their houses in Roussillon because it was "important for Our service and for conserving [Roussillon] in Our obedience."[80] This order implicitly acknowledged the threat that Catalan influence might pose.

It took some time for the order to be implemented. The Religieux Carmes Deschausses de Perpignan were, for example, attached to a mother house in Aquitaine in March 1661, and the Capucins of Roussillon were attached to Toulouse the next month. That the purpose of these reorganizations was francisation is clear in a letter from Louis XIV to the Provincial des Jacobins d'Occitanie on 21 May 1666:

Judging it important to Our service to accustom, as much as is possible, the Catalan monks of the Frères Prêcheurs of Perpignan to the language and customs of the French clerics, We are writing this letter to you in order to inform you that Our intention is that henceforth when Catalan novices of that house in Perpignan have made their profession, you will send them to the other houses of your order situated in Our kingdom.[81]

The attaching of most of the convents and orders of Roussillon to houses in France served in the long term to achieve some of the goals that the French had set. The clergy eventually looked less and less to Catalonia for spiritual guidance and became theologically incorporated into the French church.[82]

The most important step taken by Louis XIV to reduce the dependence of Roussillon on Catalan ecclesiastical structures was establishment of a seminary in Perpignan. In order for a cleric to be able to serve the province properly, the priest would have to speak Catalan. However, most men with clerical aspirations who were able to speak Catalan did not understand French sufficiently to attend a seminary in France. Thus, despite all the French prohibitions to the contrary, the clergy of Roussillon had either to receive their training in Catalonia or remain woefully ignorant in many important spiritual matters. The French tried a variety of mechanisms to alleviate this problem and to eliminate the need for travel to Catalonia, including regular ecclesiastical visitations, teaching Catalan to the French clergy, training Roussillonnais clergy in the French language, and cultivating certain leading clerics for the pro-French cause. In 1682, a seminary was established in Narbonne where all the Roussillonnais clergy could be taught. Instruction was conducted in French, however, so the problem remained. The Catalan clergy of France needed to be trained in France using the Catalan language. Louis Habert de Montmor, a native of Paris and the bishop in Perpignan from 1682 until his death in 1695, pushed for the creation of a seminary to sever completely and finally all institutional ties between the churches of Roussillon and Catalonia. Louis XIV was informed by Montmor "that Ecclesiastical discipline in his diocese suffers terribly because there is no seminary where those who highly respect the Church may be formed in piety and the conduct of souls."[83] In 1690, Louis recognized the validity of Montmor's arguments and created a seminary in Perpignan, under the control of the Jesuits. Once training began in Perpignan, providing a pro-French instruction in Catalan to the clergy of the province, the clerical resistance to francisation gradually declined.[84]

The Bishop

One change in the religious patterns of the province that was brought about by the annexation, although not by any conscious decision, was the removal of the bishopric of Perpignan from the Catalan sphere of influence. Prior to 1640, when the revolt of the Catalans began, the bishopric of Perpignan had been considered a stopping point for clerics on the way to better positions elsewhere in Catalonia. This meant that the energies and ambitions of the bishop were focused upon the rest of the Catalan nation, and on how best to position himself for successions further south. From 1599 to 1641, there were, for example, twelve different bishops of Perpignan, with an average tenure of only three and a half years apiece. After the French annexed the province, the bishopric entered a new circle of influence. The bishop would no longer seek advancement in the Catalan clergy, but among the French. The result of this change was that the bishop was no longer focused upon the Catalan world, which was now useless to him professionally, but upon the Gallican church hierarchy. Being cut off from the Catalan clerical orbit also meant that bishops were much less likely to be Catalans themselves, but rather French. The first bishop of Perpignan after the annexation was an immigrant from Barcelona, Vicenç de Margarit, but all other bishops during the Old Regime were French. Thus, the highest levels of the Roussillonnais church fell under French influence rather early, and this influence slowly percolated throughout the whole of the church in Roussillon. Refocusing the attention of the bishop of Perpignan on Paris meant that the rest of the province's clerical hierarchy eventually became similarly focused.

A conscious ratification of this decision was made on 27 May 1678, when Louis XIV moved the diocese of Perpignan from the sufferance of Tarragona, in Catalonia, and placed it under the sufferance of the archbishop of Narbonne. The French justified this decision, which was made without the pope's consent, based upon two lines of reasoning. First, the French claimed that the diocese of Perpignan had been wrongly attached to Tarragona. In the sixteenth century, Clement VIII Aldobrandini had, at Spanish insistence, removed Perpignan from the sufferance of Narbonne and attached it to Tarragona. Thus, according to the French, the connection to Tarragona was an innovation, and tradition dictated that Perpignan belonged under the sufferance of Narbonne. (The bull of 1591 had, in fact, merely ratified what had been a long-established practice). The second justification used to defend the French rearrangement was based upon the Gallican liberties of the French church. Since the king was believed to have nearly complete control of the church in France, the realignment of the diocese of Perpignan needed no other justification than the king's will. The effect of this change was to formalize the shift in focus undertaken by the bishopric. In religious matters, Perpignan, and thus Roussillon, would look to France, not Spanish Catalonia, for guidance.[85]

Another minor step toward consolidation of French power in the Roussillonnais church was the recognition of Louis's right to nominate the bishop. The king of France had possessed the right to nominate bishops in his kingdom since the concordat between Francis I and Leo X Medici in 1515. Pope Alexander VII Chigi, who had a strong dislike for France, denied that this permission was automatically extended to all new French acquisitions. That is, Alexander held that Louis XIV had the right to name only those bishops whose dioceses had been under the control of Francis I and had remained French until Louis' reign. Any new territories, such as Roussillon, were not granted to Louis' nomination, but remained under papal control. This disagreement persisted throughout Alexander's life, keeping the diocese of Roussillon without a bishop. Clement IX Rospigliosi, Alexander's successor, reached a compromise with the French, allowing Louis the right to name the bishop of Perpignan in April 1668. Once Louis XIV was allowed to nominate bishops, he proceeded to select firmly pro-French individuals who implemented his policies of francisation among the clergy of the province.[86]

The bishop, selected by the king and responsible to the French government, was very active in promoting assimilation within the province of Roussillon. Frequent episcopal visits were undertaken to discover clergy who were opposed to the French, who were then often exiled. Louis Habert de Montmor, who held the bishopric from 1680 until his death in 1695, published his own book to assist the ecclesiastics of Roussillon. Among his advice were such injunctions as "hold in horror secular affairs" and commands to inquire in confession if a penitent "has carried out the ordinances of the Church and the king."[87] Jean Hervé Basan de Flamenville, bishop from 1695 until his death in 1721, held regular meetings every Saturday morning with all aspiring priests in order to train them and encourage them in obedience and loyalty. Since the clerics of Roussillon were the most opposed to the French presence, strong encouragement from the bishops of Perpignan was necessary to attenuate that hostility.[88]

Clerical Reorganization

Removing dissident clerics from the province, either by transfer or exile, was an approach to assimilation that was quite effective when properly employed. The most celebrated case of this type occurred even before the Peace of the Pyrenees. In 1652, Francesc de Sagarra exiled Anne-Marie Antigo, abbess of Sainte-Claire in Perpignan, from the province for her anti-French sentiment. Expulsions continued throughout the reign of Louis XIV, although with decreasing frequency as resistance lessened. In 1666, for example, Louvois had a priest named Sousias transferred to another diocese because "he is a man whose spirit is troubled and whose life is black with crimes."[89] Whether transferring or exiling those individuals who opposed the rule of the French in Roussillon, the government policy of banishment played a role in gradually silencing the vocal opposition of the lower clergy to the French presence.

Another tactic proposed by Louis XIV to control anti-French sentiment among the clergy was the reorganization of the religious hierarchies in the province, placing regular clergy under the control of the bishop and his delegates. It was thought that by placing the regular orders beneath the bishop's control, the latter could work to exclude Catalan sentiment from the monasteries and abbeys of Roussillon, and thereby increase pro-French sentiment throughout the province generally. The French planned to carry this reorganization to the most ancient and important monastic foundations in the province, hoping in this manner to reduce their resistance to francisation. To alter the structure of the elite of Roussillon's religious life so radically was, however, not practical, and plans that were too brazen were never implemented. In 1684, Louis proposed, for example, to transfer all the members of Saint-Michel de Cuxa, an ancient and prestigious house, to Perpignan and convert them into canons of the Cathedral of Saint-Jean. The monks protested vigorously against this reorganization, and it was never carried out. Although the French could not boldly attack the leading monasteries of Roussillon, throughout the reign of Louis XIV a variety of reorganization was carried out for monastic establishments of lesser importance. Pope Alexander VII Chigi attached the convent of Sainte-Claire in Perpignan to the *ordinaire* in 1664. This decision removed it from the jurisdiction of the Observants and gave the bishop much greater control over the convent. This led to a storm of protests, and it wasn't until 1667 that the issue was finally resolved in favor of the bishop. In another case, Louis XIV attached the abbey of Notre-Dame-la-Royale in Perpignan to the office of the bishop of Perpignan, with a great deal less controversy. By asserting the control of the bishop over the abbeys of Roussillon, and by ensuring that the king nominated that bishop, the French created another mechanism by which they assimilated the religious of the province and culled Catalan influence from the Church.[90]

Still another policy used by the French to help their customs and values become instilled in the population was the introduction of the French and Francophiles into the higher levels of church administration in Roussillon. It was hoped that by promoting only pro-French individuals into the upper clergy, those leaders would encourage francisation among the lower ranks of the church by example and exhortation. The men appointed as Bishop in the reign of Louis XIV were Vincenç de Margarit, Jean-Louis de Breuil, Jean-Baptiste d'Estampes, Louis Habert de Montmor, and Jean-Hervé Basan de Flamenville. The first of these men was a pro-French immigrant from Barcelona, and the other four were all from France. The important abbeys of Nôtre-Dame d'Arles-sur-Tech and Saint-Michel de Cuxa were given as rewards for loyalty to the loyal Catalans Pere Pont and Monpalau. In addition, at least two inquisitors in Roussillon were Frenchmen, brought in from outside the province to administer this position, as was at least one abbot of Saint-Martin-de-Canigou, Pierre Poudroux. Like most of the French religious reforms, these efforts were eventually considered successful, since the clergy came to accept French rule.[91]

Since Louis XIV was often at odds with the pope, regardless of who filled that office, the claims and struggles of the Roussillonnais clergy against the French were almost invariably supported by the Holy See. In order to reduce this foreign interference, the Sovereign Council repeatedly prohibited all instructions from outside France from being executed without the authorization of the intendant. Papal bulls had to be registered with the Sovereign Council before their publication or proclamation, and orders from the heads of orders were to be ignored unless specifically endorsed by the French *provinciaux* of the order. In this way the French hoped to minimize outside interference in their province and thus achieve the francisation of the clergy without opposition.[92]

In addition to all the preceding administrative reforms and reorganizations, the Sovereign Council was not reluctant to bring clergy to trial for crimes against the state. Dozens of clergy were tried during Louis' reign, generally for crimes that were directed against the French presence in the province. In 1667, for example, the rector of the parish church in Saint-Laurent de Cerdans was convicted for refusing to pay *droits de rente* due the king, which the priest claimed were illegal levies. Joan Pagès, a priest in Saint-Laurent de Cerdans, was tried and on 7 June 1672 was put to death for aiding the Angelets, who were rebels against the French government. Among the many other clerics also tried and convicted for complicity with the rebels were the abbot of Saint-Genis des Fontaines, both the abbot and the prior of Arles, and the rector at Prunet. Another abbot of Arles was imprisoned for taking orders from Gerona, in Catalonia, and encouraging others to do so as well. Dozens of lower clerics were brought to trial for smuggling salt and refusing to pay the various taxes due the French government. The goal of the Sovereign Council in dealing with the clergy was to eliminate the leaders of the resistance to French rule, after which, they believed, the remainder of the clerical population, even if unhappy, would acquiesce in accepting French policies and rule.[93]

One final method employed by the local elites and the Parisian authorities in attempting to dominate and control the attitudes among the religious of the province was the favor shown the Jesuit order in Roussillon. At the time of annexation, there were no Jesuits in Roussillon. When the order was introduced into the province, their members were drawn exclusively from France and thus had no Catalan sentiment in their order. Because the Jesuits were exclusively French and worked hard to further royal goals in the province, the order was highly favored by the Sovereign Council and the pro-French elite of Roussillon. They were granted lands and buildings by the king; Ramon de Trobat donated an altar piece that cost 1,050 livres, de Broca left them his home in his will, the governors chose their confessors from among the Jesuits, and they were granted the privilege of running a seminary and a college in Perpignan. These numerous gifts and favors served two purposes in assimilating the clergy. First, the Jesuits became wealthy due to the patronage of the government and leading citizens. This wealth, in turn, meant that they were a leading force among the clerics of Roussillon and were therefore influential in spreading pro-French sentiment. The largess of the French also served as an example, demonstrating to the other orders in Roussillon how to succeed, at least in material terms. Since the province was separated from Catalonia, few donations would come from the Principat to support pro-Catalan clergy. The government was persecuting and eliminating the anti-French citizens within Roussillon, so that group would also be unable to provide financial support to the church. Thus, if a religious establishment wished to receive gifts or income, its only real hope was to please the French and their supporters, since that group now controlled the financial resources of Roussillon.[94]

CULTURAL POLICIES

In addition to political reorganizations, the utilization of Catalan nobles, and the implementation of innovative religious policies to encourage indirectly obedience to the French crown and promote the adoption of French culture, the French also instituted policies designed to overtly encourage the acceptance of the French language, mores, laws, and attitudes. Both short-term plans, such as introducing Frenchmen into local government and demanding that the Perpignannais wear French clothes, and long-term schemes, such as creating schools and subtly favoring the French language, were combined in the French efforts to create new loyalties and identities in Roussillon.

Education

Among the most important of all French policies undertaken in Roussillon were the various attempts by the king and the Sovereign Council to create institutions for educating the Roussillonnais in the French language and culture. The first attempt to implement this policy took place at the post-secondary level. In 1661, Louis XIV created a Jesuit college in Perpignan to teach grammar, humanities, and rhetoric. The mission of this institution was to educate the sons of the middle class of the city. By shaping the values of the influential middle class through education, Louis XIV hoped to induce them to accept French culture and rule. Louvois addressed separate letters to the intendant and Sovereign Council in which he stressed the crown's desire for the Roussillonnais to accept a French education: "It would be a very good service to the King if you would insinuate to the Catalans that it would be very agreeable to His Majesty for them to send their children to the Jesuit College to be instructed."[95] To emphasize further the importance of this new institution, it was repeatedly favored over the extant secular university, which had existed since 1349 and was completely Catalan in curriculum, language, and outlook. In 1662, for example, the grammar classes at the university were transferred to the Jesuit College. Assigning the Jesuit College primacy in language studies was a clear sign that it was the favored school in the region and that the French language was the vehicle of social advancement. Ambitious students would, quite naturally, want to attend this prestigious institution, and would therefore learn French values while studying there.[96]

One major problem confronting the Jesuits in their attempts to provide a French-language secondary education in Roussillon was the fact that few students understood French, since it was never spoken in the homes of Perpignan. The Sovereign Council decided that attempting to assimilate the region would be far easier if French was widely understood; indeed, acculturation would be impossible otherwise. It was therefore decided that educating the children of Perpignan in French offered the best hope of implanting the language in the province. As children grew up speaking French, they would surely become increasingly aligned with French culture, values, and governance.

The first step toward the instruction of the young in Roussillon was taken in September 1663, when Louis XIV authorized the Benedictine order of Notre Dame de Beziers to establish a school in Perpignan. The goal of the school was explicitly aligned with acculturation. The teachers were "to apply themselves to everyone's satisfaction in the instruction of the young daughters of the bourgeois and inhabitants of that city [Perpignan] in respect, and to teach them morals and the French language."[97] This idea of providing an education for girls was forward-looking but was designed from practical considerations. In Roussillon, as in most of Europe, mothers served as the earliest and most important transmitters of culture for each succeeding generation. If the Roussillonnais were to be successfully acculturated, it would be necessary to implant French language and customs in a generation of women. Once they had accepted French values, those values would then be passed on to their children, thus achieving French long-term goals. Since Perpignan was the cultural and political center of the province, having the Benedictine nuns educate the girls of the leading families of Perpignan clearly demonstrated the French long-term commitment to the acculturation of Roussillon.[98]

The educational efforts undertaken by the Benedictines were, from the French point of view, relatively successful but limited in scope. One small convent school teaching girls was ultimately restricted in how much it could accomplish. The successes of the Benedictines, coupled with the great need that still existed in Perpignan, prompted a proposal from the intendant, Étienne Carlier. Late in 1671 he wrote to Louvois, suggesting that the consuls of Perpignan be required to establish schools to teach their children. Among the required topics of instruction would be, of course, the French language. Indeed, the teaching of French was clearly the primary goal of the schools, as was acknowledged in Louvois's response to the idea: "[T]he proposal you made to require the consuls of Perpignan to establish some lower schools to teach the French language to the children has been approved by His Majesty, and I am sending you a letter to encourage this goal."[99] Louvois was unconcerned about the other courses of instruction, but he wanted to ensure that French was taught in order to strengthen loyalty to the government. Carlier was encouraged by the response from Paris, and early in 1672 the Sovereign Council, under his direction, required all the villages in Roussillon to create these local schools and to provide a means for funding them. The issue of funding came to be the most pressing concern in the establishment of the schools. Neither Paris nor the Sovereign Council would fund the local schools. Leaving the entire financial burden upon the small villages of the province meant that few were ever created. In fact, only four were established under this ordinance—one in Perpignan and three in other parts of the province. The small number of schools established was disappointing, but it still remains that four more centers for the acculturation of the young had been created. These educational efforts of 1671 and 1672 brought the French a bit closer to their ultimate goal of assimilating the Roussillonnais into the French state and nation.[100]

The next step in the educational endeavors undertaken by the Sovereign Council in Roussillon was begun in 1682, with laws demanding the creation of free schools. The intendant Ramon de Trobat had, in 1681, proposed to Louis XIV that each town in Roussillon be compelled to create a primary school to teach its children French, a plan similar to Carlier's earlier proposal. To ensure that the whole population, regardless of social or economic position, experienced the acculturating effects of this effort, the schools were to be compulsory and without cost to the student, and were to be funded by each town. It was in making the schools obligatory and free that Trobat differed from Carlier's outline. The government in Paris believed this to be a good proposal, and commanded Trobat: "[T]o enjoin the consuls of this very faithful town of Perpignan and of the others of the province to establish royal schools in each of these towns in order to teach the children the French language, Christian doctrine, reading, writing, arithmetic, and the principles of the Latin language."[101] Louis XIV was explicit in identifying these schools as mechanisms to inculcate loyalty and engender francisation. He wrote to the Sovereign Council that the purpose of these institutions was to have children grow up in "the fear of God, obedience to their prince, submission to the laws, respect for the magistrates, love for their country, and the practice of honest and virtuous actions."[102] Thus the purpose of educating the Roussillonnais was to mold good citizens; literacy and knowledge were simply means to that end, but not considered important in themselves. The grand plan of a free and compulsory education being provided in every town in Roussillon fell almost completely short in reality. Perpignan, as the capital of the province, did create a school in compliance with Trobat's plan, but only under his constant prodding and with money supplied by the Sovereign Council. No other town acted upon the ordinance in the reign of Louis XIV, despite repeated prodding from the Sovereign Council and intendants.[103]

Despite the limited implementation of educational reforms at the primary level in Roussillon, these schools were important mechanisms of assimilation in the province. They slowly diffused the French language into Perpignan, especially among the wealthier classes. As the capital gradually evolved a dual cultural identity, the rest of the province was carried along with, although always slightly behind, the capital. To the very limited extent that acculturation was achieved in the Old Regime, the school systems played a great role in that success.

Another important step in acculturating the Roussillonnais was the establishment of a mechanism by which French law could be taught to aspiring jurists. The Roussillonnais had, since the annexation, continued to teach and study the Catalan constitutions and laws at the University of Perpignan. This was partly due to the fact that the Catalan-speaking professors knew no other juridical traditions and partly to the fact that no French jurists possessed the language capabilities to teach in Perpignan. The university's emphasis on Catalan law and customs was also due in part to the university's culturally conservative outlook.

As the French language became more widely known in Perpignan, it became possible to begin French legal instruction. In 1684, the first professor of French law in Perpignan, Jean-Jacques Fornier, was appointed. Several aspects of his appointment indicate the importance placed upon this position by both the Sovereign Council and Louis XIV.

First, Fornier and his successors earned 800 livres per year to teach French law in Perpignan. The university professors of canon and civil law earned, by contrast, only 200 livres apiece each year. By paying him such a high wage, the government emphasized the importance of the professor of French law and of his subject. To further stress his importance, Fornier was not attached to the university, which was not favored by the Sovereign Council. Instead, the professor of French law taught his subject at the Hôtel de Ville until at least 1702. By establishing the professor in such an accessible site, the government ensured that many jurists could attend his lectures. Still another special distinction granted to the professor of French law in Perpignan was the limited nature of his charge. Most of those who taught French law in France were required to teach all the ordinances of Louis XIV and those of his predecessors, their reconciliation with one another, the usages of fiefs and other generalities, and the jurisprudence of *Parlements*. In Perpignan, by contrast, the professor had only to teach the French law contained in the ordinance of April 1667. A final mark of distinction is seen in the fact that four of the six professors during the reign of Louis XIV sat on the Sovereign Council as full councillors.

Despite these many advantages and distinctions, the government had a difficult time establishing a solid program of French law. Fornier himself held the job only a short time, and then was succeeded by a Perpignannais lawyer, Vaguer. That a Catalan with poor training in both the French language and French law was given this position is a measure of the difficulties confronting the government in filling this position. Vaguer was himself succeeded by another Catalan, Rafel de Ortega i Closells, who held the position for one year. Jacques Sicre, from Montpellier, then took the position for two years. After he resigned in 1694, the intendant was unable to find any replacement for four years, during which time the post remained vacant. Fesquet then came from Toulouse to accept the position; his tenure marks the point at which the position became a valuable tool for assimilation. He did a good job, but died in 1702, after only four years. He was followed by Pere Collares for six years, and then Louis Fornier occupied the post from 1708 to 1752. Once the position became stabilized in the late 1690s, the professor of French law became important in the acculturation of the Perpignannais. To encourage further the study of French law, the Sovereign Council offered cash rewards to those who earned a degree. Since studying French law was a mechanism to obtain advancement and favors in society, it became more commonly studied and gradually supplanted the Catalan *Usatges* in the province as the conceptual basis of rights and resistance. In this manner, the professor of French law became an important character in the acculturation of Roussillon.[104]

To control further the educational processes in Roussillon, the Sovereign Council repeatedly forbade all persons from studying abroad. Unless one obtained explicit permission from the Sovereign Council, which was difficult to do, it was illegal to study at any university outside France. Before 1659, it had been common for young men to travel to Barcelona and study at the university there. That school, however, emphasized the *Usatges* and traditional Catalan laws and customs. After studying these ideas for some years, the impressionable young Roussillonnais might return to the province in an effort to defend the constitutions against French encroachment. After several such incidents, the French issued their injunction against foreign studies, intending to stanch the flow of young scholars to Barcelona and redirect them to Perpignan or Narbonne. The plan was never completely effective but did serve to reduce the number of students going to Barcelona, and therefore diminished the impact of Catalan higher education on Roussillon.[105]

Linguistic Policies

One policy encouraged by the French in their plan for linguistic assimilation was the encouragement of the local clergy to deliver their sermons in French. Religion was extremely important to the Roussillonnais, and if the church endorsed the French language, that would be an important advantage for the government in the quest for acculturation. The use of the French language was, however, unknown outside Perpignan, and rare even within the city throughout the whole reign of Louis XIV. One significant reason that the clergy would not use French in conducting Mass was that the secular clergy of Roussillon did not speak French, and thus could not use it to lead a Mass. Further, sincere priests who wished to provide a meaningful Mass for their parishioners had to preach in Catalan, since most worshipers did not understand French. Finally, many of the clergy who were natives of Roussillon quite simply did not like the French. Indeed, the indigenous clergy were one of the most strident opponents of French government in the reign of Louis XIV, and therefore they would not, even if they could, employ French in their ecclesiastical offices. Even in the most prosperous and pro-French quarter of the capital, the parish of Saint-Jean, it was rare to hear services in French. It was not, for example, until 1676 that the first sermon in French was given at the Cathedral of Saint-Jean in Perpignan, and it remained uncommon enough to merit comment throughout the reign of Louis XIV. The use of French by the clergy would have provided a major endorsement for acculturation, but it simply did not occur in the reign of Louis XIV.[106]

Rather than simply recommending or encouraging the study of the French language, or relying upon the good offices of the Church, the king began to insist upon the knowledge and use of French in a variety of endeavors. Knowledge of French became a requirement for graduation from the University of Perpignan, for example. This decision was made not only to spread the French language among the educated classes but also to acculturate the university itself, which was a bulwark of Catalan conservatism. Language studies improved throughout the last four decades of the seventeenth century. Immediately after the annexation of Roussillon, most students received a mark of "doesn't understand" or "mediocre understanding" on their French exams. By the 1690s, "very good" became the most common grade on language exams. The French policy did, obviously, have an influence on shaping the linguistic patterns of the intellectual elite of the province. Once the elite spoke French, they could understand French culture and laws, which would then make possible the acceptance of those laws. Gradually assimilating the elite of Roussillon led the way for the rest of the province to accept the French domination of the province.[107]

In addition to requiring all students at the university to be proficient in French, the French in 1682 placed further restrictions on the population of Roussillon as a whole.

[U]nless they demonstrate by their certificates that they speak, understand, and write the French language sufficiently, no one will be admitted to charges nor receive any degree of honour, neither degrees from the rectors of the university of that town [Perpignan], nor from college of the notaries, procurers, surgeons, apothecaries, or others, nor will any of the other [guilds] of other arts and crafts receive them into their colleges and bodies.[108]

Thus, according to the letter of the law, no good job in the province was available to those who refused to learn French. The law was rarely enforced in the reign of Louis XIV. In some cases, such as the university, French was indeed a prerequisite for matriculation. Certain government positions also required a minimal comprehension of French, at least in theory. In confirming Pere Joan Guardia as archdeacon of the Conflent, the intendant noted that the priest "understands and speaks sufficient French,"[109] although there were other, more important, considerations in his appointment. In most cases, however, the little linguistic acculturation that did occur was achieved by informal means, and not by laws such as these.[110]

As Louis XIV's reign progressed and French control of Roussillon became more secure, the government moved to completely proscribe Catalan in public life. Despite the many educational, religious, legislative, and cultural efforts of the French to introduce their language into common use in the province, it was still considered an alien language. Catalan continued to be employed in private life and public records. Shopkeepers' accounts, ecclesiastical records, notarial registers. judicial proceedings, tax settlements, and even much of the business of the Sovereign Council continued to be recorded and conducted solely in Catalan until 1676. Believing that acculturation would not progress until the Roussillonnais accepted the French language, Louis XIV saw that no real progress was being made toward the integration of French into common life. Therefore, on 8 February 1700, he decreed that "all the procedures and public acts which will be made in these lands [Roussillon] will be couched in the French language."[111] In explaining his reasoning, the king said that using Catalan was "distasteful and is in any event contrary to Our Authority, the honour of the French nation, and even the inclination of the inhabitants of these lands."[112] Despite his great optimism that the Roussillonnais wanted to be delivered from their native tongue, Louis was to be disappointed with the impact of his Act. Very little change occurred due to this edict, as evidenced by the fact that variations on this Act were reissued throughout the reign. Paris continued to receive reports from Perpignan that little compliance was forthcoming, and the overwhelming portion of everyday business in the province continued to be conducted in Catalan.[113]

The evolution of the role of the French language in Roussillon is a good microcosm of the general pattern of assimilation established by the French in Roussillon. To disseminate the knowledge of their language, the French government began with a small college that was supposedly designed to supplement the existing Catalan university but was in fact a tool to undermine the older institution. Gradually, other educational reforms were added that first offered the possibility of learning the French language, and later demanded knowledge of it. In the same way, the general pattern of assimilation established by the French was one of subverting and co-opting local institutions, insinuating French laws, practices, and values into the region, and only after several decades demanding that the population embrace those innovations.

Another type of cultural policy practiced by France to further assimilation was the introduction of Frenchmen from outside the province into the administration of Roussillon. The hereditary governors of the province, the Dukes of Noailles, were, for example, natives of the region near Paris. The Noailles were, however, rarely in Roussillon and had little to do with the daily administration of the province. More important were the lieutenants general, intendants, and members of the Sovereign Council, positions that also had many Frenchmen among their ranks. The five lieutenant governors who served under Louis XIV, de Chouppes, Châtillon, Chazeron, Quinson, and Fimarcon, were all native Frenchmen from beyond the borders of Roussillon. Roussillon had seven intendants during the reign of Louis XIV, and all of those men were from outside the province, although Ramon de Trobat was a Catalan from Barcelona. The Sovereign Council during Louis's reign embraced twenty-eight councillors. Of those, at least seven were completely non-Catalan subjects, and another eight were Catalan émigrés. Only one member of the Sovereign

Council came from a family that is known to have lived in Roussillon before the Peace of the Pyrenees. The goal of the French in introducing these outsiders into Roussillon was to minimize the influence of Catalan customs and laws by diluting them with the inclusion of French values, perspectives, and legal structures.

The introduction of Frenchmen into Roussillon was of limited effectiveness over the short term in changing the cultural or legal systems of Roussillon. Even though many of them were immigrants, twenty-one members of the Sovereign Council were Catalan by birth and education. Moreover, the lower levels of the provincial administration were filled almost exclusively with Catalans, either native Roussillonnais or immigrants. To work effectively in Roussillon, an official would have to understand Catalan. Very few French would have such proficiency, for Catalan was, then as now, a relatively little-known language of no great importance in international economics or politics. Further, learning that language just to obtain a minor position in a culturally alien provincial administration would be extremely unappealing to most Frenchmen. Thus only the Roussillonnais or Catalan immigrants would possess both the qualifications and desire to serve in Roussillon, and so it is not surprising that the lower levels of government in Roussillon were staffed almost exclusively with Catalans. Since the entire lower structures of the legal and administrative systems were staffed by men with Catalan backgrounds, those systems were run almost exclusively by standards derived from Catalan practices. Even the court of last resort, the Sovereign Council, was staffed primarily by Catalans who lacked any training in French law. There were at least twelve trained jurists on the Sovereign Council, but ten of them received their training in Catalan Law in Barcelona or Perpignan. And, of the other sixteen members of the Sovereign Council, eleven were Catalan. Thus the judicial background of the majority of the Sovereign Council was in Catalan law and practice. Their decisions would, in most cases, be based on common Catalan practices. Indeed, Catalan traditions became so ingrained in Roussillon, despite French efforts to eradicate them, that understanding Catalan law became virtually a prerequisite for an efficient councillor. Intendant Ramon de Trobat, for example, when asked to recommend a new councillor following the death of Josep de Martí in 1689, could recommend no one: "The Frenchmen who aspire to this charge possess neither the knowledge nor experience of the laws of this region, nor of the written laws, which I believe are necessary to fill the post well."[114] The Secretary of War did work actively to introduce non-Catalan Frenchmen into the upper levels of the administration of Roussillon throughout the reign of Louis XIV. These men did have some small successes in encouraging the adoption of French law, but most French successes would be found elsewhere.

The French pursued their goal of acculturation in a variety of ways, one of which was attempting to eliminate Catalan festivals and observances and replace them with French ones. A central point of Catalan cultural identity in the seventeenth century was the feast of Saint George, patron saint of Catalonia, which fell on 23 April. The French sought to move the Roussillonnais away from the observance of this festival, since it reinforced the sense of a common cultural identity on both sides of the border. As early as 1667 the French began to encourage the celebration of the feast of Saint Louis, which occurred on 25 August, as a substitute for that of Saint George. Despite annual observances by the Sovereign Council and the bishop of Perpignan, the festival did not become an important element of the Roussillonnais religious calendar. In a similar manner, other festivals and religious observances were prohibited when they reinforced cultural ties with Catalonia. In March 1672, for example, the Sovereign Council prohibited the clerics of Perpignan from conducting religious services timed to coincide with Masses in the Principat, all of which were designed to beseech God to end terrible flooding throughout Spanish and French Catalonia. Later, in 1691, intendant Ramon de Trobat requested that Louvois put an end to an annual festival in Roussillon that was celebrated throughout Catalonia. Like so many other French reforms, these attempts to regulate the cultural holidays of the Roussillonnais accomplished little toward the goal of acculturating the province.[115]

Immediately after the annexation, Louis XIV ordered the residents of Perpignan to cease wearing Catalan fashions and to begin dressing in the French manner. Louis explicitly stated that since the Perpignannais were residents of the provincial capital, they should set the example of acculturation for the rest of Roussillon. Whether this would have been an effective mechanism of acculturation is moot, since this edict, like many aimed at forced adoption of French culture, remained a dead letter despite repeated proclamations.[116]

Among the most important mechanisms for inducing the Catalans to accept French rule in the province were the repeated reassurances offered that their privileges, traditions, laws, and usages would be respected. This pledge was enshrined in Article 55 of the Treaty of the Pyrenees: "[A]ll the Catalans and other inhabitants of the province will remain or be re-established in the possession and peaceful enjoyment of all their goods, honours, dignities, privileges, franchises, rights, exemptions, constitutions, and liberties."[117]

After signing this treaty in 1659, Louis repeatedly issued public proclamations and private instructions which stressed the importance of Catalan traditions. Relations with the church, for example, should be "of the same sort and manner that have been previously practiced by the Royal Council of Catalonia when the Counties of Roussillon and the Conflent were under the power of the Catholic King without changing anything or innovating for any reason or under any pretext whatsoever."[118] Two years later, the injunction to observe local custom in ecclesiastical relations was repeated:

"[T]he local usages and constitutions must be punctually observed."[119] Louis did not, however, limit these directives to merely religious questions, but extended them to all legal issues: "The intention of His Majesty is that following the Constitutions of Catalonia and local usages," the Sovereign Council was to decide the issues before them.[120] Throughout the reign of Louis XIV, such assurances were repeatedly offered the Roussillonnais. It appears, however, that these assurances were offered solely to placate the Catalans, and not because the king intended to honor his promises. Almost every communication in which Paris confirmed the precedence of local customs contained a proviso that local customs should be honored only when those customs agreed with French law or when French law was silent on an issue.[121]

Joined to these rather insincere assurances of good faith was the implementation of Catalan law in fact. For much of Louis XIV's reign, most provincial officers were Catalans with little experience in French judicial practices. Thus, most people's legal experiences were within the Catalan tradition. Despite the insincerity of the government's promises to respect Catalan law, much of that legal tradition did linger for decades in Roussillon. The promises of Louis XIV, combined with the gradual displacement of Catalan legal traditions, helped to make French rule palatable to many of the Roussillonnais. [122]

Another institution created by the French government in an effort to acculturate the Roussillonnais was the Hôpital Général. This new hospital was created in 1686, and joined to the existing Hôpital de la Miséricorde, a much older institution. The new creation was designed to administer poor relief and take care of the orphans in the city of Perpignan. This was an attempt to connect the idea of charity with the French government, which would then cause the French to be implicitly associated with positive Christian virtues, thus gaining the French more respect among the Roussillonnais.[123]

In February 1663, Louis XIV annulled all prejudicial distinctions between the French and Roussillonnais throughout the province. After Spain reacquired Roussillon in 1493, a series of laws had been issued that prohibited the French and their descendants from holding any municipal offices in the province. After the Peace of the Pyrenees in 1659, the Roussillonnais pointed to these laws to deny attempts by Frenchmen to hold municipal offices. Indeed, any native Catalan who seemed too pro-French might be barred as being of French extraction. If the French were ever to be accepted in Roussillon, all legal barriers to equality had to be removed. The inhabitants were slow to accept this imposed equality and continued to find new legal bases for discrimination. As late as 1702, the king had to issue edicts stating that all grants of nobility and honor were equal throughout Roussillon, regardless of the language in which they were written. By forcing the Roussillonnais to accept the French as political equals, the government planted the seeds of social and cultural acceptance as well.[124]

These cultural policies constituted the most direct assaults the French undertook against the Catalan identity in Roussillon. Attempting to supplant the language by teaching French, trying to introduce new festivals, forcing the acceptance of Frenchmen in government offices, and eventually proscribing the Catalan costume and language – these were the policies of the French in their overt campaign of cultural assimilation in the province. While some of these policies may have contributed to the success of the French in politically assimilating the province, they played very little role in acculturating the province, as evidenced by the fact that Roussillon retained a distinctly Catalan identity throughout the old regime.

Political innovation and alterations of traditional institutions, employment of the Catalan elite, religious re-structuring, cultural imperialism, economic advantages, and various military displays—these were the methods the French employed in their efforts to achieve their two goals in Roussillon. The first goal, political assimilation, was reached by the French due to the interaction of these various techniques. The other goal, acculturation, was never achieved in any significant degree during the reign of Louis XIV. To explain the reasons for the successes and failures the French experienced in Roussillon, the variety of motivations and methods of resistance to the French must first be examined.

Chapter 4
Resistance

MOTIVATIONS FOR RESISTANCE

Policies designed to bring Roussillon within the economic, social, political, legal, and religious orbit of France were generally unpopular with the native Roussillonnais and met with resistance. The inhabitants of the province justified this resistance in a variety of ways. They used the political argument that the government was violating the *Usatges* and the royal promises to respect them. The overt attempts by the French government to acculturate the province led to arguments that defense of the Catalan cultural heritage justified resistance to government directives. French religious policies led the Roussillonnais to view their new masters as poor Christians, which again excused disobedience. Certain individuals suffered economically from the French presence in Roussillon and were therefore justified in their dissatisfaction. The Spanish government and residents of the Principat also provided money, arms, and refuge to those who resisted the central government in the province. In addition to these reasons for resistance, the Roussillonnais possessed a long tradition of resistance to authorities espousing centralization and an intense hatred for the French.

Political

One of the most important justifications for resisting Louis XIV's actions in Roussillon was a perception by the Roussillonnais that traditional Catalan rights were being violated by French policies. Many of the institutions introduced by the French government into the province were viewed by the inhabitants as clear usurpations of the traditional *Usatges* of Catalonia. According to the Constitutions of Catalonia, no new taxes could be levied upon Roussillon nor could any new political institutions be created without the explicit approval of the *Corts* of Roussillon, a representative body. Because the *Corts* was not called, the legitimacy of the French was denied by many Roussillonnais, especially those outside Perpignan and its environs.

The foremost example of Roussillonnais hostility toward French fiscal and political reforms in the province was the reaction against a salt tax, the *gabelle*, established in November 1661. The Constitutions of Catalonia set out a process by which new taxes could be introduced; this process involved the *Corts* of Roussillon and protracted negotiations between crown and subjects. Moreover, clear evidence that the *gabelle* was patently illegal could be found in the *Usatges*, which had explicitly forbidden such taxes on salt since at least 1283.[125] The apparent French contempt for the rights of the Catalans, especially in the matter of the *gabelle*, led to open revolt in 1663. This rebellion, the revolt of the Angelets, involved thousands of people and lasted for over fifteen years, a testimony to the depth of Roussillonnais feeling on the issue. Indeed, even leading Frenchmen recognized that the *gabelle* was becoming a major stumbling block to the assimilation of the province. On 24 April 1669, Vauban wrote to Louvois that "it remains true that no one could invent a better means to make French domination odious and execrable to foreigners than in establishing the *gabelle* in Roussillon."[126] The Catalans, more than simply rejecting the fiscal burdens created by new French taxes and bureaucracies, were profoundly offended by the illegal methods by which the French imposed these innovations.

In addition to the illegal nature of taxes, the residents of Roussillon pointed to many other French violations of the Consitutions of Catalonia. Non-Catalans could not, for example, hold clerical offices anywhere in Catalonia. Despite this prohibition, the king encouraged native Frenchmen to serve in the church in Roussillon. The *Usatges* had a 400-year-old ban on foreigners holding any governmental office in Catalonia. This law was repeatedly violated by the Sovereign Council and Louis XIV in their efforts to control the province.[127]

The French used various arguments to justify their actions in Roussillon. One common defense popular among the pro-French Catalans was the assertion that the Sovereign Council was the functional equivalent of the *Corts*, and thus any laws or levies registered by the Sovereign Council were as valid as those approved by a *Corts*. Many Roussillonnais rejected this view by pointing out that the Sovereign Council was not a new version of the old *Corts*, but was rather the image of the old Royal Council of Perpignan. In fact, many of the members of the old body had been transferred to the new. The Royal Council of Perpignan was an institution completely distinct from the *Corts*, and thus its successor could have no claim to the role of the *Corts*. Therefore, the Sovereign Council was not the *Corts*, which still had to be called and addressed by the monarch if new levies or institutions, including the Sovereign Council, were to be legal.[128]

Another argument used by the French government to legitimize the imposition of new taxes and bureaucracies was the assertion that Roussillon was not Catalan at all, but French. It had been wrongly wrenched from the French in 878, when Guifredo the Hairy, Count of Barcelona, seized the province. The Treaty of Bayonne of 1462 had provided Louis XI the right to reoccupy Perpignan and Collioure, and that king then seized all of Roussillon by right of conquest and heredity. The French were again wronged in 1493, when the Aragonese re-took the province. The cession of Roussillon to the French in 1659 was only the redress of centuries of wrongs—heredity, conquest, and natural frontiers all dictating that Roussillon had always rightfully belonged to France. Thus, any appeals to Catalan law by the Roussillonnais were void, because that law had been an illegal imposition, and the French monarch had every moral and legal right to ignore it. The Roussillonnais pointed out, in turn, that Charles the Bald first separated Languedoc and Roussillon in 865, before Guifredo moved in. Moreover, all hereditary claims to Roussillon had been explicitly abandoned in 1258, when the French kings gave up their claims on the Carolingian Spanish marches. The return of the province to Aragon in 1493 was also legitimized by a French treaty, and followed the illegal French seizure of 1462. Any claims the French kings ever had to Roussillon they had repeatedly repudiated, and so were in no position to claim special rights in legal matters.[129]

Other French apologists, especially trained French jurists, claimed that the approval by the *Corts* was granted implicitly when the French were invited to assist the Catalan rebellion in 1640. The French Catalans, however, pointed out that in the Accords of Péronne, Louis XIII had explicitly agreed to observe all the usages and customs of the Constitution of Catalonia, specifically including the rights of the *Corts*. Further, Article 55 of the Peace of the Pyrenees replaced any implicit agreement that might have existed between France and the Catalan people with an explicit one: "All the Catalans and other inhabitants of the province will remain or be re-established in the possession and peaceful enjoyment of all their goods, honours, dignities, privileges, franchises, rights, exemptions, constitutions, and liberties."[130] To reinforce further the idea that the French would respect the Constitution of the Catalans, Louis XIV had issued an edict at Montpellier on 6 January 1660, which promised to maintain all the privileges of Roussillon, then newly acquired. The traditional rights of the Catalans to a *Corts* had clearly not been sacrificed, and thus any innovations were to be considered illegal until such time as a *Corts* was called.[131]

Finally, some people in Paris and Perpignan simply asserted that the province was conquered in war, and thus old practices and customs were swept aside in victory, permitting Louis XIV to treat his new subjects in any manner he chose. These claims were similarly referred to the Treaty of Péronne and the Peace of the Pyrenees. The Catalans had invited Louis XIII to be their ruler; he did not conquer them. And, even if the French were victorious conquerors, their monarchs had still bound themselves to respect traditional Catalan usages in several edicts. Whether Roussillon was conquered or not was irrelevant to the Roussillonnais. Two kings had agreed to respect their constitutions, and the monarch was now failing to abide by his promises.

Many Roussillonnais, then, felt that their traditional political rights were being violated. This in turn led some inhabitants to resist the French government in Roussillon. Those who took up arms to resist the French, together with those who plotted to do so, were usually motivated by a desire to secure the traditional rights they had long enjoyed and now saw threatened. Active resistance to France often involved co-operation with and plotting in favor of Spain. This was necessary because resistance to France was clearly an overwhelming task, and there was no hope of success without foreign assistance. Spanish promises of assistance were accompanied by pledges to observe faithfully the *Usatges*. Even those inhabitants who did not react violently to the French presence often justified their resistance in terms of Catalan political liberties. When the French provincial intendant imposed a new method for the election of town consuls or a new tax was introduced, for example, the residents of many towns signed petitions decrying such innovations as illegal and a violation of traditional rights. The French attempts at imposing a new legal and political system in Roussillon, while ultimately successful in achieving political assimilation, also provided the basis for active and passive resistance to those reforms.[132]

Cultural

In addition to the defense of political traditions, the Roussillonnais also justified resistance to assimilation on the grounds of preserving their cultural and linguistic heritage. The French were trying to eradicate the Catalan culture in Roussillon and were quite explicit in their goals. One example frequently cited by the Roussillonnais as an assault on their cultural heritage was the mistreatment by the French of the faculty and students of the University of Perpignan. The university served as a center of traditional Catalan values in the province, and so the French sought either to reform or to eliminate it. Among the various indignities the school suffered were the creation of the new professor of French law as an independent scholar, the establishment of the Jesuit college, and repeated prosecutions of university faculty by the government and French sympathizers. The ultimate indignity was the banishment of the university faculty from their quarters, which were then used to house the mint. As a result of this expulsion, the school suffered severely, struggling to find new chambers, and the faculty of medicine had to be completely disbanded for lack of space. Many Roussillonnais believed that all of these troubles were visited upon the university because it refused to serve as an agent of assimilation in the province, a view that was essentially correct.[133]

The observations of Vauban, the celebrated military engineer, provide a better example of French cultural imperialism. He observed one traditional Catalan winter festival during a visit to the province, and labeled the celebration a "Sabat." To compare, even implicitly, such a profoundly Catholic people as the Roussillonnais to witches and devil-worshippers was one of the most vile insults possible. The French were attempting to eradicate Catalan culture and populate the province with Frenchmen. In the face of such open hostility to their way of life, the Roussillonnais felt justified in rejecting French attempts to impose new values and language in the province.[134]

Religious

Another type of justification for resistance to the French presence in Roussillon was the practice of religion. There existed basic differences between the Roussillonnais and their French masters in theology and church organization. The former were, since the days of Philip II, more ultramontane than the French in their beliefs. The ultramontanes believed that God, represented by the pope, represented the ultimate authority to whom man must answer. The dictates of God, and therefore those of the pope, must have precedence over all other commitments or obligations, whether international or intranational. This conception of religious hierarchy stood in direct contrast to the French views on the Gallican liberties of the church. The French would agree that the dictates of God demand precedence over all other commitments man may have. However, they considered the monarch as God's anointed representative, who acts as an intermediary for his subjects. Therefore, a man's duty is to follow the will of his prince, and thereby obey God. A chasm thus existed between France and its newly acquired province in theological explanations of religious structures and civic obligations.

This ultramontane-Gallican split was particularly important in shaping both groups' views of one another. The French monarchy had long asserted the rights of the Gallican church and worked to gain freedom from papal influence. The views of the Catalan church undermined the political and religious power that the kings had struggled to create. Ultramontane views were therefore a challenge not only to the ecclesiastical hierarchy of France, but to the existing political structures as well. The Roussillonnais, for their part, felt themselves to be far better Roman Catholics than the French, who seemed to reject papal supremacy and tolerate heresy. That the French rejected the primacy of the Pope was, to the ultramontanist Roussillonnais, *prima facie* evidence that the French rejected the will of God. Having rejected God's sovereignty, the French government had destroyed the obligations that bound subject to monarch. Moreover, it was the duty of good Christians to struggle against heresy, and thus the Roussillonnais were not only justified, but obligated, to resist the French.

The abhorrence of Protestantism was another compelling justification for resistance to French. The inhabitants of Roussillon blamed the French for introducing heretics into the province through army and governmental service, a problem that had never existed before the French acquisition. The French were well aware that the Roussillonnais were stridently opposed to heresy. The Catalan opposition to heresy was so strong that it was enshrined as the first law of the *Usatges*, which stated: "No layman will be tolerated to dispute the Catholic Faith in public or in private; and whosoever contravenes this order will be excommunicated when he appears before his bishop, not only without forgiveness, but also as one suspected of the highest heresy."[135] The government was well aware of this firm opposition to heresy and offered repeated reassurances. The Duke of Noailles offered the Catalans a confirmation of French support for the Catholic Church during one of his many campaigns in the Principat: "[A]nd as the Province of Catalonia is one of those in Europe which holds heresy in the greatest horror, do not doubt that his Divine Majesty will continue to serve as the protector and defender of the Catholic Religion alone."[136] Despite their awareness, the French never fully appreciated the extent of the antipathy for Protestants, both Calvinist and Lutheran, that existed in Roussillon. The depth of this feeling is demonstrated in an anonymous letter presented to the Sovereign Council in 1691. "[Satan] opened the gates of Hell, dispatching his emissaries Luther, Zwingli, and Calvin, who formed a formidable league of all his disciples; but it is this which is deplorable and worthy of Catholic arms: heresy has bedazzled some Catholics, who are more demonstrative in the publication abroad than the observance of the bull *Cena Domini Contre Fautores Hereticorum*."[137] Just as Vauban had earlier compared a Catalan festival to a witches' Sabat, so too did the Roussillonnais implicitly associate the French government with demons from hell. The French were seen as responsible for tolerating Protestantism and, still worse, encouraging its spread to Roussillon by transferring heretical troops to the province.

The most common means by which Protestants entered Roussillon, at least in the opinion of the Roussillonnais, was by being stationed there on army service. There are many accounts and complaints from the citizens of the province, who repeatedly requested that no more Protestants be dispatched into Roussillon. One compelling example comes from Saint Laurent des Cerdans, where a company of infantry had been stationed by Chamilly.

[O]n the 23rd of this month, the people being assembled in the church in order to pray that God might turn aside a great storm, lightning struck within, and two men were killed . . . and about twenty others wounded. . . . We are worried that nothing will reach the Crown of God, who is angered by the irreverence which is common to soldiers lodged in churches, particularly since there are among our troops several who are heretics.[138]

This type of complaint did have a substantial basis in fact, for there was a large number of Protestant soldiers stationed in the province. In one list of abjurations, for example, at least fifty-one of the new Catholics had come to Roussillon to fulfill their military duties. Many of these men were from Germany, but the majority were from France, reinforcing the Roussillonnais idea that France was a source of a Protestant plague. In a pay record dating from 1688, sixty-three of sixty-eight enlisted men in the German Surbeck Regiment were Protestants. These men came from across Germany, Sweden, Denmark, Hungary, and Finland, adding anti-foreign sentiment to the already extant hatred for Protestants. The depth of the Roussillonnais religious sentiment was demonstrated in 1703, when many residents of the province joined the French army to put down a Huguenot rebellion in Languedoc. In explaining their motivation, the intendant of Roussillon wrote that they "are all persuaded that they are fighting for the Catholic Faith, and that if they risk their lives, those who die will be martyrs."[139] The government thus recognized that the presence of Protestant troops was a serious problem, threatening the peace of the province. In an attempt to alleviate this situation, the French employed a priest solely to convert these Protestant troops.[140]

Other French Protestants came to Roussillon in an attempt to reach lands that might be more hospitable to their religious beliefs. In 1668, soon after the annexation, the Consuls of Perpignan were prompted to write the following prohibition to forestall such difficulties: "For the conservation and increase of the Holy Catholic Faith, it is necessary to prevent heretics and those who are not in union with the Church from having their residence in the present town."[141] The following year, a man named de Brun, a preacher of the French Reformed Church, was arrested for attempting to convert Catholics to Protestantism in Salces. Confirming the worst suspicions of the Roussillonnais, de Brun had been appointed *commis de la foraine* in that town by the French authorities. Thus, by sending Protestants to Roussillon, the French were held to be indirectly responsible for proselytization on behalf of heretics. A final example dates from 1686, when seven persons were arrested for attempting to leave the country. The Sovereign Council appointed Isidore de Prat to investigate and found that they were Protestants from Languedoc fleeing through Roussillon on their way to England. In every instance in which civilian Protestants were discovered in the province, they were quickly condemned as heretics and punished, usually by being sentenced to the galleys. It still remained, however, that the French were held responsible for the initial introduction of Protestantism and its continued presence in Roussillon. While military imperatives precluded the complete exclusion of Protestant troops from the region, efforts were made to address the problem of both civilian and

military Protestants angering the Roussillonnais. Despite the efforts undertaken by the French, the presence of Protestants, which was explicitly
associated with French rule, provided another basis by which inhabitants
justified resistance to the king.[142]

Economic

While Roussillon as a whole benefited economically from the French
presence, individual residents of the province could justify resistance to the
French because their commercial patterns had been disrupted. After Roussillon
passed to the French in 1659, they severely circumscribed trade between Iberia
and the province. Since Spain, and the Principat in particular, had been the
primary economic focus of Roussillon for centuries, the new prohibitions
caused traumatic disruptions in the local economy. The residents of the Carol
Valley had long traded wood down the river into the Cerdanya. Now, however,
that traditional pattern was halted by French intervention, forcing the Carolans
to cultivate other trading partners and exploit new resources in order to
maintain their economic status. This behavior was repeated throughout
Roussillon, as long-established trading relationships were sacrificed by the
French to international political imperatives. One significant result of this
disruption was discontent among the Roussillonnais. If the new injunctions
were obeyed, tensions were produced as new economic patterns were tirelessly
created. The residents of Roussillon, even if they profited from the French
initiatives in the province, harbored some resentment for the disruption that
change caused. If the injunctions were ignored, tensions were still created as
the disobedient were labelled smugglers by the government. Thus, whether the
government was obeyed or not, whether profits were made or lost, the French
presence created at least some tensions for most of the residents of Roussillon,
who had long relied on trade with Catalonia for economic survival.[143]

The seizures of goods and lands from disloyal Roussillonnais by the
French also provided a motivation for resistance. Don Tomàs de Banyuls
originally served France but became dissatisfied and fled to Spain, losing all
his goods and property in Roussillon as a result. Don Ramon de Çagarriga
was suspected of disloyalty by the French, and all his goods were seized. Pere
Angel Descallar was another dispossessed Roussillonnais and his goods were
taken by Conti for anti-French activities. Among other inhabitants who
suffered economic loss at the hands of the French were Antoni Generès, Don
Emanuel d'Oms, and Don Ramon de Moncada. Individuals were not the only
ones to be dispossessed of their lands and goods, however. The property of the
monastery of Saint Antoine in Perpignan, for example, was transferred by
Louis XIV to the Enseignantes de Notre Dame to create the girls' school. To
fortify the citadel of Perpignan, the cemetery and a chapel of Notre Dame de La
Real were destroyed by Vauban, along with other personal and religious
properties. Confiscations by the French, whether to achieve other goals or

simply to punish disloyalty, created hostility within the province, a sentiment which could serve to justify resistance to the French. Many individuals who were dispossessed, even those who themselves fled to Spain, left various unhappy relatives in the province. Men who remained in the province frequently became active opponents of the French regime due, in part, to dissatisfaction with the way in which their relations had been treated. At least four of these dispossessed individuals were, for example, related to young men who were later condemned to death by the French for revolt and conspiracy against the crown. In the same way, seizing properties from religious houses served to alienate further the clergy, the majority of whom had loathed the French since before the annexation. The dispossession of property, money, and goods from individuals and institutions was, for some Roussillonnais, another legitimate justification for resistance to the French.[144]

When the Roussillonnais pointed to taxes as a justification for resistance, it was because those taxes were considered illegal, not because the levies were too high. There is very little evidence that the residents of Roussillon opposed the French policies of assimilation due to the fiscal burden of taxes levied from Versailles. Taxes were never popular in the early modern period, and the Roussillonnais were no more eager to pay them than any other early modern European. But the Roussillonnais, despite their dislike for France, did not attempt to justify resistance by claiming that French taxes were ruining the economy. An example of this behavior can been seen in the resistance to the *gabelle*. After five years of open rebellion to that tax in Roussillon, the French offered the rebels a greatly reduced price on salt. Despite this fiscal incentive to end the revolt, the rebels continued to fight, claiming the levy was fundamentally illegal. The payment of taxes was not, therefore, a justification for the Roussillonnais to oppose the French monarchy except when those taxes were perceived to be illegal impositions on the province.

Foreign Intervention
Foreign intervention was another factor that encouraged resistance to the French presence in Roussillon. Both Spain and the pope stimulated, with varying intensity, resistance to French authority in Roussillon. The Spanish viceroys of Catalonia typically offered material aid to the rebels in the Vallespir, and fomented and supported conspiracies and isolated acts of resistance in other areas of the province. The revolt of the Angelets, a twenty-year-long revolt against the *gabelle* and other French violations of the *Usatges*, was strongly encouraged by the Spanish. Money was provided, refuge in Catalonia given, arms were supplied, and other forms of support and aid offered to the rebels by Spanish officials. In a similar manner, the Spanish viceroy of Catalonia, the Count of San German, offered to dispatch troops to support a series of anti-French conspiracies in 1674. Furthermore, Spanish

spies were infiltrated throughout the province, the better to foment such conspiracies and to encourage resistance to France.[145]

The Spanish also encouraged resistance through military actions against the French. Most of the period between the Peace of the Pyrenees and the War of the Spanish Succession was marked by fighting between France and Spain, and Spanish armies regularly made forays into Roussillon. These repeated incursions were encouraging to the Roussillonnais, who hoped for a return to Spain and reunification with the Principat. Even after 1701, when the Spanish government was allied to that of France, the residents of Catalonia and their local governments continued to support actions hostile to the French interests. In 1702, for example, the *viguier* of the French Cerdagne was murdered by seven men from the Spanish Cerdaña, of whom only two could even be found by the local authorities in Puigcerda. And once those two were apprehended, the Catalan leaders of Puigcerda refused to allow them to be returned to France for trial.[146]

The papacy was the second major foreign power to encourage resistance to the French. Throughout the reign of Louis XIV, Rome was generally at odds with the French monarch. The pope repeatedly denied the government's right to intervene in ecclesiastical affairs, excommunicated pro-French Roussillonnais, and lent support to the resistance the clergy offered France. In 1673, the bull *Incana Domini* excommunicated Josep de Trobat for accepting a benefice from Louis XIV which Clement X Altieri had given to Emanuel Oyonarte. Another pro-French leader who was excommunicated was Jeroni Lléopart, who became embroiled in a dispute with the cathedral chapter of Perpignan. As late as 1713, Rome was continuing to protest French actions in Roussillon, claiming the Church possessed all the rights in the province that it enjoyed before annexation. The constant tensions between the papacy and Paris lent support to the anti-French activities in Roussillon. The papacy was generally sympathetic to claims and complaints against the French, and rarely moved to discipline those clergy who refused to co-operate with the French government. Knowing that Rome would almost invariably support the Catalans encouraged and justified their resistance to France, and further reinforced the negative impressions the Roussillonnais had of French religious convictions.[147]

Historical

The Roussillonnais had a long history of attachment to Iberia, and this, too, encouraged resistance to francisation. The province had been, with few interruptions, linked to Catalonia and Iberia since the fall of the Roman Empire, and these thousand years of association and co-operation formed certain habits, attitudes, and preferences among the Roussillonnais. Thus, the people naturally looked toward Spain for guidance, even when France ruled the province. Examples of this attitude were common throughout the reign of

Louis XIV. When the king was to visit Perpignan in April 1660, for example, the consuls of the city assumed that he would make his processional entry in the same manner as Emperor Charles V. Louis disabused them of such an idea, in part because he wished to break with Spanish precedents in the province. There are several letters from intendants to the Secretary of State for War explaining that many Roussillonnais served in the armies of Spain out of habit, rather than from any profound disloyalty to France. A printed declaration of the Sovereign Council that prohibited service in Spanish armies acknowledged this fact: "The liaison that Roussillon has had for a very long time with Spain, and the natural disposition of the majority of the inhabitants of the mountains to serve as Miquelets."[148] The intendants believed that some number of the inhabitants who fought against France did so because their families had long served in Spanish armies. Such habits were not only difficult to break, but dangerous. Whether an individual fought against Louis XIV incidently or purposefully, it was an unacceptable example of resistance to the French government. At the annexation, the majority of the population viewed Spain as the rightful rulers of Roussillon, and that attitude de-legitimized the French rule in the region until such patterns of thought were reshaped.[149]

The Roussillonnais possessed a historical loathing of the French as a people, and this also fostered resistance to francisation. The Roussillonnais often referred to Frenchmen as *gavatxos*, a highly pejorative term designed to offend French sensibilities. The residents of the province had long harbored this resentment toward France, its culture, and its language. Many laws had been passed during the period of Spanish domination that explicitly precluded Frenchmen from holding office, barred French from use in official documents, and restrained French mercantile activities within Roussillon. It was with this traditional dislike of the French that France obtained Roussillon in 1659.

Exacerbating the traditional antipathy of the Roussillonnais toward the French were the excesses committed by French soldiers in the province. The governors, intendants, and Sovereign Council spent much of their time attempting to punish soldiers and pacify indignant townsmen when those two groups came into conflict. There were frequent murders and attacks committed by, or at least blamed on, soldiers stationed throughout the region. In addition, theft, destruction of property and livestock, corruption of young women, and maltreatment of civic officials were among the many disorders attributed to the garrisons of Roussillon.[150]

SOURCES OF RESISTANCE

Just as there was a variety of motivations and justifications for resistance in Roussillon, those who resisted French rule represented all classes and social strata of the province. The social and economic elite, the secular and regular clergies, the peasants of the mountains, municipal administrations, and even the Sovereign Council offered resistance to French policies at different times and to varying degrees.

Resistance from the Roussillonnais elite was usually offered by young people from families predating the French annexation. These local notables, both male and female, were often motivated by legal arguments favoring the *Usatges* and other Catalan rights. This group suffered the greatest political and economic loss from the French annexation. The lands that were seized, the nobles who were exiled, the money confiscated, and the rights abrogated—all these were taken from the native elite of Roussillon for the benefit of others. Thus, with both political and economic motivation to resist French authority, the native young notables often became leaders in movements to eject the French, even when those movements represented popular opinions and attracted a large following from the lower classes.

The other social group that provided the leadership for anti-French sentiment and activities in Roussillon was the clergy, both regular and secular. Everyone in Roussillon was aware that the priests of the province were hostile to France. The clergy's motivation for resistance to Louis XIV often centered on religious issues. The French were seen as poor Christians who forfeited their right to rule through consorting with heretical soldiers and infidel Turks. Furthermore, since the clergy were the most literate group in Roussillon, the priests understood more of the *Usatges* and rights of Catalonia than most other people. Their detailed knowledge of those rights also meant that the clergy best understood how French actions violated them, which made the clergy the natural defenders of the Constitutions of Catalonia. The clergy were the primary source of Catalan influence in Roussillon and the social focus of the villages. Thus, the Church served to shape the opinions of the residents, and often worked to ensure that those opinions were negative. Some clergymen preached, for example, that it was not a sin to kill a collector of French taxes. Others allowed their churches to serve as arms depots for rebels, and many participated in salt smuggling in defiance of royal edicts. In every major conspiracy and rebellion against the French, at least one priest was a central figure.

The residents of Roussillon, the peasants and lower classes of the villages and towns, also offered resistance to the French. Just as the notables and clergy offered leadership, the peasants served as the ranks of the rebel armies. Indeed, one primary motivation for their resistance was the leadership of the higher social orders. The peasants were conditioned to follow their priest and the local notable, and received most of their knowledge of the world from those two sources. When both of those groups agreed on a course of action, the typical peasant was little able to resist. In addition, many peasants suffered economically from the French annexation of Roussillon and came to dislike the French as a result. One particularly common form of resistance by the Roussillonnais, smuggling, was practiced almost exclusively by this lowest social class. Accustomed to trade with the Principat, the Roussillonnais often continued their commerce despite French prohibitions. Thus the lowest social orders joined the first and second estates in their resistance to French policies of assimilation.

Other sources of occasional resistance to French policies were the various governmental organs in Roussillon. Consuls of villages, royal officials, and even the Sovereign Council offered mild resistance to French actions. Generally, the resistance took the form of a written protest, or, at most, delay in executing an edict. The Sovereign Council, for example, sometimes put off registering certain edicts because members feared the laws would exacerbate tensions in the province. As the primary agent of assimilation in Roussillon, the Sovereign Council often resisted particular decisions from Paris government to further the overall goals of political assimilation and acculturation. The village officials, somewhat less attached to Paris, more often complained about policy decisions as their form of protest, requesting that troops be moved or a tax reduced. While the resistance offered by the governmental institutions in Roussillon was generally mild, it was in some ways the most significant.

In sum, resistance to the French in Roussillon was justified by various motivations. Political and legal arguments, based on Catalan customs and the *Usatges*, demonstrated that the French were violating not only traditional rights but also French promises to accept these rights. French policies of acculturation invited cultural justifications of resistance. The French sought to erase Catalan influences from Roussillon and the residents felt obliged to defend their way of life. Catalan religious views served further to reinforce negative attitudes and justify the rejection of French rule. Louis XIV sought to limit the authority of the pope, a practice suspect to the Roussillonnais. The king was further accused by the residents of consorting with heretics. By engaging in these two practices, the king had forfeited his divine anointment, the Roussillonnais argued, and resistance to an errant monarch was not only justifiable, but righteous. The fact that both the pope and the Spanish were, for the first several decades after annexation, generally hostile to Louis XIV provided the Roussillonnais with more encouragement to resistance. The Spanish offered money, arms, and occasionally soldiers to help the cause of resistance. The pope implicitly approved resistance by offering bulls and proclamations attacking the same French actions that rebels and other anti-French forces protested. The French occupation of Roussillon also disturbed conventional economic patterns by introducing new trading regulations, trading companies, customs duties, and prohibitions against trade. These attempts to alter the way in which people made their livelihoods offered yet another justification for resisting French assimilation and rule. Finally, their traditional attachment to Iberia and antipathy for France reinforced other Roussillonnais grounds for complaint and resistance.

Resistance to French policies of assimilation and acculturation came from a variety of social groups. Leadership usually emerged from the native social elites and the clergy, and the lower classes provided a broad base of support and recruits for anti-French activities. The government itself, through its many local institutions, occasionally offered resistance as well. The sum of these motivations and social groupings was a plethora of activities directed against the French presence in Roussillon. The most dramatic forms of resistance, and the most severely punished, were open rebellion and conspiracy to deliver the province to foreign powers.

Chapter 5
Rebellion, Conspiracy, and Espionage

Most of the resistance to the French annexation of Roussillon took place in the first two decades of Louis XIV's personal reign, 1661–1680. Often this resistance was expressed actively and violently, especially during the first twenty years of French rule. There were conspiracies to surrender key strong points to Spain, plots that had the active involvement and support of many leading citizens. An open rebellion erupted in the Vallespir in 1663 and ranged into other regions of the province by 1668. In addition to mass of dissent, there were acts of violence and resistance directed against the French by individuals acting alone. Central to the examination of all these acts of resistance, both corporate and individual, is the fact that 1680 marks a watershed in the history of the province. All the group acts of resistance occurred and were terminated before that year, as were all the serious individual acts of defiance. The little resistance directed against France after 1680 failed to generate any popular support and was viewed as more nuisance than threat by the Sovereign Council. An examination of the forms of open resistance against France in Roussillon reveals that French governance was initially unpopular, and that France ultimately succeeded in making that same governance palatable.

THE ASSASSINATION OF DON EMANUEL DE SANT-DIONÍS

The first instance of active resistance to French rule in newly annexed Roussillon was the murder of Don Emanuel de Sant-Dionís on 20 December 1661. That evening, the Sovereign Council received information that a murder had been committed in Perpignan. Nicolas de Manalt, a councillor of the Sovereign Council, was dispatched with Pere Aymerich, a bailiff of the court, to conduct an investigation. They proceeded to a house owned by Honofre del Fau on a street near the intendant's residence. This house was rented by Don

Emanuel de Sant-Dionís i Pol, a Catalan native of Roussillon and an officer in the French army. In a front room of that house Manalt found the body of Sant-Dionís. He had been stabbed fifty-two times, and his skull had been shattered by a hammer blow. After Aymerich had three times given the requisite injunction, "Don Emanuel de Sant-Dionís, the King bids you rise,"[151] Sant-Dionís was declared dead by an act of murder.

Suspicion for the officer's death immediately fell upon two individuals, Teresa de Camprodon and Ramon de Monfar. An order for their arrest was quickly issued. Teresa de Camprodon i d'Armengol was twenty years old when Sant-Dionís was murdered and the daughter of one of the most senior noble houses in Roussillon. Moreover, she was the wife of her uncle, Francesc de Foix-Béarn i Descamps, the head of the oldest and most respected native noble family in Roussillon. Her brother Josep was married to Narcissa de Sant-Dionís, the daughter of the dead officer. Despite this pedigree, she was immediately suspected by the Sovereign Council because it was widely known that she had been the lover of Sant-Dionís, and the house in which he was found had been their rendezvous.[152]

Ramon de Monfar was a monk and *capiscol* at the abbey of Arles in the Vallespir. Monfar, however, was usually to be found in Perpignan, where he enjoyed a luxurious lifestyle, which included long visits with the leading citizens of city and the company of several prominent young women. Teresa de Camprodon was frequently seen in his company, thus linking the two as suspects. Casting further suspicion upon him was the fact that after the body of Sant-Dionís was discovered, Monfar immediately fled to Spain, where he remained for the rest of life. These associations and behavior caused the Sovereign Council to suspect him of complicity in the murder.

Teresa de Camprodon was arrested and interrogated, but she revealed nothing, even under judicial torture. An official explanation of the murder was nevertheless issued, stating that Emanuel de Sant-Dionís, who had a reputation for being short-tempered, had seen Camprodon in the company of Monfar and confronted her. The three of them then returned to the lovers' house where, following an arranged plan, Monfar murdered Sant-Dionís with the aid and approval of Camprodon. Monfar's sudden flight to Spain offered the damning proof of his guilt that could not be obtained by a confession from Camprodon. On 13 May 1662, Teresa de Camprodon was led to the Place de la Loge in Perpignan and before the assembled notables of the province, was there decapitated for her role in the murder of Emanuel de Sant-Dionís.[153]

The execution of Camprodon stirred resentment among the local nobility for several reasons. Camprodon and her husband Foix-Béarn were among the most respected nobility of Roussillon, and their status seemed to have been ignored as the Sovereign Council imposed judgments upon the woman, with little regard for local sensitivity. The composition of the Sovereign Council gave further reasons for discontent. The death sentence had been exacted by a panel consisting of a Frenchman, seven immigrants from Spain, and only one native of the province, an indication that local sensibilities were apparently unimportant to the new government. Further, Sant-Dionís was rude, abusive, and often violent, and few of the notables mourned his passing. None would have blamed Camprodon for killing him. However, the primary reason that many nobles stood in silent support of Camprodon at her execution was that she was seen as a martyr for Roussillon.

It was widely believed in the seventeenth century that Camprodon and Monfar were involved in organizing and encouraging resistance to the French in Roussillon. Emanuel de Sant-Dionís, although born in Perpignan, was thoroughly pro-French and an officer in the French army. It was assumed by most nobles that he had befriended Camprodon in an attempt to gather information on the dissidents, which he would then pass on to his superiors. This information, which would include the names of many leading nobles, would prove damaging to both the resistance movement and the indigenous nobility as a class. To protect their friends and allies, Camprodon and Monfar, with others to assist them, lured Sant-Dionís to a rendezvous, where he was murdered to prevent the incriminating information from reaching the government.

There is strong circumstantial evidence to support this explanation of the murder of Sant-Dionís. At the execution, the nobility surrounded Francesc de Foix-Béarn in a show of solidarity that was extremely unusual for the execution of a notable public figure. Traditionally, he should have stood alone, with the other nobles far removed from him. To ally themselves with him in this manner was to share his shame or, perhaps, her cause. Among those surrounding Foix-Béarn that day were Emanuel Descallar, Carles de Banyuls, Francesc de Llar, and Josep de la Trinxeria, all of whom became involved in later plots and rebellions against the French.[154]

Monfar was a monk in Arles-sur-Tech, in the Vallespir, a village and region that were centers of anti-French agitation for at least three decades. The people and officials of Arles were repeatedly punished in the seventeenth century for anti-French activity. These attitudes of resistance were often transmitted and encouraged by the priests of the town. That Monfar was a monk, an occupation that usually stood in opposition to France, and was from a town and abbey that typically was quite hostile to the French gives weight to this explanation of the murder. Immediately after the murder, the prior of Arles personally gave permission to Monfar to travel to Barcelona, a visit that provided his escape. Monfar's frequent visits to Perpignan can be explained as trips that served as vehicles of communication between conspirators in Perpignan and those in the Vallespir. Moreover, in conducting the murder investigation, the Sovereign Council investigated several priests closely, although no charges were brought against them in connection with the murder. These priests were all close associates of Monfar's, and several of them are known to have been active in later plots against French rule. It is quite possible that Monfar was fully part of this tradition of clerical anti-French activity in Roussillon.

Another individual to flee the province upon the arrest of Camprodon was her brother, Josep. Although born in Perpignan and married to the daughter of Sant-Dionís, also a Roussillonnais, he moved to Gerona, in the Principat, after his sister's arrest. He remained there until at least 1667, after the investigations had ended, before returning to Roussillon. While Josep eventually resigned himself to French rule in the province, his son, Don Aleix Josep de Camprodon, joined the armies of the Archduke Charles during the War of the Spanish Succession. It is again highly suggestive that the brother of the condemned should flee Roussillon, and her nephew take up arms for Catalan liberties and nationalism.[155]

In investigating the murder of Sant-Dionís, the Sovereign Council turned up evidence of a conspiracy, or at least a vastly different explanation from the one publicly offered. The only person who witnessed any events in connection with the murder saw five or six men coming from the house very late, after the murder was believed to have been committed. Furthermore, giving the lie to its official explanation, the Sovereign Council suspected far more people were involved in the murder than simply Camprodon and Monfar.

The investigations conducted by the Sovereign Council lasted until at least the spring of 1664, nearly two years after Camprodon was executed. In the course of the probe, many men were investigated for complicity. Among these were Joan Marset, J. Beaufort, Bruno Gelabert, Josep Mardeu, and Bernat d'Oms. Marset, for example, was condemned to the galleys for seven years for his involvement in the murder. Charles Macqueron, the intendant, expelled d'Oms from Roussillon for life on an unspecified charge stemming from the murder investigation. D'Oms, a priest, went to Barcelona, where he rejoined his family, the majority of whom had fled Roussillon at the Peace of the Pyrenees. The d'Oms family in Roussillon and Spain was constantly involved in agitation against the French, including plots to turn Collioure over to the Spanish, and encouraging plans for Spanish invasions. It is highly suggestive that an anti-French subversive from a family of known conspirators was somehow connected with the murder of Sant-Dionís. If the official explanation of the murder as a lovers' quarrel were correct, these men could not have possibly have been guilty of participating in the murder. Thus the continued investigations of the Sovereign Council indicate that its official explanation was not true, and that members believed other individuals were involved in the murder.[156]

While concrete evidence of a plot against the French has never been found, circumstantial evidence suggests that anti-French activities were being planned. The evidence, provided by an eyewitness and the Sovereign Council's prolonged investigations, indicates that many people were involved, not

simply two lovers. The association of Camprodon with a host of people who
were later condemned for resisting the Bourbon monarchs lends further support
to the conspiracy theory. The Roussillonnais at the time of the murder
believed that it was the work of an anti-French conspiracy, and there is
abundant evidence that they were correct.

REVOLT OF THE ANGELETS

The most important act of resistance to French rule in Roussillon
was the revolt of the Angelets, a rebellion that lasted from 1661 until 1679
and was prompted by the French tax on salt. In France, everyone was required
to purchase their salt from licensed vendors, and in this way the government
could collect a tax on it, known as the *gabelle*. The *gabelle* was introduced to
Roussillon in November 1661, over the protests of the inhabitants of the
province. The Roussillonnais resisted the tax not because of the financial
burden it imposed, but because the tax on salt was a clear violation of the
Usatges, which had explicitly prohibited such a levy since the *Corts* of
Montçó in 1283. Because the French were obviously violating the Constitutions of Catalonia, which they had sworn to respect, opposition to the
gabelle soon erupted into full rebellion.[157]

Those who opposed the imposition of the salt tax repeatedly stressed
that their quarrel was to defend the *Usatges* and that their loyalty to the king
was still solid, even if it was, in fact, quite weak. Once resistance to the
gabelle escalated to open organized rebellion, the most common battle cry of
the rebels, "Long live the king and the land, Death to the *gabelle* and to
traitors,"[158] continued to emphasize that the goal of the struggle was to defend
traditional Catalan rights. This conception of the *gabelle* as an illegal
imposition was shared by the consuls of Perpignan, who protested in 1661
that the *gabelle* was a clear violation of the privileges of the city and of the
Usatges. The village of Ceret, in the Vallespir, decided in February 1662 to
add its protests to those of Perpignan, Canet, and Collioure in opposing the
gabelle. The reluctance of the towns of the province to accept this new
imposition was shared by Louis XIV's own local representatives, the Sovereign Council, which initially refused to register the edict. It was only upon
insistent urging from the Secretary of War that the council relented and
reluctantly registered the edict.[159]

In addition to the legal arguments, ethnic tensions contributed to
armed opposition to the salt tax. The tax farm in Roussillon was given to
Pierre-Paul Riquet, who was also director of the tax farm in Languedoc. Riquet
employed his agents from the former region to collect taxes in Roussillon,
further insulting the inhabitants. The tax was now being collected by
gavatxos, contemptuous foreigners. Part of the resistance to the *gabelle*
stemmed from the fact that the tax seemed to be imposed and collected by
outsiders, a problem recognized in Paris. Colbert wrote to Riquet on 25

October 1669: "I am not satisfied with your clerks in Roussillon; it is impossible that their poor conduct has not contributed to the disorders that arrive there daily."[160] The facts that the Roussillonnais considered the *gabelle* an illegal imposition and that Frenchmen were collecting the tax led to extreme tensions in the region, which ultimately exploded into open armed rebellion.

Since the *gabelle* was seen as illegal and salt could be easily transported from Spain, Roussillon's traditional source of it, smuggling became quite common; indeed, it was normal. Most smuggling occurred in the Vallespir, where Saint-Laurent de Cerdans and Prats-de-Mollo became vital centers of the illegal trade in salt from Cardona. Although the officers of the *gabelle* intercepted and seized large quantities of illegal salt in this region, the *gabelle* nearly always went unpaid in the Vallespir. The inhabitants of the Vallespir quickly learned not to hide their illicit salt in their own homes as house searches by the officers of the *gabelle* became common. To combat smuggling and determine who was involved in the illegal trade in salt, local village officials were ordered to undertake investigations in their localities. Such local inquests invariably failed to produce criminals, as all the residents participated in a conspiracy of silence or misdirection.

Failure to stop the smuggling led the inspectors of the *gabelle* to become increasingly heavy-handed, arbitrarily assigning blame, indicting whole towns, and carrying out unannounced surprise searches. Hostility toward the *gabelle* and its officers grew as the incidents mounted, and soon there was violence. In January 1663, for example, several guards of the *gabelle* intercepted a group of Roussillonnais smuggling salt into the Vallespir. According to the local residents, the guards of the *gabelle* opened fire, killing two men. After the convoy was disrupted and prisoners were taken, a three other men were said to have been killed in the camp of the guards of the *gabelle*. The tax guards disputed this version of events, claiming that the smugglers fired first and denying any deaths in camp. The Sovereign Council dismissed the charges of murdering prisoners, but found that the *gabelle* guards had acted provocatively. As a result, one guard was condemned to death, and another three were sentenced to the galleys.[161]

Incidents like these led to increasing hostility on the part of the Roussillonnais. On 4 August 1663, for example, Jean Mouise, *lieutenant du procureur principal du Vallespir*, accompanied by his assistant and four guards, arrested Antoine Vigo and several other smugglers in Saint-Laurent de Cerdans and began the journey back to Perpignan with his prisoners. Church bells were rung in outrage. Soon a fifty to sixty armed men gathered and began to follow the men of the *gabelle*. The tax collectors were overtaken at Arles-sur-Tech, where they had stopped for the evening. In the bloody confrontation that followed, all six of the employees of the *gabelle* were killed, and the prisoners were freed. A subsequent investigation by the Sovereign Council found no witnesses at all in Saint-Laurent de Cerdans or Arles-sur-Tech. Francesc de Sagarra was dispatched by the Sovereign Council to investigate the incident. In the trials that followed, eight men were condemned to death, and another fifty-one were sent to the galleys for life, effectively sentencing them to death as well. Most of the condemned were from Saint-Laurent de Cerdans, establishing a pattern that was to be followed throughout the next two decades. In cases of doubt and when individual culpability could not be determined, an entire village where a crime had been committed would be punished, and all likely suspects were assumed to be guilty.[162]

These sporadic and spontaneous acts of personal resistance gradually coalesced around charismatic young leaders, men who elevated the resistance to the salt tax into open rebellion. The rebels, called *Angelets de la Terra* (Angels of the Land), enjoyed many advantages over the royal troops in the struggle. The land itself was important to the rebels. The mountainous areas of Roussillon, where the Angelets operated, was perfect for guerrilla warfare. The long, narrow valleys made it difficult to move large numbers of troops after the rebels, and allowed small groups of men to check much larger units. Intendant Charles Macqueron explained this to Colbert, perhaps exaggerating slightly when reporting that "there are several places in these mountains where six men can bar the passage of two thousand."[163] The rebels possessed the additional advantage of an intimate knowledge of the land, since they had spent their entire lives in the Vallespir. Residents also were aware of the disposition of the royal troops, who were garrisoned at fixed points, allowing the Angelets to strike and retreat at will.

The Angelets received the active assistance of most of the populace in their struggle. Farmers provided food, priests often allowed churches to be used as meeting centers and weapons depots, civic leaders offered warning of French movements and plans, and other citizens offered arms, shelter, money, or skills as they were needed. In the many investigations of the Sovereign Council into the rebellion, its members repeatedly concluded that nearly everyone in the Vallespir was involved, either by taking up arms or supporting those who did. Condemnations and fines were levied on whole villages or areas, with a rare explicit exception made for a single individual when necessary.

Another advantage enjoyed by the rebels was the proximity of the Spanish border and France's difficulty in sealing it. The French catalogued at least thirty-nine major passes of military importance along the border between Roussillon and Catalonia. In addition, there were many more minor passes, not particularly useful in time of war, but quite adequate for the passage of rebels through the frontier. Unable to deploy the thousands of soldiers necessary to completely seal the border with Spain, the French were compelled to allow the frontier to remain porous. The open border meant that the rebels could, should they become hard-pressed, retreat into Spanish Catalonia. Once in Spain, the rebels enjoyed still more advantages. Since Madrid and Paris were constantly at odds throughout the seventeenth century, the Spanish government actively encouraged the rebellion in Roussillon. The viceroys of Catalonia provided arms, money, and training to the rebels to ensure their continued resistance to Louis XIV. Étienne Carlier, the provincial intendant in Roussillon, described the Angelet rebellion as a "revolt which is fomented daily by the artifices of the Spanish and their adherents,"[164] and offered many specific examples of their interference. Spanish aid came from a variety of sources and took many forms. The Catalan residents of the Principat, for example, provided food, shelter, and medical care for the rebels from Roussillon. The viceroy of Catalonia tacitly assisted the Angelets by permitting them to cross the frontier at will. The Spanish viceroys also offered some help openly. Spanish funds were given to the Roussillonnais rebels, elements of the Spanish army in Catalonia occasionally entered Roussillon to co-operate with the rebels, and many of the rebellion's leaders were offered positions in the Spanish army as a reward for their services.[165]

As the revolt evolved, the rebels gained sympathy across the province, and armed supporters from throughout the Tech and Tet valleys. The rebels represented a cross-section of Roussillonnais society, with muleteers, petty merchants, laborers, and members of similar lower-class occupations filling their ranks. The resistance was led, however, by the leading citizens of the province. The sons of the nobility and local notables planned and executed the strategy of the rebels. These leaders were also in correspondence with leading citizens of Perpignan, indicating that there was a great deal of sympathy for the rebels throughout Roussillon.

The Angelets were led by a group of young notables from the rural areas of southern and central Roussillon. The chief of these rebels was Josep de la Trinxeria. He was a local leader in Prats-de-Mollo, at the upper end of the Vallespir. His father had been granted the lowest grade of nobility by King Philip of Spain in 1640, just as the revolt of the Catalans was erupting. Josep de la Trinxeria became involved in the revolt when, sometime in 1667, an unannounced search of his home by the officers of the *gabelle* uncovered about twenty-five livres' worth of untaxed salt. The inspectors, however, valued it at sixty-six livres and demanded immediate payment of taxes and penalties. Trinxeria, who believed the *gabelle* to be fundamentally illegal, was enraged by this gross extortion, and this event pushed him to become the foremost leader of the Angelets in the province for the duration of their struggle.[166]

The revolt of the Angelets was spread into the Tet valley by Joan Miquel Mestre, *Lo Hereu Just de Ballestaví* (the True Heir of Bellestaví), a godparent to one of Trinxeria's children. Some historians believe that Miquel Mestre was driven primarily by fiscal motives, desiring a cheaper price on salt such as had been offered to the residents of the Vallespir in 1668.[167] This seems unlikely, as he continued to reject such offers from the French officials, and ignored pardons and financial incentives in order to continue the struggle. Other Angelet leaders included Jaume and Damià Noell, Lambert Manera, who was killed in combat with the French in 1675, the priest Joan Pagès, Emanuel de Llupià, and Josep Boneu, who often aided Trinxeria in the tactical planning of the raids they undertook.[168]

In the seventeenth century, churches were the primary social centers for communities and the forum for the exchange and dissemination of ideas. Since it was at the churches that much discussion of the Angelet movement occurred, the clergy of the region were of necessity well informed about the resistance. Due to their knowledge, the clergy could have been of great use to the French government in suppressing the revolt, both in exhorting parishioners to forsake violence and in providing names and locations of key conspirators. Most of the priests of the Vallespir, however, were rural Roussillonnais and fully supported the Angelets. Indeed, the priests, often the most literate members of a rural community, generally served in positions of leadership in the rebellion, exhorting parishioners to resistance, drawing up formal lists of demands for the government, and providing communication between groups of rebels.

The name Angelet is a derivation of "angel" in both Catalan and French, implying a sense of divine favor or mission on the part of the rebels. The name was originally applied because the royal troops claimed the rebels fell from the sky, and then disappeared without a trace after inflicting their damage. The divine favor implicit in such a label was immediately apparent to all parties, and the name was quickly embraced by the resistance. The priests and peasants usually referred to the rebels as Angelets. Louvois, Colbert, and the Sovereign Council, however, pointedly avoided doing so, usually preferring the terms *Miquelet* or rebels, or simply referring to disorders in the province. On those occasions that an intendant did use the term *Angelet*, he usually prefaced it with "so-called," or a similarly disparaging remark. The lower clergy, however, actively enhanced this vision of the rebels as God's messengers. In some cases their sermons stated that killing an officer of the *gabelle* was not a mortal sin, as murder normally would be.[169] In addition to moral and spiritual support, the clergy also provided material support to the rebels, allowing them to use churches and monasteries as safe houses, depots for weapons and salt, and meeting places. Notre-Dame de Corral and Saint-Michel de Cabrenes were foremost among these strongholds.

All of this clerical activity in favor of the rebels was not unnoticed by the Sovereign Council. The abbot of Saint-Genis des Fontaines was arrested for aiding the Angelets, and Joan Pagès, a priest in Saint-Laurent de Cerdans, was executed on 7 June 1672 for complicity with the rebels. Another priest, Jaume Ubert, was indicted for giving aid to the rebels.[170]

All of the clergy in the Vallespir did not join the Angelet rebellion, and the king had a few clerical supporters in that region. For example, Pere

Pont, abbot of Notre-Dame d'Arles-sur-Tech from 1661 to 1684, aided the intendant in re-establishing the *gabelle* in 1671, after it had been suppressed by the rebels. Two years later, an examining committee from the Sovereign Council received testimony from the consuls of Arles that Pont "has always exhorted and commanded us as a group and individually, in public and in private, to be most vigilant and punctual to do the service of the King, our lord (may God protect him), and to obey the orders given us by Monsieur de Boisredon, governor of the Fort des Bains, in all matters concerning the service of His Majesty."[171] Pont's behavior is perhaps explained in part by the fact that he, unlike most residents of the Vallespir, was an immigrant to Roussillon. Pont and his brother Rafel had fled Barcelona when the Peace of the Pyrenees was signed and were rewarded with positions in Louis' administration in Roussillon. Because Pont's position had been granted by Louis XIV, and he had no local ties to Josep de la Trinxeria and the other inhabitants, he remained faithful to the monarch's policies.[172]

The year 1667 is usually offered as the date when resistance to the *gabelle* became a full-scale revolt. Not only was that the year in which Trinxeria took up the standard of rebellion, but the first significant military action between the French and the Angelets occurred in 1667. On 12 May 1667, the Angelets won a pitched battle with the troops of the *gabelle* at Pas de Fangas, killing five commissioners. The creation of a military force capable of taking the field against the soldiers of the *gabelle* was obviously the work of a widespread and well-organized movement. The capability to win the day further indicated that the rebels were not only well equipped, but also well led. On 2 July of that same year, the rebels ambushed the *sous-viguier* of the Vallespir and killed him. This action convinced the Sovereign Council that more was occurring in the Vallespir than isolated acts of violence; the government acknowledged that open rebellion had erupted. As a result, the Angelets were, as a group, declared enemies of the king and a price was placed upon their heads.[173]

The fact that open insurrection had erupted meant that more than narrowly local issues were at stake; rebellion was an issue important enough that the government in Paris took notice of what was occurring. Throughout 1667 and 1668, however, the Sovereign Council and the intendant, Charles Macqueron, were at odds over how best to deal with the rebels. The council wished to offer an amnesty, followed by fines on villages that continued to support the rebels. Macqueron, however, wanted to request 5,000 or 6,000 more troops from Paris and garrison them throughout the Vallespir in order to crush dissent. The Catalans on the Sovereign Council warned him that his solution would only further excite tensions in the province, as it was too difficult to employ troops against the rebels. The French ministers, receiving conflicting advice from their agents in the province, delayed making any real decisions, but issued a steady stream of advice and requests for information. On

2 March 1668, for example, Colbert wrote to Riquet, telling the *gabelle* farmer that he might consider offering a pardon to rebels who would "deliver their companions into the hands of justice." The first two years of the rebellion therefore passed with no definite plan of action having been agreed upon by the government.[174]

While pursuing a negotiated settlement with the rebels, including offering the proposed amnesty, the intendant, Sovereign Council, and Riquet were also attempting to place military pressure on the insurgents. Francesc de Sagarra, a councillor of the Sovereign Council, personally undertook to lead military operations against the rebels of the Vallespir in 1668. On 15 September Sagarra, with fellow councillors Francesc de Martí and Ramon de Trobat, was riding at the head of a company of cavalry from Arles-sur-Tech toward Prats-de-Mollo. At Pas-du-Loup they were set upon by a group of *Angelets*, who killed 10 percent of the soldiers and seriously wounded an additional 10 percent. The officials and their remaining troops barely escaped back to Arles with their lives. The town was then besieged by the rebels for nine days, and in response the militia was called out and 150 regular troops were dispatched from Perpignan to convey the councillors back to the capital in safety.[175]

Compelling evidence that the Angelet revolt was not purely fiscal in nature was offered in 1668. That year the first of many settlements was offered the communities of the Vallespir, none of which ended the uprising. For example, on 23 December 1668, an agreement was reached between Pierre Paul Riquet and the representatives of the communities. There were to be no more house searches for illegal salt, and twice a year the whole of the Vallespir would purchase 300 *minots* of salt from the licensed vendor in Prats-de-Mollo at a price of 6 *réaux d'argent* per *minot*, with payment due six months after purchase. This salt was to be divided among the entire valley in any manner the valley decided. The communities also agreed to make no more attacks upon convoys carrying legal salt or *gabelle* officers. The Sovereign Council supported this arrangement by offering an almost general amnesty to the Angelets, with only the most notorious leaders being excepted. This agreement was clearly a tacit agreement to allow smuggling, as the quantities indicated in the agreement were insufficient to supply the entire Vallespir. The price was also an excellent one, and the rest of the province vigorously protested against the favoritism being shown the rebellious region. Despite these excellent terms, the Angelets remained in the field, continuing their violence against the *gabelle* in defense of the *Usatges*.[176]

The events of 1668, including Sagarra's defeat and the failed attempt at conciliation, had two important effects. First, in Roussillon, parts of the Conflent valley openly joined the Angelet cause, thus spreading the rebellion into the valley of the Tet. The second was that in Paris the government became concerned over the handling of the situation and accepted Macqueron's recourse to arms. Louvois rebuked the Sovereign Council for allowing "the Miquelets and people of the Vallespir" to commit unpunished acts of violence against the officers of the *gabelle*. Since Sagarra's defeat seemed to demonstrate that the military forces available locally were either insufficient for or incapable of quelling the uprising, it was determined in Paris that more troops had to be dispatched to the province. In order that the Sovereign Council might put down the rebellion, Louvois dispatched 4,000 additional troops to Roussillon on 16 November 1668 to aid the local government.[177]

Despite an increased military presence, the Angelet problem continued, and the government in Paris grew increasingly displeased with the conduct of the intendant, Sovereign Council, and Riquet. Louvois wrote the Sovereign Council on 1 January 1669, complaining that negotiations only exacerbated the problem. In a separate letter to the intendant, Charles Macqueron, Louvois reiterated his insistence that the revolt be suppressed, and believed that the arrival of royal troops would finally crush the Angelet rebellion. At the same time, he also encouraged the intendant to offer another general pardon.[178] Macqueron shared, and probably informed, Louvois' view that negotiations only worsened the problems in Roussillon. In the spring of the same year, Macqueron explained to Louvois "The insolence of the Miquelets and communities of the Conflent is a result of the indulgence shown to those in the Vallespir. . . . [T]he Catalans are not at all reduced by gentleness and forgiveness; controlling them it is necessary to keep them in awe with rectitude and authority."[179] These suggestions of increased military pressure, a single favorable tax applied throughout the province, and a general pardon reveal that Louvois and Macqueron still did not completely comprehend the reasons behind the rebellion, since no effort was made to address the Catalans' concerns over the violation of their rights.

On 20 February of the same year, Louvois proposed another possible solution to the crisis that would, he believed, go a long way toward ending the rebellion. He wrote to the Sovereign Council that it should attempt to recruit Josep de la Trinxeria and his comrades as officers of the Royal-Roussillon infantry regiment. The rebels would thus be allowed to exercise their native genius for military affairs and would hold positions of prestige, while the government would gain able guerrilla leaders and end a vexing problem. However, since commissions in the French army held no appeal for Trinxeria and the other rebel leaders, Louvois again demonstrated that he did not fully comprehend the nature and motivation of the rebellion in Roussillon.[180]

In March 1669, the Sovereign Council again offered an amnesty to all Angelets who would renounce violence and cease all activities against the *gabelle*. The Sovereign Council made this amnesty known by printing hundreds of copies of the declaration in Catalan and posting them throughout the Vallespir and Conflent regions. This offer was not widely accepted by the rebels, and the uprising continued.[181]

Riquet journeyed to Roussillon in April 1669 to determine the best method for ending the rebellion. He wrote to Pesenas that "these people are in such a state of rebellion that I have returned without having won their minds in the least." He went on to place at least part of the blame for the lack of results on the Sovereign Council, claiming that "the jealousies which have long existed among the eight or ten people who comprise the Sovereign Council" were partially responsible for the lack of success in suppressing the Angelet movement.[182]

In August, Louvois again wrote to the Sovereign Council, saying that the rebels had been virtually unopposed for two years and that he was becoming increasingly unhappy with the state of affairs:

His Majesty has resolved to severely punish these disorders, and in order to achieve this end, to dispatch to Roussillon a considerable number of troops in case the disorders continue. I beseech you to make me aware of any new developments in this matter, and moreover, to apply with great care all the severity of justice in order to punish the authors of these developments, assuring me that the example you make will stop the disorders.[183]

Colbert informed Riquet on 25 October 1669 that the latter was to "go there and put it [the province] in order once and for all, if it is possible; otherwise the king will be obliged to send troops to severely punish the guilty, which will not be good for your farm."[184] These instructions were followed by the dispatch of a further 6,000 troops to the intendant, Charles Macqueron, to be used in suppressing the revolt. The ministers had struck the definitive note on governmental policy toward the Angelets—severity. Any reconciliations or amnesties would henceforth operate only in tandem with large military operations and severe punishments throughout the Vallespir.[185]

Colbert was prompted to write the Sovereign Council in November 1669, encouraging them to work harder at suppressing the rebellion and reiterating the need to punish those responsible. Colbert was especially insistent that the crimes against the officers of the *gabelle* not be treated as special cases. He was emphatic that they should instead be prosecuted just as any other crime, thus implicitly denying the political component of the rebellion:

Since it is of extreme importance not to distinguish the punishment of violences which have been committed by the Miquelets towards those who are employed in the collection of taxes in Roussillon, I beseech you to work tirelessly to prosecute the guilty to the full extent of the law, making others content to adhere to their duty by the example you set and by fear of a similar punishment, which will deter them from committing similar disorders.[186]

In a separate letter sent at the same time to Macqueron, Colbert was obviously displeased that this insurrection was dragging on and again emphasized strong deterrent punishments: "[G]ive all your attention to arresting Just and his accomplices, so that you may severely punish them; and if you encounter difficulties which are too great and bar you, or the communities are taking part in these disorders, it will be good if you would send me recommendations concerning what measures the King might take."[187] Throughout most of 1669, despite repeated exhortations by the ministers in Paris, little was done to contain the rebellion, which dragged on for another decade.

On 22 January 1670, Joan Miquel Mestre and a companion were on the road to the village of Camprodon when they were captured by the French during a routine patrol of the upper Tech valley. They were then escorted by royal soldiers to Prats-de-Mollo, the nearest sizable town. When news of this capture reached Trinxeria, he organized a raid on the city, capturing the wife and children of the governor of Prats-de-Mollo, Arnaud de Belsunce. Trinxeria threatened to execute his hostages unless Miquel Mestre was released, and the governor of the town quickly freed his captives. The Sovereign Council believed that the hostages were taken merely as excuses, enabling the governor to free the prisoner without reprisals from Perpignan. Prats-de-Mollo had long been a center of the Angelet movement, and as leader of the town, the governor probably shared his citizens' sentiments.[188]

The French sent in troops to pursue Trinxeria, and in the ensuing combat, Lieutenant-General Josep d'Ardena, the Comte d'Ille, was killed. This was a serious blow to the French, as Ardena had been a significant French supporter in the Vallespir and a leading figure among the nobility of the province. This incident, according to Colbert, finally persuaded Paris that the rebellion was too serious for the local authorities to suppress without assistance, an opinion Louvois had begun to form in 1668. As a result, a detachment of French line troops under the command of Chamilly was sent into Roussillon to combat the Angelets and "force them to do their duty."[189] Colbert informed the Sovereign Council of the king's decision, and demanded repression.

The new sedition which has arrived at Prats-de-Mollo appeared too criminal to the King to remain unpunished, and as His Majesty has considered that it would be difficult to compel the atonement which he is due unless he dispatched troops to Roussillon, He has made a decision to do this, and forthwith sent all the orders necessary to dispatch a considerable corps. It is now up to you to examine, together with Macqueron, the means by which the seditious may be easily seized so that a punishment may be meted out to them which is so severe that that land will forever obey His Majesty.[190]

Despite Colbert's demands for punishments that would frighten the Roussillonnais into compliance, and regardless of the increasing number of soldiers, the rebellion continued at full strength.

The military high point of the revolt for the Angelets came in the spring of 1670, when they invested Ceret, a town of approximately 2,000 residents that controlled the entrance the Vallespir. The siege was begun on 31 March and concluded three days later, giving the Angelets complete control of Roussillon's second-largest town, and of the whole Vallespir. Chamilly was soon dispatched from Perpignan with 4,000 soldiers, and on 5 May a pitched battle was fought at Col de Regina. The Angelets were driven off, and Ceret was relieved.[191]

Soldiers were then garrisoned throughout the Vallespir and parts of the Conflent, and many executions and banishments followed as the Sovereign Council finally moved in the manner that Macqueron and Paris had been demanding for years. A trial was held *in absentia* for the leaders of the rebellion, and Trinxeria, Damià Noell, Miquel Mestre, Antoni Font, Pau Gallant, Lluch Manent, Francisco Manent, March Manent, Pau Vert, Hyacintho Caualler, and Abdon Tarrius were among many condemned as "stubbornly disobedient and weak, rebels, unfaithful, and traitors to the royal majesty of the King our lord, and to all the Province of Roussillon, Conflent, and the adjacent lands of the Cerdagne."[192] In the massive inquests that followed, the Sovereign Council meted out punishment across the Vallespir. Forty-two communities from the Vallespir and Conflent were found guilty of corporate complicity with the Angelets, and punished accordingly. These punishments included fines of up to 3,500 livres for Prats-de-Mollo, and 1,600 livres apiece for Arles-sur-Tech and Saint Laurent de Cerdans. Many other villages of the valleys were also fined considerable sums for aiding the Angelet rebellion. In addition, the *Gent* of thirteen places, including the city of Perpignan, were indicted as a body for aiding the rebels, and the *consuls* of seven villages were singled out for special condemnation. A further 416 named individuals, including priors, rectors, abbots, middle-class property owners, and craftsmen were found guilty of providing some form of assistance to the Angelets, and fined or punished. Those receiving the most severe fines were Jeroni Parayra, consul of Tallet, who was assessed a penalty of 200 livres, and Josep Brusi, dit Jacoÿat, who was to pay an incredible 1,650 livres. The French authorities further ordered the village of Pi to be completely razed for its part in supporting the rebels before and during the battle of Col de Regina.[193]

The government was not wholly punitive, however. The fines and punishments were issued with another general pardon, forgiving all those who would renounce violence. The Sovereign Council also sought to encourage obedience to the government by using the many fines to indemnify and reward those who had suffered at the hands of the rebels. Men who had not given in to local pressures but had remained loyal to Louis XIV received rewards, sometimes quite generous. The rebellion continued well beyond these events, but the scale of rebel operations would never again reach such threatening proportions, and the Angelets were thereafter more usually a nuisance than a serious threat.[194]

Among those exiled in the mass punishments of 1670 was Emanuel Descallar of Villefranche-de-Conflent, who was exiled to Spanish Catalonia on 20 December. This was the second time he had been exiled for anti-French sentiments. In 1654, when the French were occupying Roussillon, he had been sent to Barcelona for opposing their presence. He returned to Villefranche from that exile in 1659. His sentence of 1670 was lifted on 9 January 1672, after he had paid a bail of 300 livres. However, he did not return to Ville-franche for another year, when he became involved in another major conspiracy against French rule.[195]

The defeat at Ceret changed the scale of the Angelets' operations, but it by no means stopped them. On 9 April 1671, for example, Joan del Trull, second consul of Prats-de-Mollo, was killed by Trinxeria for collaboration with the French against the rebels, demonstrating that the movement was still very much alive. That an important political figure of the Vallespir would collaborate with the French also indicates, however, that the tide was turning against the rebellion, and popular support was beginning to erode.[196]

Evidently the actions and bearing of the men of the *gabelle* were still offensive to the inhabitants or Roussillon, for in March 1672, the men of the town of Argeles rioted and attacked the officers of the *gabelle* while the latter were seizing a quantity of illegal salt from a home. Screaming "Kill! kill! kill!" the mob beat and shot the guards, leaving at least one dead. The spontaneous nature of this rebellion is reminiscent of the earlier anti-*gabelle* movement, since it did not involve a planned attack on the part of the rebels. This illustrates the slow demise of the Angelet movement. Eleven years of fighting had accomplished nothing of substance, and the government was still willing to be fairly generous in attempts to find a compromise. The inhabi-tants of the region had resigned themselves to paying an illegal tax, but the overbearing actions of contemptuous foreigners could still provoke them to violence.[197]

In 1672 Arles-sur-Tech, one of the centers of Angelet activity in the Vallespir, petitioned the king for the restoration of its privileges, which had been suspended in the investigations of 1670. The king, through Louvois, returned the matter to local jurisdiction to be decided by the Sovereign Council. That body recommended that the honors and privileges of the town be restored, and the king did so. This indicates the reduction of tensions in the valley; for a major center of the rebellion to have regained its honor from the king indicates that it was no longer considered a hotbed of sedition. If a major center of the rebellion had withdrawn active support for the movement, it was clearly weakening.[198]

A minor international incident occurred due to the Angelet rebellion in the spring of 1672. A priest named Joan Pagès had been leading the rebels and had fled to Spain to avoid arrest. The Spanish allowed him a parish at Massanet de Cabrenys, near the border, and from that village he continued to incite and organize rebel activities. The Sovereign Council, determined to make an example of Pagès, had him seized in Spain and returned to Roussillon. In retaliation for this arrest, the Spanish arrested the grandson of Don Josep de Fontanella, *president à mortier* of the Sovereign Council, and the son of Don Francesc de Martí, a councillor on the Sovereign Council, both of whom were in Barcelona. The Sovereign Council was unhappy at this reprisal and petitioned Louis XIV for relief. Messages were dispatched, and the two men were soon released from custody in Barcelona. Pagès was executed on 7 June 1672.[199]

Although the Angelet movement seemed to be slowly weakening in the rural regions of the province, the rebellion was still far from over. In both 1672 and 1673, the terms of the settlement of 1668 were reissued in an attempt to pacify the rebellious regions. That the Sovereign Council again attempted a peaceful solution that included compromise on the government's part indicates that a significant level of discontent and violence still existed.[200]

In 1674, Emanuel de Llupià led a contingent of 400 men in a raid against the French at the Fort des Bains near Arles-sur-Tech. That such a sizable unit could be brought to bear again indicates that the Angelet movement was still thriving in the Vallespir, despite all French efforts to eradicate it. On 14 April 1674, Josep de la Trinxeria was condemned to death *in absentia* by the Sovereign Council for his role in leading the Angelet insurrection. This, once again demonstrated that the Sovereign Council was still hunting down the leaders of the rebellion in an attempt to crush it.[201]

The Angelet rising against the *gabelle* finally died after the Peace of Nijmegen in 1679, when the Spanish government agreed to stop supporting the Angelets with sanctuaries, money, and supplies. Support within Roussillon for the Angelets had also eroded by this time as French efforts to crush the rebellion finally took their toll in the province. The French had reduced by attrition the number of supporters able to take up arms against them. Further, the peace settlements offered by the French were generous, and, since French victory was seemingly inevitable, it was better to seize a generous peace than have a harsh one imposed. Without the support of Spain or the majority of the inhabitants of Roussillon, the rebels could no longer sustain their efforts against France.[202]

After the Angelet rebellion was finally put down, the French government repeatedly tried unsuccessfully to recruit Trinxeria as an officer in its Royal-Roussillon regiment. Trinxeria accepted a lieutenancy in the Spanish *Miquelet* infantry in 1673, later rising to become a colonel.[203]

Once the rebellion of the Angelets was suppressed, local officials were anxious to prevent a recurrence of the violence, demonstrating that an accommodation had been reached rather than a real settlement of the issues. When a new tax farmer was appointed to Roussillon in 1685, Intendant Trobat wrote a letter in May requesting that "concerning the sale of salt, the new *fermier* leave things in the same state in which he finds them, maintaining the reduction of prices according to the treaties made with the inhabitants of the frontier."[204] That Trobat's motive was the avoidance of any recurrence of violence is evidenced in the same letter, in which he condemned the former tax farmer for attempting to repeal the settlements that had been reached in Roussillon. Louvois agreed, writing in June of the same year that no changes should be made in the practices of selling and distributing salt unless those alterations were first discussed with the intendant.

Even though the Angelet rebellion was ultimately suppressed, salt smuggling continued, as evidenced by the continuing records of prosecutions for this crime. As late as 1702, for example, priests in the cathedral church of Perpignan were arrested for possession of untaxed salt. This incident does not, however, necessarily indicate a continued resistance to French rule. It could quite easily be interpreted as men attempting to save money by avoiding the payment of taxes, since there was no legal or philosophical justification known to be attached to these later acts.[205]

An interesting parallel to the Angelet revolt occurred in the western end of the Pyrenees mountains. An uprising against the *gabelle* took place in and around Bearn from April 1664 until August 1665. This uprising was called the Audijos uprising, after Bernard d'Audijos, its leader. He was a petty noble of the region and he and his band employed guerrilla tactics against French troops. Spain played a minor role in this anti-*gabelle* movement, serving as a haven for the rebels and offering assistance when possible. The Audijos revolt was a typical reaction against the salt tax in the reign of Louis XIV. Despite the superficial similarities between the revolt in Bearn and that in Roussillon, the differences point out the unique nature of the Angelet rebellion. Two points of contrast are especially clear. First, typical anti-*gabelle* risings lasted for a year or two, and then either dissipated or were crushed. The revolt of the Angelets, however, lasted almost two decades. Second, most revolts against the *gabelle* were generally popular among the residents of region but rarely gained real material support in the face of a French military presence. Again the Roussillonnais were distinctive. The Vallespir and much of the Conflent provided active material support, havens, and bases for recruitment to the rebels throughout much of the 1660s and 1670s. These two major differences between other tax revolts and the Angelet rebellion underscore Roussillonnais resistance to France. Most other anti-tax rebellions were financial in nature and sought a diminution in the tax, whereas the Angelets made an appeal to Catalan law and custom, an appeal with which many Roussillonnais agreed.[206]

By the judicious combination of military force, negotiated compromises, and a great deal of patience, the French suppressed the Angelet rebellion after a decade of struggle. When this revolt ended in 1679, it marked the completion of France's goal of political assimilation. After the Peace of Nijmegen in 1679, there were no more popular displays against French rule in Roussillon. There were still individuals who acted against the French government, sometimes for political reasons and sometimes from hope of personal gain. There were still acts of violence and resistance in the province, but these were usually spontaneous responses to individual incidents, not part of a pattern of dissatisfaction with French rule in general. The permanent withdrawal of Trinxeria into Spain in 1679 marks the point at which the few anti-French Roussillonnais and the pro-French factions both recognized that the province was safely part of the French political system.

THE CONSPIRACIES OF 1674

In 1674, coinciding with the French war against the Dutch, groups of citizens in Villefranche-de-Conflent, Perpignan, and other smaller villages developed an elaborate plot to throw open their cities to Spanish troops and thus free themselves from French rule. Their plan had been carefully worked out with the Count of San German, Spanish viceroy of Catalonia and, through him, Josep de la Trinxeria. Joan Boixó, the brother of a priest in Forques, was a student residing in Barcelona, and under pretense of visiting his relatives, had served as the messenger between the Roussillonnais and the Spanish over the course of many months. Contact between the conspiring groups within Roussillon was usually maintained by Josep Tixedas, who frequently traveled from Perpignan to the Conflent.

Emanuel de Llupià, a Roussillonnais who had been driven from the province by the French twenty-two years earlier, was to infiltrate from Spain with over 500 picked Spanish and Catalan soldiers and wait at Arles-sur-Tech. The viceroy was to mass a troop of 30,000 men near the border, to be moved on Perpignan at the opportune moment. On 16 March, Friday of Holy Passion Week, Trinxeria would provide a strong diversionary attack on the French, forcing reinforcements to be rushed into the Vallespir. During this distraction, Llupià and his men would proceed to Villefranche while the Spanish soldiers marched through Maureillas and Ille-sur-Tech to Perpignan, and in both cities the conspirators would be waiting to throw open their cities. If everything went well, the viceroy was to follow these successes by moving Spanish troops into the Cerdagne and occupying the rest of French Catalonia. The reunification of Catalonia would then be accomplished, and the boldness of the move would leave the French no option but to negotiate the return of Roussillon to Spain.

Among those leading the conspiracy in Villefranche-de-Conflent were Emanuel Descallar i de Soler, a twenty-six-year-old "gentleman of illustrious birth who has many illustrious ancestors,"[207] and who had previously been exiled for aiding the Angelet insurrection; his cousin Francesc de Llar; Carles de Banyuls, Seigneur de Nyer, whose father, Tomàs de Banyuls, had been expelled in 1652 for rebelling against the French; Joan Soler, the second consul of Villefranche; and Emanuel Boixó, a priest at Forques who had often spied on French military movements for the Spanish. The parallel plot developed in Perpignan included Josep Tixedas, formerly a member of Noailles's personal guard; Francesc Puig i Terrats, a lawyer; Francesc Ça Cirera, a leading citizen of Perpignan; Josep Vilaroja, a notary; Josep Gelcen, a lawyer; Macià Tixedas, brother of Josep and a cavalry officer in the French army; and Antoni Ribet, a former consul of Perpignan.

At Villefranche, the conspirators planned a procession for the evening of Holy Thursday. Francesc de Llar asked the head of the French garrison in the town, Parlan de Saignes, if the 200 soldiers garrisoned in Villefranche would serve as torch bearers for the procession. Coincidentally with de Llar's request, Lieutenant-General Le Bret, commander of French forces in Roussillon, had sent for another two companies of troops because the Spanish were massing troops at Puigcerda. The conspirators thought they had been discovered, and many of them fled for Spain during the night of 21 March. The following morning several more guilty Roussillonnais fled the province. The sudden exodus of the town's leading citizens aroused suspicions in Le Bret's mind. At the same time, a Spanish army that had been advancing on Pla de les Llençades suddenly withdrew. In parallel to these developments, the conspirators were also betrayed by Agnès de Llar, cousin of Francesc de Llar, who was involved with de Saignes. In order to advance herself in his affections, she revealed everything she could uncover about the conspiracy. The news from Saignes about the conspiracy then gave substance to the suspicions of Le Bret.[208]

It should be noted that some modern scholars have rejected Agnès de Llar's involvement in discovering the conspiracy.[209] It is claimed, for example, that her father, Carles de Llar, was not actively involved in the plot, and therefore Agnès could have learned nothing. Considering the extremely close nature of family relationships in small towns in early modern Europe, it is highly unlikely that Carles de Llar, even if not plotting, knew nothing of the conspiracy. In the close quarters of the family circles, it is quite likely that Agnès de Llar overheard a great deal of the plans that were made. The documents issued by the Sovereign Council implicate her, moreover. The Sovereign Council explicitly stated that de Saignes had been warned of a plot by an inhabitant, and later named her as that informant.[210]

Having discovered the plot only days before its execution, the Sovereign Council moved rapidly to seize the conspirators. A councillor, Fructus de Quéralt, was dispatched to Villefranche to conduct investigations on the spot. In the home of Jeroni Prats was found a signed document that outlined the entire conspiracy. As the enormity of the plot became apparent, two more councillors, Francesc de Martí and Isidore de Prat, were also sent to aid the investigations. In the course of their probe, the councillors were approached by Josep Bordes, a theology student from Prades. He offered to testify in return for immunity, an offer that was accepted. As the investigations proceeded, dozens of suspects were arrested, gradually revealing a large conspiracy spreading across much of the upper Conflent. Josep Puig of Corneilla, at least twenty men of Pi and Sahorra, two consuls of Prades, and residents of Fulla, Las Illas, and Oletta were among those implicated.[211]

When secrecy was broken, Emanuel Descallar, unlike many of his fellow conspirators, refused to flee to Spain. He was arrested and taken to the citadel in Perpignan, where he underwent judicial torture. Under this duress he confirmed everything, including his own role in the plot. On 26 April 1674, Emanuel Descallar was executed for lèse-majesté, with several other members of his family. Carles de Llar, one of the few members of the de Llar family still in Roussillon, was tried for his role in the conspiracy. Both Bordes and Descallar, with testimonies extracted under very different circumstances, agreed that Carles de Llar was not involved in the plots. Despite these assurances, he was found guilty, and on 4 May received the garrot. The rest of the de Llar family, excepting Agnès, was banished from Roussillon, and Agnès was imprisoned in a convent.

In the course of the investigations in Villefranche, Le Bret began to uncover signs that a parallel plot had developed in Perpignan, and moved to arrest conspirators there. Josep Tixedas was detained on suspicion in the capital, although nothing could be proven against him. At this arrest, Josep Vilaroja became frightened, and, in return for immunity, he revealed details of the plot in the capital. He confirmed that Tixedas was one of the men who maintained contact with the Spanish viceroy, and revealed the names of many other conspirators as well. Among those implicated were leading citizens of the city, including Josep Rossell, a doctor of philosophy, Joan Cossana, commander of Saint Antoine de Vienne in Perpignan, and Antoni Garau, a *docteur en droit*. As in Villefranche, some the conspirators in Perpignan feld to Spain, while others were captured and tried.[212]

Emanuel Boixó was denied clerical immunity and was executed at the Plaça de la Llotja in Perpignan. Josep Tixedas was garroted on 16 May, and his brother Macià was executed in front of the cathedral and then beheaded. Puig i Terrats was questioned and tortured at great length, revealed everything, including his own role as leader in the Perpignan conspiracy, and was executed on 19 May. The head of Macià Tixedas was displayed in Perpignan as a warning. In the same way, the heads of Descallar, Joan Soler, and Carles de Llar were displayed outside Villefranche for some years as a caution to future rebels. Agnès de Llar, despite a pardon received from Louvois in October 1674, was shunned by everyone she knew. Most of her neighbors viewed her as a traitor to Catalonia and to her family, de Saignes did not marry her and was transferred away from Villefranche, and she had neither the means nor knowledge to move away from the Conflent. As a result, she took holy orders and remained in a convent for the rest of her life.[213]

Among those who had fled to Spain was Emanuel de Llupià, who continued to fight against France for the rest of his life, becoming a knight of the Order of Alcantara, an officer of artillery, and vice governor of Catalonia. Carles de Banyuls also fled to Spain, and was executed in effigy in Roussillon. All of his property and goods were seized by the Sovereign Council. His wife, the daughter of Lieutenant-General Josep d'Ardena, remained in Roussillon, and all of her husband's property was eventually transferred to her. The marquisate of Montferrer was created for her in April 1675, in recognition of the loyalty displayed by her and her father. [214]

The leaders of the conspiracies had either been executed or had fled the country within a few weeks of their discovery. The Sovereign Council, however, was determined to root out all culpable individuals so that they might not plot again. The Sovereign Council continued to hunt for remaining enemies of the state for three years. In July 1677, it registered an edict from the king granting a pardon to the remaining conspirators, who were minor players. Occasional interest was shown in the conspiracies until 1679, when the issue was finally laid to rest.[215]

The conspiracies of 1674, like the Angelet rebellion, mark the turning point for the French presence in Roussillon. Early in the 1670s, antipathy toward France was so great that the leading citizens risked their lives in an effort to drive the French from Roussillon. The immediate, forceful, and violent reaction of the government indicated that anti-French sentiment was perceived as a real threat to French policies in the province. For the next several years, the government continued to live in the shadow of the conspiracies, striving to eliminate the conspirators and fearing their appeal. By 1679, however, the conspiracies had become merely a historical issue, and the threat of conspiracy had become theoretical. Once again, 1679 can be seen as marking the point by which the French had achieved their goals.

INDIVIDUAL ACTS OF RESISTANCE

In addition to the resistance offered by groups of people as evidenced in the Camprodon affair, the Angelet rebellion, and the conspiracies of 1674, the French were also often the targets of acts of resistance undertaken by individuals. The most common forms of resistance included passing intelligence to the Spanish, joining Spanish armies to fight against France, and attempting to subvert the loyalty of French troops in the province. These individual acts of defiance were the only form of open resistance found in Roussillon after the 1670s, the time by which most Roussillonnais had come to accept French rule.

One such spy case developed into a serious incident in 1677 in the village of Massenette. The commandant of the fort at Bellegarde, Saint-André, received reports that an inhabitant of that village had been spying on French activities in Roussillon for the Spanish. Two companies from the Regiment d'Anjou were dispatched on 1 December to arrest the man and return him to Bellegarde for questioning. When the troops arrived at the village, the inhabitants became enraged and began firing shots at them and then charged the soldiers. Seven or eight French soldiers were killed, and more were wounded. In addition, the townsmen captured about forty of the soldiers and sent them to Barcelona as prisoners.[216]

The situation was very different later in the reign of Louis XIV, after most Roussillonnais became accommodated to French rule. In 1690, for example, a new commandant of Bellegarde, de Bruelh, arrested a man from Agullane on suspicion of spying for the Spanish. Intendant Trobat personally investigated the charges and decided that "there is neither suspicion nor appearance that any person of quality has entered into these negotiations, nor even a resident of the area."[217] Trobat went on to qualify his statement by adding that one or two smugglers might have aided the spy.[218]

Two year later, in 1692, Antoni Alverny of Collioure and Rafel Percer of Banyuls-de-Maresme were found guilty of passing intelligence to the Spanish. The Sovereign Council sentenced them to corporal punishment and heavy fines. In 1707, Nicolas Couloumier, a *clerc de procureur*, was condemned to serve six years in the galleys for attempting to help a cavalry officer escape. These rebels' intention was to provide intelligence to the enemy about the state of defenses in Roussillon.[219]

The difference between the incident in 1677 and later ones is striking. The first example illustrates the tense atmosphere in Roussillon before 1680. That the commandant felt it necessary to dispatch 100 men to arrest a single spy reveals that he was concerned about the possibility of popular assistance being provided to the suspect. The fact that those two companies were insufficient to arrest the spy indicates not only that the commandant was correct, but also that he in fact underestimated the depth of anti-French sentiment. The later incidents were clearly the acts of single individuals, without community support. A crime that led to such explosive results in 1677 was punished only by beating and fines fifteen years later. Resistance to France had not disappeared even by the end of Louis XIV's reign. The striking change in the outcomes of the spying incidents, however, indicates that activities directed against the French presence became exceptional and were perceived as relatively non-threatening by the government.

Another method of resistance by which individuals expressed their dissatisfaction with and opposition to French rule was by actively aiding the Spanish armies. This aid could take the form of providing intelligence, as previously discussed, but more active assistance was also a possibility. Many Roussillonnais, for example, joined the Spanish army to fight against France. The military unit into which most Roussillonnais enrolled was the Spanish mountain fusiliers, which spent most of its existence fighting the Pyrenees mountains. According to the Duke of Noailles, these men were very successful at "destroying little by little our armies."[220] These emigrés were so successful that the governor was inspired to create his own fusilier unit from the ranks of loyal Roussillonnais, which was then used against Spanish armies in Catalonia. Most of the Roussillonnais that are known to have joined the Spanish army did so by deserting from the French army. Upon being con-scripted, many residents chose to fight against the French army rather than with it, and so deserted to Spain.[221]

A different way in which some Roussillonnais offered assistance to the Spanish was to offer shelter and food to the Spanish forces when they were in Roussillon. Joan Bonet and Josep Vilanova, two young men of the Vallespir, were convicted of fighting with the invading Spanish armies late in 1674. As did other forms of active resistance, aiding the Spanish through military service declined after the first two decades of French rule in Roussil-lon, and it became especially rare for the Roussillonnais to offer any assistance to invading Spanish armies after 1680.[222]

Individuals also demonstrated resistance to France by attempting to subvert the French garrisons in Roussillon. Except for the conspiracies of Villefranche and Perpignan, most plots against French positions were conducted by one or two people, and relied on bribery or seduction, rather than military action and Spanish intervention. For example, coincident with but independent of the great conspiracies of 1674, Marie Guitart developed a plot against Fort des Bains. Acting on her own initiative, she attempted to induce several soldiers of that fortress into throwing open its gates if a Spanish army approached. The disorganized nature of her plot and the indiscretion of her advances led to her intentions being discovered by the commandant, and she was tried and executed for treason.[223]

Throughout the first two decades after the annexation of Roussillon to France, the inhabitants of the province had recourse to a variety of methods of open resistance to Louis XIV's rule. There were various conspiracies, most notably those involving Teresa de Camprodon, the notables of Villefranche, and several leading citizens of Perpignan. Open rebellion through the Vallespir and, at times, parts of the Conflent also evidence the hostility felt for France by the Roussillonnais. Many people did not participate in these group acts of dissent, yet still undertook individual acts of violence against French interests in Roussillon. It is notable, however, that most people who acted against the

French did so before 1680, and every significant threat to French rule occurred before that year. Acts of violence against France continued after 1680 but never received popular support, and, more significant, were never considered to be a threat by the French after that period. Thus, the open resistance to France in Roussillon indicates the initial level of antipathy to the French and implicitly confirms that the French were ultimately successful in incorporating Roussillon into the French polity.

Chapter 6

Other Forms of Resistance to French Rule

In addition to revolts, conspiracies, and espionage, French rule in Roussillon was also resisted by less violent activities such as non-payment of taxes, refusing to associate with French immigrants, harassing French officials, and a variety of other means. Leading nobles and other persons of means emigrated throughout the first years after the French annexation. The lower clergy of the province demonstrated hostility to their new masters by rejecting French appointees, appealing to foreign clerical hierarchies, and aiding and encouraging the peasants to resist the French government. The peasants also resisted French rule in Roussillon. They maintained their economic contacts with Catalonia, openly discriminated against French neighbors, and were generally slow to pay their taxes. Even the municipal and provincial governments at times demonstrated some form of resistance by refusing to implement certain laws and edicts from Paris. All of these groups engaged in resistance, often for diverse reasons and to differing degrees, but all ultimately came to accept French rule in Roussillon, even while rejecting French culture.

EMIGRATION
One of the first forms of resistance displayed by the Roussillonnais after the Peace of the Pyrenees was emigration from the province to Spanish Catalonia. There are no precise data concerning the number of persons who fled Roussillon, but it is estimated that approximately 2,000 people left the province after it was ceded to France. The most important source of this emigration was the rural nobility, men such as the Baron Alemany de Cervellon, the Baron de Saint-Marsal, the Comte de Plaisance, the Seigneur de Llupia, and the Vicomte de Juch. Another, only slightly less important group that experienced a significant emigration was the bourgeoisie of Perpignan. Many members of both groups moved to Spain rather than accept French rule over Roussillon. As life under French domination became unbearable, other

disaffected French Catalans moved to Spanish Catalonia. Among the most notable examples of these later emigrants were those fleeing the sentence of French courts. Ramon de Monfar, Josep de Camprodon, Josep de la Trinxeria, Emanuel de Llupia, Carles de Banyuls, and Josep Gelcen were some of those who fled to Spain because of legal proceedings instituted against them. The first group of emigrants and those who left later usually moved to be near their families in the Principat. Nearly every Catalan of any social standing had relatives on both sides of the frontier, and so would have kinsmen who would take him in. Emigration as a form of resistance actually proved to be a benefit to the French. Many unhappy Roussillonnais left the province and no longer challenged the French or stirred up sentiment against them. On the whole, the emigrants were of little concern to France, as the exiles gradually became involved in Spanish politics and were absorbed by Iberian Catalan concerns.[224]

THE CLERGY

The lower clergy of Roussillon were the social group most stridently opposed to the French presence in the province and most diligent in resisting that presence. In addition to open rebellion and conspiracy against the French, the clergy engaged in several significant types of resistance. Frenchmen and pro-French Catalans within the church's hierarchy were often the focus of defiance, the indigenous clergy seeking to undermine them whenever possible. Churchmen in opposition to France also made appeals to extra-territorial religious establishments in Spain and Rome, and those hierarchies in turn supported and encouraged resistance to France. The clergy also demonstrated resistance to France by encouraging, tacitly and explicitly, resistance on the part of the other inhabitants of Roussillon. Finally, the clergy resisted France by ignoring, circumventing, and condemning the political structures and leaders established by Louis XIV in the province. Clerical resistance to the French control of Roussillon was very strong, but ultimately it proved to be only an irritant to the French. The province was assimilated into the French political system despite clerical protests, and the clergy themselves were gradually transformed through persuasion and punishment into a basically loyal social group.

Resistance to French Appointees

One way in which the clergy displayed hostility toward the French without open rebellion was by constantly challenging the bishop, a prelate chosen by France. The first bishop chosen by Louis XIV, Don Vicenç de Margarit i de Biure, was a Catalan and former bishop of Barcelona. Despite these credentials, his selection was challenged by the Cathedral Chapter of Saint Jean, and he was never popular among most of the clergy of his diocese. The monks of the Church de la Real in Perpignan, for example, refused to allow Margarit to examine their accounts when he was bishop. In a similar manner, every bishop appointed by Louis XIV had to contend with intransigence on the part of his clergy, and the records of the Sovereign Council are full of injunctions ordering recalcitrant clergy to comply with the various commands of the bishops. The French wished the bishop to serve as an agent of assimilation and acculturation, and so that office became a focus for resistance and hostility from the clergy.[225]

Any Frenchman or pro-French Catalan who held a religious office in Roussillon could, and often did, became an object of clerical hostility. Jean Louis de Brueil, a Frenchman, was named Grand Inquisitor of Roussillon in 1663. The Cathedral Chapter of Elne immediately protested to the Sovereign Council and Rome against his selection. Despite the injunctions of the Sovereign Council, which reinforced his appointment and ordered the priests to accept him, the chapter consistently questioned his authority. In 1669, for example, it accused him of having "expressly contradicted scripture"[226] in order to extract questionable tithes. The same year the Dominicans in Perpignan were engaged in a theological dispute with Brueil, demonstrating his unpopularity with the regular and secular clergy. Louvois recognized the effects this subtle opposition was having and cautioned the Sovereign Council that "it is necessary, as much as possible, to avoid divisions among the clergy in a region such as Roussillon"[227] and encouraged them to reconcile the pro- and anti-French factions. Despite the efforts of the Sovereign Council to encourage his acceptance, Brueil continued to be unpopular in the province until his death.[228]

Another individual who represented the pro-French faction in Roussillon and was therefore held suspect by the clergy was Jeroni Lléopart, *vicaire capitulaire* of the diocese. Lléopart was an emigrant from Barcelona who had fought for France from 1639 to 1640, and later spent three years at the court in Paris. After the French annexation of Roussillon, the canons of the cathedral chapter of Elne appointed Vilaroja to the secretariat of the *vicaire capitulaire*. Lléopart, representing the pro-French faction of the church, promptly fired Vilaroja, who was from the anti-French group. On two occasions in late February 1663, the cathedral chapter demanded the reinstatement of Vilaroja, asserting that Lléopart had usurped the chapter's rights in firing him. Members further protested his use of the title *vicaire general apostolique*, which implied that he was the single head of the diocese. Lléopart rejected the idea that he had infringed on their prerogatives and argued that, canonically, in the absence of a bishop, he was the chief religious leader of the diocese. Unwilling to accept this intransigence, the cathedral chapter escalated the conflict.

The canons wrote to Rome for adjudication of the controversy. In their correspondence, they introduced a third complaint, that Lléopart had been using the seal of the *vicaire capitulaire* in those situations where the seal of the cathedral chapter was required, effectively usurping their power. Pope

Alexander VII Chigi, being hostile toward Louis XIV and France for many reasons, supported the canons in all their complaints. As a result, in early 1664, the canons deposed Lléopart and installed Francesc de Quéralt, brother of Fructus de Quéralt, a member of the Sovereign Council.

Lléopart was furious at such treatment and appealed to the Sovereign Council. On 2 May 1664, the Sovereign Council issued an *arrêt* requesting that both men stop performing their duties until the problem could be resolved. Since he was fairly well assured of a favorable judgment, Lléopart accepted this solution. Queralt and the cathedral chapter, on the other hand, refused this provisional settlement. In consequence, the Sovereign Council reinstated Lléopart until such time as the situation would be ultimately resolved.

Francesc de Quéralt then heightened the conflict still further, excommunicating Francesc de Sagarra, Francesc de Martí, two *hussiers*, and an *alguazil* of the Sovereign Council. As this challenge to French authority continued to escalate, the struggle became of increasing interest to the entire city of Perpignan. The Sovereign Council met on 21 May and condemned Francesc de Quéralt, Sebastien Garriga, arch-deacon of the cathedral chapter, and Pugsesch, *curé* of St. Jean for their opposition. News of this condemnation was leaked to the anti-French group before its public proclamation, many believe by Fructus de Quéralt.

On the morning of 22 May, Francesc de Quéralt excommunicated the entire Sovereign Council and repeated the action later that day from the chair of the cathedral. This infuriated the council, which issued an edict banishing Francesc de Quéralt, Garriga, and Pugsesch. The banishment orders were given to Châtillon, the lieutenant-governor, who was to enforce them. Châtillon, seeking to avoid further inflaming the situation, sought a conference with Intendant Charles Macqueron and the *avocats généreaux* of the Sovereign Council, Ramon de Trobat and Francesc de Martí.

Word again leaked out, and the morning of 23 May found the three clerics barricaded in the cathedral of St. Jean, armed with pistols and carbines. They claimed that they were protecting clerical immunity against French encroachments. Châtillon did not want to send his soldiers to storm the cathedral, and so the Sovereign Council dispatched Ramon de Trobat to Paris to apprise the king of the situation.

When Charles Macqueron, the intendant, went into the cathedral to celebrate Mass, the service was halted. Francesc de Quéralt announced that the presence of Macqueron had corrupted the Host, and the Mass could not be celebrated. A short time later, a papal decision arrived that condemned Lléopart, declaring him to be a criminal for appealing to the Sovereign Council. The council, in its turn, annulled that papal decree and condemned the three leaders for appealing to Rome. On 8 August 1664, the king ordered Châtillon to follow any instructions given to him by the Sovereign Council.

Having been given a completely free hand to resolve the situation, the Sovereign Council was now dealing from a position of considerable strength. This information reached the conspirators, and they reluctantly backed down. Lléopart was confirmed in the position as *vicaire capitulaire*, which he held until 1669. The anti-French clerics apologized to the government, and, in some cases, even came to accept the French presence in Roussillon. Indeed, Francesc de Quéralt became the *vicaire général* for the new bishop, Vicenç de Margarit in 1669.

Since the *vicaire capitulaire* was, in the absence of a bishop, the Church's most prominent symbol of the pro-French Catalans, Lléopart remained a focus of discontent for the anti-French clergy. In the summer of 1666, he became involved in a dispute with the university, which was often a locus of anti-French sentiment. The rector of the university, Llorens Carrera, came to blows with a *canon bénéficier* named Sirvent, and the latter was injured. Lléopart, acting as the self-proclaimed head of the church in Roussillon, excommunicated Carrera. At that, the chancellor of the university, Michel Vilardell, excommunicated Lléopart for violating university privileges.

The canons of the cathedral chapter were divided on whom to support, with the division mirroring attitudes toward France. The Catalan nationalists declared Lléopart deposed and announced that Garriga was the acting *vicaire capitulaire*. The Sovereign Council told both men to restrain themselves until the situation could be sorted out. Lléopart's years in Paris ensured his continued success, as can be seen from the support he was given by Louvois. The latter minister told the Sovereign Council that Lléopart was to retain his position. Garriga then became more conciliatory toward the French. As a reward, in 1673 he was awarded the post of *vicaire général* for a French bishop, Jean-Louis de Brueil, with the blessings of the Sovereign Council.[229]

Another similar case involved Josep de Trobat, brother of Ramon de Trobat. When Lléopart died in 1671, Josep de Trobat was appointed his successor as *grande sacristain*. At the same time, however, Emanuel Oyonarte traveled to Rome, obtaining a papal bull in April 1672 that awarded him that position. Upon Oyonarte's return in the spring of 1673, his actions were discovered. As punishment, the French government banished him from the province and asserted that the royal orders took precedence over the papal ones. On the morning of Holy Thursday of 1673, placards that declared Josep de Trobat excommunicated were in place on every church door in Perpignan. The excommunication, dated 27 February 1673, was passed on Trobat for appealing a clerical matter to secular judges.

The Sovereign Council, which could not allow its authority to be challenged in this manner, called together the leading pro-French theologians and canonical jurists of the province. This group, selected by Sovereign Council to ensure a favourable judgment, reveals the clerical bases of support for France in Roussillon. The Jesuits, France's staunchest supporters in

Roussillon, were disproportionately represented. It is not surprising that this group found in favor of Josep de Trobat, declaring the excommunication to be without foundation and therefore completely void.[230]

In addition to the cases involving Brueil, Lléopart, and Trobat, there were a number of similar but less significant episodes in Roussillon. Throughout the first two decades of French rule in the province, clerical benefices were repeatedly contested by pro- and anti-French claimants. Typically, when a vacancy occurred in the Church hierarchy, the Sovereign Council would appoint an individual to that position, and the Papal Court would appoint a different person to the same office. When two such claimants existed for a position, the clergy of Roussillon usually supported the priest who was appointed by Rome in order to oppose the Sovereign Council. The conclusion in such cases was, however, invariable: The Sovereign Council ensured that its claimant obtained the position. Josep Balba, for example, obtained Papal bulls awarding him a benefice already granted to Jean-Baptiste Chiavari by the Sovereign Council. It was Chiavari who retained the position.[231]

Another example of clerical resistance to the French government and its appointees in Roussillon is the behavior of the nuns of Sainte Claire de la Passion in Perpignan. Unlike the preceding examples, these women were not confronting an individual representative of French authority but rather opposed the general concept of French control.

Sainte Claire de la Passion, founded in 1270, was highly esteemed throughout Catalonia. During the struggle with Spain in the 1650s, however, Francesc de Sagarra had exiled twenty of the cloistered nuns of the house to Gerona and Barcelona for anti-French sentiment and activity. When Queen Anne of France was in Perpignan on 10 April 1660, the abbess of St. Claire implored the queen to allow the exiles to return. The queen agreed, intervened on the behalf of the exiles, and obtained their return on 25 May. Within the ecclesiastical hierarchy of Roussillon, the Clarisses were under the spiritual authority of the Franciscans of Perpignan. As a result of the French policies of acculturation, the Franciscan monastery came to be staffed by French monks. The nuns, led by a returned exile named Anne-Marie Antigo, claimed that Franciscan supervision put them in spiritual jeopardy, since none of the friars could understand the Catalan of the nuns' confessions. Certainly there were few Catalans among the Franciscans, but it was widely accepted in the seventeenth century that the nuns simply wanted to avoid associations with the pro-French monks. As a result, in 1664 the nuns of Sainte Claire appealed to the pope, requesting that he place them under the authority of *ordinaire* of the diocese. The result of such a move would be to place the Clarisses under the jurisdiction of the secular clergy in Roussillon, the arm of the Roussillonnais church that was most active in resisting French authority. The conflict thus became an anti-French protest with three facets: The nuns emphasized the Catalan over the French language, they appealed to the Papal Court in Rome over the Sovereign Council or Paris, and they wished to join the more hostile secular clergy in the province.

Pope Alexander VII Chigi, a committed opponent of Louis XIV and all French policies, agreed with the Clarisses and on 17 July 1665 placed them under the supervision of the *ordinaire*. The Sovereign Council denied the validity of the change, insisting that the Franciscans were the legitimate authorities to supervise the nuns. This conflict between French Gallicanism and papal ultramontanism was finally resolved by a compromise between the king of France and Alexander's successor, Pope Clement IX Rospigliosi. In 1667 the king agreed to allow the Clarisses to remain under the jurisdiction of the *ordinaire*. The monarch, however, was given authority to name the bishop of Perpignan, who in turn selected the *ordinaire*. The nuns of Sainte Claire de la Passion had thus won their point, and greatly inconvenienced the French, but ultimately were able to impose no real compromises or restrictions upon the French.[232]

Appealing to Non-French Hierarchies

Another form of resistance undertaken by the clergy of Roussillon was appealing to and encouraging intervention by ecclesiastical authorities from outside France. The two most important of these foreign religious authorities were the Catholic Church in Spanish Catalonia and the Papal Court at Rome. There were several important religious houses in the province that were controlled by Spanish mother houses. At the time of annexation, every major religious establishment in Roussillon answered to a Catalan mother house. Many of those were reassigned to French mother houses. Some of these monasteries, however, could not be so easily removed from Catalan influence. Saint Genis des Fontaines, for example, was long an important center of resistance to French rule. This presidency of this monastery was, however, under the nomination of the Abbey of Montserrat in Spanish Catalonia, which meant that Catalan theological and cultural traditions continued to be introduced into Roussillon through Saint Genis. Since Montserrat possessed the right of nomination of the presidency, the French had no mechanism by which to shape policies in this influential monastery, and so it served as a vehicle of foreign intervention in Roussillon.[233]

In addition to monasteries that served as extensions of houses in the Principat, parts of the secular clergy in Roussillon were under the direct jurisdiction of Spanish bishops. The Diocese of Urgel encompassed the whole of the French Cerdagne. Thus the entire clerical hierarchy of that area was appointed by and answered to a Catalan from Spain. This led, quite predictably, to many conflicts between the Sovereign Council and the bishop of Urgel over appointments, policies, and loyalties among the clergy. As in the case of Saint Genis, the Cerdanyol parishes were directly subject to foreign control and served as conduits by which Catalan identity and culture were transmitted from the Principat to Roussillon.

In addition to Catalan influence reaching into Roussillon, many Roussillonnais clergy went to Spanish Catalonia to study and take orders. Despite repeated prohibitions and prosecutions on the part of the Sovereign Council, significant numbers of clergy traveled to the Principat to obtain theological training and to receive orders, and then returned to Roussillon to serve the residents of the province. These illicit voyages to Spain were not simply individual actions of discontent and resistance, but were encouraged by the ecclesiastical hierarchy of Roussillon. The abbot of Arles, for example, was arrested for encouraging those who desired to become monks to travel to Barcelona for training and investiture. Receiving clerical training in the Principat evidenced resistance to both goals of France for Roussillon. Disobedience to explicit French proclamations demonstrated resistance to the French desire for political assimilation, and Catalan religious training was in direct opposition to French plans for acculturation. [234]

In addition to Spanish Catalonia, the other major foreign influence that the Roussillonnais accepted as an act of resistance was that of Rome. Most of the popes during the reign of Louis XIV were hostile to France, and so might have viewed opposition to French actions in Roussillon as a means of burdening the king. The disputes involving Lléopart and Quéralt, Trobat and Oyonarte, Chiavary and Balba, and the Clarisses all provide examples both of the willingness of the clergy to appeal to Rome and of the pope's favorable disposition toward the anti-French faction in Roussillon. Another example of the pope's hostility to France is found in the long delay in recognizing French ecclesiastical reorganization. The French placed Perpignan under the sufferance of the archbishop of Narbonne in 1678, but for at least six more years the pope refused to acknowledge the French decision. In a similar manner, the Holy See waited until ten years after annexation before finally allowing Louis XIV the right to choose the bishops of Perpignan. As late as 1713, the pope was proving difficult for the French, claiming that rights he enjoyed in Iberia should be granted in Roussillon as well. [235]

Encouraging Resistance by the Roussillonnais

Still another mechanism by which the clergy of Roussillon demonstrated resistance to French rule was through the encouragement of resistance to France among their parishioners. The most celebrated cases of this type of resistance occurred during the Angelet rebellion. In addition to the several priests who were active in leading military operations against the French, many others encouraged the Roussillonnais not to pay the *gabelle*, stored illegal salt in their churches, and refused to co-operate with French inquests in their villages. The investigations of the Sovereign Council repeatedly indicted large numbers of clerics in the Vallespir, including parish priests, priors, abbots, and rectors. There were also many priests who fell into disfavor with the French, not for complicity with any rebellion but for general opposition to France. The head of the Franciscans in Villefranche, for example, was exiled in 1666 because he was "a man whose spirit is inquiet, and life black with crime;"[236] that is, he preached against the French. Clerical encouragement of resistance and sermons vilifying the French were particularly important forms of resistance in Roussillon. The church was, for most individuals of seventeenth-century Roussillon, the primary source of information about politics, economics, and culture. Since the priests were the transmitters of that information, the hostility they felt to France was transferred to their parishioners. Clerical opposition to France, especially when the ecclesiastics encouraged the opposition of others, was therefore one of the most significant forms of resistance in French Roussillon. [237]

Harassment of Government Structures and Personnel

An additional form of resistance undertaken by the clergy in Roussillon was disobedience to and harassment of French political officials in Roussillon. One common example of this type of resistance was refusing to pay taxes. Most of the clergy of the province exempted themselves from many of the taxes levied by the French. The *gabelle* was, of course, the most commonly ignored tax, and the clergy continued to import salt without paying the taxes into the eighteenth century. There were, however, other taxes that the clergy frequently declined to pay. Clergymen were prosecuted in the seventeenth century for refusal to pay *droits de rente*, *dons gratuits*, *douanes*, and a variety of lesser imposts throughout Roussillon.[238]

Another way in which the clergy could harass and disobey the government officials of the province was by refusing to participate in festivals and processions ordered by the political leaders. A number of legalistic excuses could be used to explain why the clergy could not take part in any particular event the government ordered. These excuses, however, did not hide the reason behind the refusals: dislike for the French and their rule. In 1683, for example, the Sovereign Council planned a processional in honor of Saint Louis as an element in its grand plan for acculturating the province. The Parisian-born bishop of Perpignan, Louis Habert de Montmor, agreed that it was a good idea, and plans were developed. When the event came, however, the priests of the parish of Saint Mathieu in Perpignan refused to participate. Their excuse was that the orders for the processional had come from the *syndic majeur* of the cathedral rather than the bishop himself. The unwillingness of the clergy to participate in festivals and processionals was important in the province because the Roussillonnais were deeply religious. The sanction of the church was the cachet necessary to legitimize the French rule in such a profoundly Catholic area. As long as the clerics refused to take part in government-sponsored activities, that sanction would be painfully absent.[239]

In addition to direct or indirect disobedience to government directives, the church also harassed government officials. Just as Josep de Trobat, Jeroni Lléopart, and other pro-French clergy were excommunicated and beleaguered by the clergy, political officials working to achieve French goals of assimilation and acculturation were also harassed. Francesc de Sagarra, *president à mortier* of the Sovereign Council, was, for example, persecuted by the Roussillonnais clergy for at least a decade. In the first decade after annexation, on at least four occasions, letters were sent to Paris condemning Sagarra for employing an Italian to practice alchemy with him. The anonymous clergymen who sent the letters accused the president and his Italian of counterfeiting, and implied that even more sinister motives lay behind the experiments. Louvois finally felt constrained to send a letter to the Sovereign Council, telling them that "in order to satisfy the public and convince everyone, he [Sagarra] is to no longer work at chemistry, and he will expel from his home Joseph, who is an Italian of such poor reputation that he is capable of corrupting even the most innocent of men who would have contact with him."[240]

Sagarra sent away the Italian, but continued his experiments with the full knowledge and consent of Paris. Indeed, Louvois occasionally asked the intendants if the experiments were meeting with any success. The clergy, however, continued to attack Sagarra, condemning his interest in chemistry as evil. Letters continued to be sent to both the Sovereign Council and Paris, demanding that action be taken against Sagarra. The intendant and Louvois both dismissed these continual complaints as nuisances, motivated by jealousy of or dislike for Sagarra. Such personal attacks on pro-French political leaders were not uncommon in the first decades after annexation, and served as yet another demonstration of clerical unhappiness with the French presence.[241]

PEASANTS

The residents of Roussillon, although usually not as hostile to France as the clergy, demonstrated resistance to French rule until the 1680s. The most common forms of resistance included discrimination against the French and their supporters, non-payment of taxes, smuggling, and maintaining illegal cultural contacts with the Principat.

The most common form of resistance displayed by the inhabitants of Roussillon was discrimination against the French in the social and political life of the province. Socially, Frenchmen who moved to the province were rarely accepted into the life of the village in which they resided, especially outside Perpignan. The villagers applied the contemptuous term *gavatxos* to Frenchmen, even neighbors within the same hamlet. Religious services were in Catalan, which thus excluded most Frenchmen from that important social element of village life. In Perpignan and the smaller towns of the province, the French were often charged more to join the craft guilds. Indeed, every element of village life was steeped not only in the Catalan language, but also

Catalan traditions and culture, creating a impediment to understanding between French immigrants and the native Roussillonnais.[242]

Barriers to political office mirrored these social prejudices. Most of the villages of Roussillon created and enforced laws prohibiting Frenchmen from holding municipal office. The Sovereign Council, Louvois, and seigneural lords repeatedly warned the inhabitants of Roussillon that any discrimination against Frenchmen was illegal. In addition, the Roussillonnais managed to use French laws to discriminate against pro-French Catalans in the province. After the annexation, for example, Louis XIV had proclaimed a law that barred from municipal office all former Spanish subjects who had not lived in Roussillon since 1663. The intent of this law was to prohibit nationalist Catalans from moving out of the Principat into the province in order to create dissension. Many towns, however, were able to use this law to discriminate against the pro-French Catalans. Since most immigrants had possessed property in Spain, many returned to Spain at some point to dispose of that property. The native Roussillonnais then asserted that these men had not lived in Roussillon since the specified date, since they had returned to Spain for a few weeks, and therefore could not hold office. The intendant recognized these arguments as excuses to discriminate against the pro-French faction and ordered the towns to stop such activities.[243]

Discrimination against Frenchmen did not occur only in small villages or to new immigrants, but extended even to the well-established French of Perpignan. A French doctor resident six years in Perpignan drew up a complaint concerning the injustice that the French faced from the Catalans in Roussillon, a complaint that the local officials indicated was true in most cases. The Sovereign Council worked to annul all forms of legal discrimination against the French, but the cultural differences between the Catalans and French continued to create social tensions throughout the reign of Louis XIV.[244]

Another form of subtle resistance to French rule by the residents of Roussillon was the mistreatment of soldiers garrisoned in the province. This torment meted out by the Roussillonnais often resulted in discontent and desertion among the troops. Louvois recognized this fact in a letter to Intendant Macqueron in which the Minister of War wrote of an infantry commander: "[T]he treatment which is given to his soldiers by the residents of Prats-de-Mollo compels them to desert."[245] There were a variety of ways by which the inhabitants of the province effected this discontent. Villages often provided the minimum food and shelter required by the government, but refused to sell any goods to or provide any services for the troops. This forced inactivity on the soldiers, since they then had no access to taverns or markets. In a similar manner, troops were generally unwelcome in parish churches, further isolating the troops from both Roussillonnais customs and the inhabitants of the region. Verbal harassment was common, especially for Protestant troops stationed in Roussillon.[246]

A related form of resistance was encouraging desertion by Roussillonnais serving in the armies of France. Many residents were conscripted into or volunteered for military service, either in the militia or in the regular army. The residents of the province were often unhappy that their relatives were fighting for France, and encouraged the soldiers to leave the armies and return home. Homesickness and desertion were common problems in all armies of all nationalities in that era, but the French government repeatedly acknowledged that the Roussillonnais were especially troublesome in that regard.

Resistance to French rule was also displayed by the Roussillonnais through an unwillingness to pay taxes. The *gabelle* was so unpopular that it led to open rebellion, but every new tax introduced by the French meet with resistance as the inhabitants refused to pay. The *capitation* of 1695, the tax on tobacco, and customs duties were all widely ignored. These taxes, like the *gabelle*, were not resisted simply on fiscal grounds, but also because they were considered to be illegal usurpations of the *Usatges*.[247]

Closely associated with non-payment of taxes as a form of resistance was smuggling, which was extremely common in Roussillon. The inhabitants of the province had traded with the Principat for centuries, and French edicts banning such commerce were widely ignored. In the last five months of 1711, for example, over 1,000 sheep were captured while being smuggled across the frontier, and many more entered Roussillon without government knowledge. The French were certainly concerned about this commerce for economic reasons. Every item or animal transported illegally across the border meant lost tax revenue for the Sovereign Council. The captured sheep, for example, brought the government over 3,800 livres when sold. Had the animals entered the province undetected, several hundred livres in tax revenue would have been lost. More important, however, the continued illegal commerce with Catalonia demonstrated a disregard for French authority and continued contacts with the Principat, undermining the French goals of assimilation and acculturation. Despite government efforts, smuggling continued across the Pyrenees throughout the Old Regime. The smuggling was conducted less for financial reasons than because it reflected the traditional pattern of commerce continuing undisrupted.[248]

A final form of resistance expressed by the inhabitants of Roussillon was the maintenance of contacts with Spanish Catalonia despite French regulations prohibiting them. The Roussillonnais continued to trade with the Principat, travel to Barcelona for secular and religious education, take trips and send letters to Catalonia to contact relatives, read books from the Spanish presses, and consider themselves to be part of Catalonia. These contacts with the Principat were important because they reinforced a single cultural identity —the Catalan. This contact between Roussillon and Spanish Catalonia is one of the primary reasons that the French did not succeed in acculturating the Roussillonnais in the reign of Louis XIV.[249]

POLITICAL RESISTANCE

The political leaders of Roussillon also demonstrated resistance to French attempts to assimilate and acculturate the province. Political resistance was found not only at the level of municipal government, which often resisted all aspects of French rule in Roussillon, but also within the Sovereign Council, which at times served as a barrier to certain policies of acculturation. Local governments demonstrated hostility to France by protesting French laws and decisions, and occasionally by refusing to obey French edicts at all. The Sovereign Council, for its part, was an impediment to acculturation because it retained Catalan legal practices and institutions, and because it delayed the implementation of several important reforms in the province.

Local Governments

One way by which municipal governments could register their disapproval of and resistance to French decisions was by protesting those decisions. The remonstrances were directed to the intendant, the Sovereign Council, Louvois, and the king, and were often joined to inaction and passive disobedience. The village of Thuir, on the plain of Roussillon, provides an illustration of this method of resistance. At the time of annexation, the village of Thuir was one of ten in which the monarch possessed seigneural rights. As a reward for faithful service, the Marquis d'Aguilar was granted the seigneural rights of the village in July 1667. The king of Aragon, however, had agreed in 1431 never to alienate the seigneural rights of Thuir, and the village demanded that the French monarch respect that former promise. The French government rejected the complaints of the residents. For the next two years, however, the residents continued to protest and refused to accept decisions and orders from Aguilar. Finally, in April of 1669, the king confirmed the Aragonese promise and reunited Thuir to the royal domain.[250]

Such protests by municipal leaders were common, although they rarely met with the same success as Thuir. The consuls of Villefranche, for example, in 1672 protested the quartering of soldiers in their town. The consuls of Perpignan complained about the ordinance of 1700 which made French the only legal language in the province. Many towns, including Perpignan, Canet, Ceret, Collioure, Alenya, and Clayra, protested the intendant's authority to elect consuls. In these and many other instances, the Sovereign Council and the royal ministers in Paris ignored the objections and continued their plans for assimilation and acculturation.[251]

The local governments of Roussillon at times went beyond remonstrances and simply refused to obey certain French mandates. Despite direct commands from the intendant or Sovereign Council, many villages remained obstinate. Most cases of this type were resolved only when the intendant obtained a royal edict that explicitly ordered the local officials to take the course of action demanded by the intendant. Very often the dispute centered on which legal system, French or Catalan, should be used in the province. Local officials rendering justice typically followed Catalan juridical precepts, with which they were familiar, and disregarded laws demanding the use of French law. Only when confronted with orders from the king did towns relent and obey the laws.

Controversies concerning judicial practices were not the only way in which resistance through disobedience was expressed. In 1672, for example, the *Hopîtal Général* in Perpignan refused to admit Protestant soldiers, despite direct orders from Intendant Carlier. It was not until instructions came from Paris that the hospital reluctantly obeyed. And laws mandating the use of the French language in commercial, judicial, and religious proceedings were ignored throughout the reign of Louis XIV. The municipal governments of Roussillon were to some degree representative of the population. In resisting French assimilation and acculturation, the local governments reflected the attitudes of most Roussillonnais toward France. [252]

The Sovereign Council

The Sovereign Council, although created by the monarch to direct the processes of assimilation and acculturation in Roussillon, also occasionally registered its dissatisfaction with French policies through the use of Catalan law. In rendering justice in Roussillon, the Sovereign Council generally followed the injunction of Louis XIV that it "examine the volumes of the Constitutions of Catalonia to extract those which seem necessary to you for the judgment of affairs . . . and the public good,"[253] and that "the local usages and constitutions must be punctually observed."[254] In writing those and similar instructions to the Sovereign Council, however, Louis was implicitly referring only to those elements of Catalan law that increased royal power, not to the entire corpus of Catalan juridical tradition. Therefore, the fact that the Sovereign Council retained the whole of the Catalan legal tradition demonstrates a resistance to acculturation on its part. This reluctance to embrace French law was disturbing to the native French serving in the province, for they recognized the opposition to acculturation among the members of the Sovereign Council. This was an important reason for the royal decision to introduce French law into the province. Despite offering courses in French law, and commanding the provincial officials to use that legal code, the Sovereign Council continued to resort to Catalan legal traditions. When a new councillor was to be appointed in 1689, for example, the intendant expressed doubts that any qualified Frenchman could be found, for the French lacked the knowledge of local laws and traditions that was necessary for the post. Ten years later, the problem still persisted, as Bishop Jean Hervé Basan de Flamenville wrote the king in 1699 that "For the last year and a half, they [the Sovereign Council] have again taken the liberty of choosing those elements of French law which suit them, without abandoning those of Catalonia which are favourable."[255] Flamenville was particularly upset because in the intervening years the monarch had more than once ordered the Sovereign Council to follow French legal practices.[256]

A form of cultural resistance closely associated with the retention of Catalan legal forms was the retention of the Catalan language by the Sovereign Council. Despite strongly worded encouragements from Louvois to begin using the French language in its proceedings, the Sovereign Council continued to use Catalan. Until Trobat's speech of 1676, Catalan was the only language used in the reports, proceedings, and records of the Sovereign Council, and that language was still being used as late as 1694. Native French officials in the province were unhappy with the reluctance of the Sovereign Council to embrace acculturation and complained to Paris repeatedly. It was these complaints and the resultant prodding from Louvois that finally resulted in French law and language being more fully incorporated into the provincial government of Roussillon.[257]

Another way in which the Sovereign Council expressed its opposition to French policies was through protesting and refusing to implement edicts from Paris. Even though the Sovereign Council was created, in part, to encourage the acculturation of Roussillon into France, the Catalan councillors sometimes opposed policies of acculturation. For example, in 1661 the royal ministers in Paris contemplated dissolving the Sovereign Council and attaching Roussillon to the jurisdiction of the *parlement* of Toulouse. The ensuing protests from the Sovereign Council followed several lines of reasoning, one of which was that the special legal and cultural identity of the Catalans must be respected. Other, more compelling, arguments were also presented, and the proposed reorganization was abandoned. Another example of the Sovereign Council's occasional resistance to royal policy also occurred in 1661, when Louis XIV extended the *gabelle* into Roussillon. The Sovereign Council protested the tax as a violation of the *Usatges* and refused to register the edict in its records. After strong urging from Paris, the councillors relented and eventually became quite vigorous in their enforcement. In 1667, Louis XIV issued an ordinance designed to unify judicial procedures throughout France. Considering this to be a threat to Catalan judicial practices, the Sovereign Council did not register this edict until June 1683, and then only because of royal prodding. A third example of the Sovereign Council delaying the implementation of royal laws is the Edict of Saint Germain. Louis issued this law in August 1670, but it was not until May 1681 that the Sovereign

Council finally implemented it in Roussillon. In explaining to Paris why it had delayed so long in implementing the edict, the Sovereign Council expressed the method by which it interpreted the laws in Roussillon: "[W]e conform to the sense as well as the letter of the laws, constitutions, and usages of this land, and, lacking those, to the laws and customs practiced by the other sovereign courts of the kingdom."[258] Although this particular explanation referred to the judgment of ecclesiastical matters, this same pattern held true in most judicial decisions in Roussillon. The Sovereign Council retained Catalan law except in those instances when Paris insisted that French norms be employed.[259]

RESISTANCE FROM THE UNIVERSITY

The University of Perpignan ranked with the clergy as the most forceful opponents of French rule in Roussillon. The university and its faculty exploited every opportunity to resist the decisions of Paris and the Sovereign Council through the harassment of their agents and obstruction of their policies. Two incidents serve to illustrate the antagonistic relationship between the government and the university in Perpignan: the establishment of the Jesuit college and the excommunication of Jeroni Lléopart.

Shortly after the annexation of Roussillon to France, the Jesuit order was introduced into the province, which led to conflict with the university. Foremost among the duties of the order was the establishment and operation of a college. The Jesuit college was created for the explicit reason of undermining the prestige and influence of the University of Perpignan, which had existed for over 300 years and was completely Catalan in curriculum, language, and outlook. Both the francophile local elites and the ministers in Paris favored the Jesuit school as part of their goal of acculturating Roussillon, and this favoritism led to resentment in the university. This resentment quickly boiled over into action. To harass the French and delay their plans, the university maintained a stream of complaints before the Sovereign Council. The opening of the Jesuit college was delayed and its functioning was impeded by disputes over questions such as the relative ceremonial status of the heads of both schools, whether the Jesuits could teach the same curriculum as the university, where the new school would be located, how students would be enrolled. and similar administrative issues. The university ultimately reached an accommodation with the Jesuit school, although the former never really accepted either the college or its French patrons.[260]

Another example of the university's resistance to French authority was its dispute with Jeroni Lléopart, the controversial *vicaire capitulaire*. On 27 July 1666, Jean Girau and Paul Gallart, both on the faculty of the university, held a debate on the teachings of Saint Thomas Aquinas. In the course of this debate, Girau asserted that Saint Thomas had retracted certain of his own propositions, as had the Dominican order and the Catholic Church as a whole. By nine o'clock that evening, Lléopart had ordered the imprisonment of both men. The chancellor of the university, Michel Vilardell, protested this action to the Sovereign Council, claiming that Lléopart had violated the privileges of the school. On 29 July, the rector of the university, Llorens Carrera, became embroiled in an argument with a *canon beneficier* named Sirvent about the affair. The two men came to blows, and Sirvent was injured. In retaliation, Lléopart excommunicated Carrera for attacking the priest. As a counter-measure, Vilardell then excommunicated Lléopart for twice violating the privileges of the university.

The canons of the cathedral chapter were divided during the controversy. Six continued to recognize Lléopart as *vicaire capitulaire* and head of the Church in Roussillon, two abstained, and the other thirteen named Sebastien Garriga *vicaire capitulaire* of the province, who promptly appealed to Rome for recognition. The Sovereign Council, strongly disliking both the university and Lléopart, ordered the latter to refrain from exercising his office until Rome had heard the matter, and ordered Garriga also to withdraw from the controversy. Lléopart appealed to Paris, and Louvois wrote a harsh letter in which he condemned the Sovereign Council for allowing the university and anti-French forces to disrupt the peace of the province. He ordered Lléopart to be confirmed in his position.[261]

Even more clearly than its disputes with the Jesuits, the university's controversy with Lléopart demonstrates how easily it could disrupt the French presence in Roussillon without open disobedience. The chancellor appealed to tradition to justify his actions against Lléopart, knowing that both the *vicaire's* personality and his position would force a strong reaction from the French. The Sovereign Council favored the university's claims because they were substantially correct according to Catalan law and because Lléopart was widely disliked. It could not, however, acknowledge the legitimacy of an attack on French policies and personnel in Roussillon. Thus, the Sovereign Council found itself at an impasse and took no action. In these two incidents, the university succeeded in demonstrating vigorous resistance to the French by first slowing and then paralyzing the provincial government.[262]

In conclusion, resistance to the French was very common in Roussillon, especially before the 1680s. Policies that were designed to promote acculturation were more often the targets of resistance than were policies of political assimilation, although resistance to the latter was certainly present as well. One of the first forms of resistance demonstrated in Roussillon was the emigration that followed the Peace of the Pyrenees. That exodus was followed by a small but significant number of exiles who left throughout the next twenty years. The clergy, peasants, and local governments demonstrated other, more important, methods of resistance during those twenty years. French laws barring contact with Catalonia were widely ignored, and commercial and religious contacts continued to flourish. Culturally, the

Chapter 7
French Success and Failure

The French were ultimately quite successful in eliminating open opposition to their rule in Roussillon. After 1680 it became clear that they had achieved one of their goals in the region, political assimilation. At the same time, however, the French failed to acculturate Roussillon. Throughout the reign of Louis XIV, and much of the Old Regime, the province retained its Catalan cultural identity, as its language, traditions, food, clothing, and social habits continued to be derived from Catalan standards.

THE ACCEPTANCE OF FRENCH RULE

The year 1680 clearly stands between two eras in the history of French Roussillon. Before that date was the revolt of the Angelets, the conspiracies in Villefranche and Perpignan, and most of the active forms of resistance to France. In addition, most of the acts of passive resistance to French rule, as distinct from French culture, occurred before 1680. After that date French political authority was secure in Roussillon, as French political symbols became increasingly common in the province, the Roussillonnais volunteered to serve in French armies, and little support was demonstrated for conspiracies against the rule of Louis XIV.

The first two decades after the annexation of Roussillon by France witnessed strong opposition both to French rule in the province and to French attempts to introduce their culture into the region. The murder of Don Emanuel de Sant-Dionís and the subsequent investigations lasted from 1661 until 1667. The Angelet rebellion began in 1661 and continued until 1679. The plots in Villefranche and Perpignan occurred in 1674, and the resulting investigations also extended until 1679. The skirmishes at Ayguatebia and Massenette in 1675 and 1677, respectively, also fell into the first twenty-year period. The clerical controversies involving Jeroni Lléopart, Jean Louis de Brueil, and Josep de Trobat all ended before 1674. The majority of Catalans who emigrated during the reign of Louis XIV did so before 1680. Intendant Étienne Carlier, writing in 1675, summed up the mood of the inhabitants during these first two decades: "[The Roussillonnais] still retain all their inclination for the Spanish, and wait for occasions to demonstrate it by enterprises or conspiracies."[263] While it would be more accurate to describe the inclination as anti-French than pro-Spanish, Carlier was essentially correct in fearing resistance to French rule in Roussillon before 1680.

The years following 1680 mark a distinct contrast with the earlier period. While the Roussillonnais still did not accept French culture, they did accept French political domination. One example of the entrenchment of French political authority in Roussillon was the change in Perpignan's coat of arms. In 1681 the consuls of the town, desiring to prove their loyalty, petitioned Louis XIV for permission to alter the arms of the town. The old design, which had been in use since at least 1346, featured the gold and red stripes of Catalonia. The new arms replaced this Catalan symbolism with *fleurs de lys*, the symbol of the French monarchy. Similar modifications were undertaken on the municipal arms of Ceret, Prades (1704), Sornià (1686), and Thuir (1684). That these governments voluntarily abandoned powerful Catalan political symbols for those of France indicates that the French were clearly seen as the real political authority in Roussillon, and that the political elite of the province had accepted them in that role.[264]

Other evidence that hostility to French rule had largely dissipated after 1680 is the number of Roussillonnais who took up arms in the service of France after that date. One striking example is found in the military service of Ille-sur-Tet. In 1690, Intendant Ramon de Trobat wrote to the Secretary of War to explain why no recruits were being found in that town. In his letter, Trobat explained that more than 200 men had already volunteered, as distinct from being conscripted, for service in French armies, a figure that represented over 10 percent of the town's total population. While not all villages in Roussillon contributed such a high proportion of their population to the war effort, there was significant participation throughout the province.

More than 7,000 men from Roussillon served in the military forces of Louis XIV in 1690. This includes 2,437 men of the Royal-Roussillon Infantry Regiment and the *fusiliers de montagne*, 516 soldiers in the Royal-Roussillon Cavalry Regiment, and more than 4,000 members of the local militia. In addition, there were Roussillonnais serving in the Noailles Regiment, as well as other French infantry units. When the militia was called up in 1690, more than 8 percent of the total population of the province were under arms and on campaign. This figure indicates that between 20 and 30 percent of the military-aged population of Roussillon was in service in 1690. In 1716, the year after the death of Louis XIV, one of every 214 residents of Perpignan was serving in the armies of France. This proportion was far higher than in towns such as Nantes, Pau, Marseille, or Bordeaux, all of which had been assimilated long before Roussillon. Such enthusiasm for the service of the king had been unknown twenty and thirty years earlier, but became unremarkable after 1680.[265]

A further demonstration that the Roussillonnais came to accept the French as the political masters of the province is seen in the lack of significant conspiracies after 1680. The Spanish government, and later the Archduke Charles, repeatedly attempted to foment conspiracies and plots among the Roussillon throughout the reign of Louis XIV. In the first two decades after annexation, the Spanish met with success, as the Angelet rebellion and the events of 1674 clearly indicate. After 1680, however, such attempts at foreign intervention were almost completely unsuccessful. In the spring of 1690, for example, a spy from the Principat was seized and revealed that the Spanish were searching to enlist Roussillonnais to seize key positions in the province. Trobat conducted a thorough investigation of these confessions, and concluded that "there is neither the suspicion nor appearance of any person of quality, nor any other inhabitant of this land, having entered into these negotiations."[266] This is, of course, in marked contrast with the events of 1674, when scores of prominent men were deeply implicated in anti-French conspiracies. Four years later, the intendant was similarly unconcerned by the possibility of the Roussillonnais aiding Spanish *Miquelets* raiding the province. Indeed, Trobat believed that the raids would further increase loyalty to France, as the residents came to blame Spain for the depredations. That Spanish conspiracies designed to drive the French from Roussillon became unappealing to the Roussillonnais testifies to the fact that the inhabitants had come to accept French rule in the province.[267]

One of the most telling indicators of French success in winning the obedience, if not the hearts, of the Roussillonnais, can be found in the closing years of the reign of Louis XIV. During the War of the Spanish Succession, Spanish Catalonia declared for the Hapsburg claimant to the Spanish throne, Archduke Charles. The French Catalans in Roussillon, however, did not demonstrate any enthusiasm for the Austrian pretender. This was true despite invasions by pro-Austrian forces and the dissemination of propaganda in the province by the archduke's supporters. Even when the war was going very badly for the Bourbon cause, Philip V was able to visit Perpignan several times without incident. There were a few speeches given in the province in favor of the Austrian claimant, and some spying conducted for the Hapsburg forces. Those actions were, however, typically carried out by Spanish Catalans who had come to the province to create trouble rather than by long time residents. For example, the *viguier* of French Cerdagne was murdered by Catalans from Spanish Cerdaña, and an immigrant from Barcelona was jailed for decrying French military successes. In all, no more than fifty or sixty native Roussillonnais are known to have taken up the cause of the archduke, a marked contrast from the anti-French sentiment of the 1660s and 1670s. This remarkable apathy, when contrasted with the intensity of the Catalan struggle in Spain, seems an excellent indicator of the success of the French in suppressing dissent within Roussillon. [268]

REASONS FOR THE SUCCESS OF POLITICAL ASSIMILATION

The explanation for France's success in politically assimilating the Roussillonnais in the reign of Louis XIV is found in French policies and the consequences, both intentional and unintentional, of those policies. The French were able to dominate militarily both Roussillon and its neighbors. This military superiority contributed to French success by making armed resistance seem futile and foreign assistance improbable. Various French policies resulted, often unintentionally, in demographic changes in Roussillon. The net effect of these changes was an increase in the number of pro-French Catalans living in the province and anti-French Catalans leaving the province for the Principat. French political decisions in Roussillon also enhanced the image of France in the province by maintaining a facade of tradition behind which change occurred. Finally, the control of Roussillon by France resulted in a stronger economy, which offered fiscal incentives for the acceptance of French rule. The key to the success of Louis XIV and his ministers in assimilating Roussillon was identified by Ramon de Trobat in a speech before the Sovereign Council: "Arms and counsel are the two pillars of the state, the two poles upon which all that is stable resides."[269] It was the judicious balance of compulsion and persuasion that resulted in the acceptance of French rule by the Roussillonnais.

Military

The military effectiveness of the French contributed significantly to their success in assimilating Roussillon into the political structure of the monarchy. The Roman Empire had assimilated many peoples into its empire because it was militarily dominant. In the same manner, Paris regularly maintained hundreds of troops in the province and possessed the ability to field armies numbering in the hundreds of thousands. French military forces were numerous and the armies of Louis XIV were widely regarded as the finest in Europe. Moreover, the French were not reluctant to employ the army, both to suppress domestic unrest and to wage war on neighboring states. The existence of a large and effective army, coupled with the will to employ it, had several important implications for the success of assimilation in Roussillon. The inhabitants gradually resigned themselves to the fact that no one, either from within or from outside the province, would ever succeed in driving the French from Roussillon. Since the French could not be expelled from the region, the people, lacking alternatives, began accommodating themselves to French rule in Roussillon. The power of the French army further meant that Spanish invasions would never be more than destructive raids. Deprived of any real hope of deliverance, the Roussillonnais came to view these raiders as enemies rather than liberators. Thus the Spanish invasions, once invited as vehicles to freedom, now alienated the inhabitants and drove them further into sympathy with and reliance upon the French.

One important result of French military superiority within the province was that all forms of active rebellion to French rule were destroyed. Military actions undertaken by the Roussillonnais against the French always ended in failure. The spontaneous risings of Massenette and Ayguatèbia resulted in harsh reprisals and mass destruction. The heads of Macía Tixedas, Emanuel Descallar, Jean Soler, and Carles de Llar were displayed for more than twenty years as reminders of the consequence of treason. Even the longest and most widely supported of all risings against the French, the Angelet rebellion, was unable to succeed in the face of French military power and patience. The French record of complete success in crushing open dissent gradually lent an aura of invincibility to their presence. Every time the Roussillonnais witnessed the execution of another unsuccessful rebel or heard about houses being razed, they became increasingly resigned to the inevitability of French rule in the province.

One problem that plagued many governments attempting to assimilate conquered regions was that of foreign intervention impeding their rule in the region. The Catalans in the fourteenth century, for example, had failed to assimilate their holdings in the Greek peninsula in part because the Florentines and Byzantines had constantly pressured them, and ultimately drove them from Greece.[270] The French, by contrast, had no enemies who were capable of driving them from Roussillon. The enemies of France in central and northern Europe had little interest in seizing the province and lacked the logistical ability to do so. Spain, on the border with France, possessed the strategic location and desire to wrest Roussillon from France, but lacked the ability. In each of its wars with France, Spain launched some incursions into Roussillon, and were driven back every time. In fact, French armies were in the Principat far more often than Spanish armies were found in Roussillon. The same pattern held true during the War of the Spanish Succession, when the Archduke Charles replaced the king of Spain as France's enemy in the eastern Pyrenees. The inhabitants of Roussillon eventually came to acknowledge the fact that foreign intervention would be no more successful than provincial rebellion in expelling the French.

Spanish invasions of Roussillon also created positive images of France as the liberator and defender of the Roussillonnais. During their invasions, the Spanish treated Roussillon as French territory, and looted the land accordingly. When the French armies drove off these Spanish raiders, the French forces were considered to be the defenders of the Roussillonnais, the Church, and Catalonia. For example, in 1675 a raiding party from Spain attacked the village of Ceret in the Vallespir, and the inhabitants appealed to the Sovereign Council for relief. Among the petitions that described the assault was one written by Sebastia Garriga, who had a few years earlier excommunicated the Sovereign Council in the dispute with Jeroni Lléopart. This staunch opponent of the French presence in Roussillon was, however, now appealing to the Sovereign Council for assistance against Spain. Describing the Spanish as "cursed; sacrilegious, criminal sons of perdition" and "painfully vicious,"[271] Garriga had reluctantly come to view the French as the defenders of the Church against the evils of the Spanish.

Military service by the Roussillonnais also contributed to the success of assimilation in Roussillon. Whether an individual was enrolled in the French army by choice or by conscription, his basic goal was to survive in order to return home. Barring desertion, one of the surest methods of survival was quick victories in the field for his army. Thus an individual, even one serving against his will, would desire his army to triumph. The same logic would apply to the friends and relatives of the soldier, who wished to see him home again. Thus, for every soldier taken from a village, a score or more of people might begin hoping for a French victory. The friendships developed in the army would provide the soldier a further motivation for his army to do well, since he would not want his comrades to be killed. The desire for military successes that was generated both in the army and in the province would naturally be transformed into some level of allegiance for the state fielding the armies. Thus, even the most hostile foes of France found their antipathy tempered when relatives were conscripted and fought for Louis XIV.

Demographic Changes

Demographic changes occurred in Roussillon after the Peace of the Pyrenees that contributed to the French success in achieving the assimilation of the province. The emigration of hundreds of anti-French Roussillonnais from the province removed one set of potentially disloyal and rebellious people. The immigration of pro-French Catalans not only served to offset the population shift, but provided a loyal base from which effective provincial administrators could be drawn. The effectiveness of French military, economic, and political policies destroyed the hostile young leadership in the province, thus further reducing the possibilities of resistance. Finally, the movement of Frenchmen into Roussillon created a toleration for the French among the previously hostile Roussillonnais and helped to acclimate the residents to French rule. These demographic changes help explain in part why France was able to politically assimilate Roussillon in the reign of Louis XIV.

The emigration of those Roussillonnais hostile to the French in Roussillon served to further the acceptance of French rule in the province. Many persons who might have otherwise become leaders of a resistance movement instead moved to the Principat, and there developed new concerns and priorities that occupied their attention. This emigration, although largest immediately after annexation, continued throughout the reign. As evidence of French military superiority mounted and the possibility of successful resistance diminished, increasing numbers of disaffected potential rebels moved to Spain. As late as 1713, Roussillonnais who were unhappy with the French government were moving to Barcelona rather than confronting the government in the province. Thus there was an movement of dissenters across the Pyrenean frontier in the seventeenth century that diluted opposition to France in Roussillon, and thereby contributed to the successful assimilation of the province.[272]

Roussillon experienced a steady immigration of Catalans from Spain throughout the reign of Louis XIV. Immediately after the Peace of the Pyrenees, leaders of the rebellion against Philip IV moved to Roussillon. Thus, men like the Marquis d'Aguilar, the Comte d'Ille, the Trobat brothers, Vincenç de Margarit, Francesc de Sagarra, and Josep de Fontanella, among many others, became residents of Roussillon. These men provided a positive example of the rewards for co-operation with the French. While some men were executed, imprisoned, exiled, or heavily fined for conspiring against the rule of Louis XIV, these immigrants were given positions of leadership, granted large sums of money, given estates, and provided titles of nobility for their efforts to secure the rule of France.

There were, in addition to these early pro-French immigrants, other Catalans who moved to Roussillon from Spain. Men such as Don Marcelino de Çagarriga, Don Josep de Camprodon, Antoni Generes, and Don Acaci de Codol who had been initially ill-disposed to France gradually returned to the province to reclaim their patrimonies. As these formerly disaffected leaders returned and acknowledged French legitimacy, they influenced other Roussillonnais to accept French rule as well. Other immigrants from Spain came to Roussillon fleeing punishment for resistance to Castile or the archduke. Their number included the bishop of Gerona, the Comte de Darnius, the governor of Peralade, and the *viguier* of Spanish Cerdaña. Since leading Spanish Catalans, with whom the Roussillonnais believed themselves to be joined, sought the aid of France, the residents of the province were further persuaded to accept French rule in Roussillon as legitimate.[273]

The pro-French emigrants served a purpose beyond simply acting as positive examples. Most of the provincial government was staffed by Catalans, either from the Principat or from Roussillon itself. These men made an enormous contribution toward the success France achieved in assimilating the province. Being Catalans by birth, they understood the culture, language, and motivation of the Roussillonnais, and could thus temper specific French policies to the province without sacrificing the intent behind those policies. At the same time, having become French by choice, the allegiance of these men was tied firmly to France, and the Principat had nothing to offer them.

They were therefore completely loyal to France and could be trusted with a degree of autonomy in governing the province. In the words of the Sovereign Council, "having been the original founders, we are the most concerned here, and possess sufficient understanding of this land to know the means necessary to attach it permanently to the crown of France."[274] It was recognized in both Paris and Perpignan that the leadership of these immigrant Catalans was critical to the success of assimilation in Roussillon. A competent and loyal leadership with ties to and an understanding of the different worlds of France and Roussillon created a buffer between the two that eventually allowed their political union.

Another important facet of French success in the assimilation of the province was the elimination of an entire generation of hostile Roussillonnais. As plots, rebellions, and other forms of open opposition were slowly eliminated, the leaders behind that resistance either were executed or fled to Spain. Rebellion, plots, and other forms of open resistance require passionate devotion, intense idealism, and torrid inspiration, qualities that are usually found among the youth of a society. It is true that in seventeenth-century Roussillon the leaders of resistance against France were generally young men and women. Teresa de Camprodon, Emanuel Descallar, Josep de la Trinxeria, Carles de Banyuls, and most of the other conspirators and rebels were under thirty years of age. By the 1680s, there were no youthful, idealistic figures remaining to serve as rallying points for the opposition. Older men had long since taken their families to Barcelona, where their children would grow up as Spanish Catalans, with their own set of struggles, and the young anti-French had also fled or been executed. Even as late as the War of the Spanish Succession, Intendant Étienne de Ponte d'Albaret wrote to Paris about loyal Roussillonnais parents and their anti-French children in the Principat. A generation of radical leadership was removed in the 1660s and 1670s, and no new leaders emerged to take its place.[275]

A final demographic component to the French success in assimilating Roussillon was the immigration of native French to Roussillon. One failure common to many states that sought to assimilate a conquered province was the lack of integration between the subject people and the rulers. The French, however, encouraged French immigration to Roussillon and allowed Catalans to advance in royal service. The many French merchants, professionals, administrators, and soldiers who moved to Roussillon played an important role in assimilating the region. Despite their initial reluctance to have contact with the new arrivals, the Roussillonnais eventually did interact with these French. As the Roussillonnais came to know more and more of the French, they became more tolerant of the French and their culture. Although the Roussillonnais did not embrace French culture, this cultural tolerance permitted the residents to tolerate French political domination as well.[276]

Political

There were, in addition to the demographic and military explanations of French success, two political considerations that contributed to the French ability to assimilate Roussillon. The first of these was the use of traditional Catalan forms, institutions, and practices by the government to disguise innovations. One way this was done was by the association of new French institutions with older, respected Catalan ones. The Sovereign Council was, for example, at its creation explicitly presented as a new incarnation of the Royal Council, which had existed for centuries. In the same way, attempts were made to associate the new *Amirauté de Collioure* with the ancient *Consulat de la Llotja de Mar*. Another way in which traditional forms were used to mask innovation was by maintaining Catalan institutions, but completely reorganizing their function and authority. Thus the intendant's control of the *pariatge, burgès honrats*, and the election of municipal consuls could be concealed by the fact that these honored traditions were retained. The maintenance of traditional forms, even without their substance, was often a highly transparent maneuver. Despite this fact, however, it contributed a great deal to the success of the French in assimilating the province, especially among the less educated, rural peasants. Those who did not fully comprehend the nature of Catalan law also did not understand the ways in which the French manipulated it, and so the French were viewed as showing some respect for the *Usatges* and Catalan tradition.

Another fact that contributed a great deal to the success of the French in assimilating Roussillon was that the French worked to address the complaints of the Roussillonnais. Soldiers and provincial officials were sometimes censured for their excessive behavior, and at least one tax collector was sentenced to death for his actions against the Roussillonnais. The demands of the Angelets were considered by the Sovereign Council, and negotiations were undertaken with the rebels. Those discussions resulted in a substantially lower salt tax than had been initially assigned the province and tacitly permitted smuggling to continue, thus recognizing the traditional economic patterns of the Roussillonnais. Except for the moments communities were actually in arms, there were very few military reprisals against dissident communities, the Sovereign Council preferring to fine and admonish rather than to raze villages. Banishment was often used as a punishment in the first instance of a crime, which lent an aura of conciliation to the government. Emanuel Descallar, for example, had been twice banished for his resistance to the French, rather than being executed at the first or even second instance. The Sovereign Council, to the frequent irritation of Louvois, continued to apply Catalan legal precedents in Roussillon, again demonstrating some measure of accommodation between the government and the residents of the province. These various compromises and conciliatory overtures illustrated to the Roussillonnais that the government was, if not completely just and receptive to all their concerns, at least willing to listen to their complaints and render justice in an evenhanded manner. [277]

The fact that the Roussillonnais were separated from the Principat also contributed to the French success in assimilating the province into the monarchy. Peter Sahlins has explained the formation of identity in the Cerdanya as the result of competing counter-identities.[278] Thus, even though the Roussillonnais and Spanish Catalans shared a common cultural heritage, they would, after 1659, define themselves as Catalans in different ways. The Roussillonnais, in asserting their culture against French centralizing and acculturating pressures, came to possess a cultural identity distinct from the Spanish Catalans, who faced different problems and pressures. As years passed, the common ground between the two groups of Catalans, especially concerning political goals, were increasingly reduced. This concept of counter-identities helps to explain, in part, why the Archduke Charles found so little appeal in Roussillon while being so popular in the Principat: The Roussillonnais had truly become French Catalans.

A final reason the French were successful in assimilating Roussillon into their political system was the economic stimulus they provided the province. The French spent hundreds of thousands of livres every year in the province, much of it paid directly to inhabitants of the province and more reaching them indirectly. In addition to simply spending money, the French undertook improvements in the infrastructure of the province. The harbor at Port-Vendres was enlarged and dredged to allow increased sea-borne commerce, capital was provided to found many new industries throughout the province, incentives were provided to stimulate agricultural trade with France, and the constant military activities permitted the growth of service industries in many towns. These many benefits of the French presence were not lost on the Roussillonnais. Under Spanish rule, the province had stagnated economically. The French had, on the whole, definitely improved the economic lot of the Roussillonnais. By improving the provincial standard of living, the French made themselves acceptable to many inhabitants, which contributed to their success.

THE FAILURE OF ACCULTURATION

The French were able to win the loyalty of the Roussillonnais, and thus accomplished their first goal for the province. Louis XIV and his ministers were, however, completely unsuccessful in achieving their goal of acculturation in Roussillon. The most immediately obvious example of this failure is seen in the lack of acceptance of the French language. Throughout the reign of Louis XIV, royal officials, ecclesiastical leaders, municipal governments, and private citizens all continued to write official letters to Paris and the Sovereign Council in Catalan, or, occasionally, Spanish. The streets of Perpignan provide another example of the failure of acculturation to penetrate even the capital of the province. During the reign of Louis XIV, at least fifty-three streets were created or renamed in Perpignan. Of those, only eight came to bear French names, and those were all streets associated with the French bureaucracy or religious foundations. Baptismal records provide further evidence that Perpignan resisted acculturation in the reign of Louis XIV. In naming their children, the parents of Perpignan very rarely gave their children French names but instead continued to use traditional Iberian names. Since Perpignan was the capital of the province and the focus of the most intense efforts at acculturation, the rural Roussillonnais were even less likely to employ French names for their children. Even among the families of the political and cultural elite, including members of the Sovereign Council and the leading pro-French nobles, names of French origin are not found among the children or grandchildren. Further, most of them continued to conduct their personal business in Catalan, not French, as indicated by contracts, wills, and other public records. This indicates that the French culture was not adopted by this cultural elite. Since acculturation was not accepted by those responsible for its promotion in the province, it is hardly surprising that French efforts at acculturation failed in Roussillon. [279]

Ample evidence can be found from later in the seventeenth century and even in the nineteenth century to indicate a failure of acculturation in the province. At the time of the French Revolution, the *Cahiers de Doléances* of many villages were in Catalan, indicating that the language was still the preferred tongue for many inhabitants. Various school administrators in nineteenth century Roussillon, then called the Departement des Pyrénées-Orientales, lamented the lack of acculturation. In 1850, one school inspector wrote that despite ruling the province for over 200 years, "the French element does not yet dominate here."[280] Eleven years later an instructor in Estagel emphasized the same theme, writing that "the maternal language is not French . . . [which] is therefore a second language that must be learned."[281] In 1889, another Roussillonnais instructor wrote that "the French language is as foreign to our young students as English, German, or Italian."[282] Louis XIV and successive French governments were unable to acculturate the Roussillonnais.

This failure of acculturation occurred despite many French attempts to encourage the use of the French language and customs. In 1661, 1662, 1663, 1672, 1682, 1684, and 1690, various educational institutions were created, including a college, grammar schools, two seminaries, and a chair of French law. The primary mission of all of these institutions was to promote the acceptance of French in Roussillon. They failed to do so, however, especially outside of Perpignan. The government's attempts to educate the Roussillonnais contributed to the successful assimilation of the province, but were generally unsuccessful in acculturating it.

The French also issued laws that explicitly required the use of French in public life and proscribed Catalan. Knowledge of French was required to graduate from the University of Perpignan and the Jesuit College. In 1682, a similar requirement was extended to all government positions in the province. After that date, men who sought to serve in any part of the provincial administration were to be able to demonstrate their ability to read and write French. The year 1700 saw a ban on the public use of Catalan. Despite these regulations and a variety of exhortations to use French, the residents of Roussillon did not embrace the language. The most pro-French church in the province, the Cathedral of Saint Jean in Perpignan, first used French in a sermon only in September 1676. Even after that date, the French language was heard only very infrequently in the cathedral. The Sovereign Council conducted its first meeting in French in November 1676. Like the cathedral, for decades after that date the Sovereign Council continued to use Catalan for most of its business. Of all the Roussillonnais, the members of the Sovereign Council possessed the most compelling reasons to accept acculturation, since their fates were tied to French rule in the province. These men, who constituted the administrative organ responsible for the local oversight of acculturation in Roussillon, did not, however, accept acculturation themselves.

Other attempts at the acculturation of Roussillon were no more successful than the linguistic and educational policies. French immigration was encouraged, but this generally had little impact on acculturation. The new arrivals were disliked not only because they were *gavatxos*, but also because French immigrants were often granted special economic privileges in the province. Thus the cultural impact of French immigrants might have been limited by resentment.

A more important limitation on the effectiveness of French immigrants as transmitters of culture was their small number. As the immigrants came to be accepted, they were often subsumed by Catalan culture, rather than injecting French culture into the province. One or two families moving to a village of several hundred residents would be hard pressed to maintain a distinct cultural identity. The constant pressures from the village demanded conformity to Catalan standards. Church services were in Catalan, and so the newly arrived French had to learn that language in order to worship and confess. Whatever trade or craft the immigrants practiced, their customers were Catalans, and so the French had to speak it to conduct their daily business. Municipal office, local festivals, courtship, and a variety of other activities required the constant use of Catalan in daily life. Thus the French who moved to Roussillon, especially those who moved to small villages, were isolated from their native culture and gradually came to accept the provincial Catalan culture. The French campaign of acculturation was, on the whole, unsuccessful in the reign of Louis XIV. Louvois and the king could not compel the acceptance of French culture, despite their efforts to do so, and the Sovereign Council and other local pro-French notables did not desire to embrace French culture. Thus Roussillon remained Catalan in the reign of Louis XIV.

CONCLUSION

France obtained the province of Roussillon in 1659, but at that time the inhabitants were not willing to accept French political domination or French culture and language. The ministers of Louis XIV therefore established two goals for the newly annexed province—to assimilate it politically and to acculturate it. A variety of political, economic, military, and religious policies were employed to reach these goals. In the governing of the province, administrators and institutions were introduced to reduce the power of or to replace completely traditional Catalan political bodies. Thus, the intendant, governor, Sovereign Council, and the *Amirauté de Collioure* were among the many innovations that undermined the political traditions of the province in order to assert French control. Louvois and Louis XIV also encouraged the immigration of loyal Catalans to Roussillon to ensure French domination in the province. The immigrants to the province had no local ties and were well rewarded by the crown. From this group were drawn the administrators who governed the province with an understanding of Catalan values and a loyalty to Louis XIV.

The Catholic Church in Roussillon was a source of great resistance to French rule, and was thus the subject of a variety of policies designed to bring it into obedience. All forms of contact with Spanish Catalonia were prohibited, French clergymen were sent into the religious houses of Roussillon, the church organization was restructured, and French religious traditions were emphasized in an attempt to create a more pro-French clergy. The French pursued several policies explicitly designed to create a French cultural identity in the province. These measures included prohibiting the public use of Catalan, establishing schools, and providing incentives for French immigration.

The encouragement of economic growth was another way in which the government of Louis XIV fostered loyalty in Roussillon. The government spent large sums of money in the province constructing fortresses, supplying the armies, and founding factories and a mint. Other stimuli were applied to the economy of Roussillon. Favorable trade policies were established for goods from the province, taxes were lowered for certain markets, harbors and roads repaired, and raw materials were purchased to assist local producers. Finally, the French employed their military forces to ensure their control of the province. Thousands of troops were dispatched to the Vallespir to crush the rebellion against the *gabelle*, key cities were heavily garrisoned as a precaution against conspiracy, massive fortresses were constructed that served, in part, to impress the Roussillonnais with the king's power, and some villages were completely razed in reprisal for acts of resistance.

Even as the French were pursuing their policies of assimilation and acculturation, many Roussillonnais were resisting the administration of the province, both through acts of violence and passive non-compliance. The murder of Don Emanuel de Sant-Dionís, the revolt of the Angelets, and the conspiracies of 1674 were the most notable incidents of violent resistance to French rule, but there were many other incidents. In addition, non-violent forms of resistance were common during the first twenty years of French rule. French clerical leaders were strongly resisted, even excommunicated, taxes went unpaid, smuggling was common, some Roussillonnais emigrated from the province, and local governments frequently protested French decisions. Despite the initial hostility of the residents, however, France achieved its first goal within twenty years. By 1680, French political control of the province was assured, and no major challenge to that control appeared after that date. At the same time, the French efforts to acculturate the province were largely unsuccessful, and even the leaders of the province most closely allied to the French government did not embrace the acculturation proposed by Paris.

The French goals of acculturation and political assimiliation were not unique to Roussillon. The frontier province of French Alsace, acquired in the reign of Louis XIII, also witnessed the extension of French absolutism during the reign of Louis XIV. Like Roussillon, it was a region with a distinct legal tradition, a different language, and a sometimes uncooperative people. The French ministers in Paris treated both provinces in a similar manner, hoping to achieve similar objectives in both. The Sovereign Council of Alsace was established in 1657, and, like its counterpart in Roussillon, helped foster the spread of French law throughout the region. Alsace provided for numerous French armies, both garrisoning the province and moving through it on the way to war. The intendants of Alsace systemized the bureaucracy there and introduced new offices and laws as they extended French power. The French were guided by a simple premise: "[T]o keep what was in use, to destroy nothing *a priori* and to maintain as much as possible the façade the people knew; to use the existing system, adapt it in the way desired . . . often changing parts of it, and always controlling it."[283] Certainly this was the twin of the policy pursued in Roussillon. The French further desired "to employ those natives won over by a show of confidence in them,"[284] again mirroring the patterns established in Roussillon.

Alsace also paralleled Roussillon in its attachment to traditional forms and resistance to certain elements of French rule. The Alsatians repeatedly appealed to the laws of the archdukes and emperors, their former rulers, and slowed the introduction of French absolutism. Towns and local officials retained many privileges of taxation and justice, even up to the Revolution, and the superificial structure of traditional institutions was respected by the French out of concern for public opinion. Protestantism was even tolerated, more or less openly, in Alsace after the Edict of Fontainebleau, again demonstrating a respect for traditional patterns of religious belief. In the same way, the French offered sympathy for the deep commitment to Catholicism on the part of the Roussillonnais, punishing Protestants to appease traditional religious sentiment in the province.

At the same time, there were significant differences between French Alsace and French Roussillon. The French were generally unable to influence significantly the bishops of Strasbourg and Basle, who had authority in the province, and thus were limited in their ability to interfere with the churches there. The bishop of Perpignan, however, was nominated by Louis XIV, and thus offered the French government some influence over the church hierarchy in Roussillon. Commercial activity was important in Alsace, and the French attempted to regulate but not prohibit trade between Alsace and the German states. Roussillon, by contrast, did not rely on commerce, and the French were able to pursue a policy that emphasized the destruction of traditional commerce with Spain without devastating the province. On the whole, the policies pursued by the government of Louis XIV in Rousillon, and the reactions to them, appear to be part of a pattern of government for border provinces: Slowly introduce change, usually under the guise of traditional forms; use the local elites to catalyze the changes; and respect, as far as possible, traditional forms and customs. In the case of Roussillon, these methods resulted in the desired political assimilation, even as acculturation was proved unnecessary.[285]

Appendix A
Illustrations

Figure 1
Catalonia in 1640

Figure 2
Towns and Villages of Roussillon

Figure 3
The Angelet Rebellion

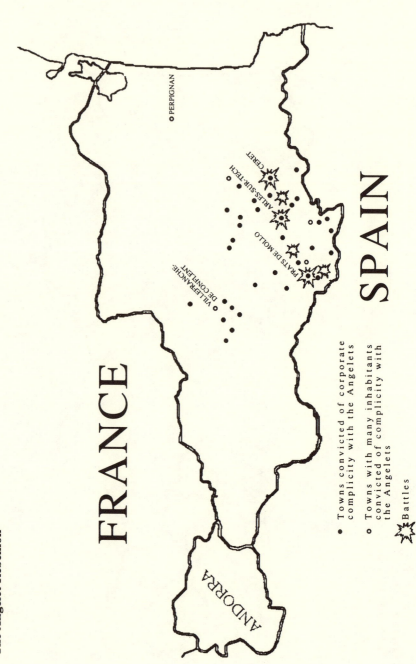

FRANCE

SPAIN

ANDORRA

● PERPIGNAN

ARLES-SUR-TECH

CERET

PRATS DE MOLLO

VILLEFRANCHE
DE CONFLENT

● Towns convicted of corporate
  complicity with the Angelets

○ Towns with many inhabitants
  convicted of complicity with
  the Angelets

✶ Battles

Table 1. Approximate Populations of Roussillonnais Towns

	1643	1670	1695	1709	1720
Arles-sur-Tech		1150		900	800
Canet	310			1150	750
Ceret	1700		2000	2500	2050
Collioure & Port Vendres	550			1300	1850
Elne	160			1100	1250
Ille-sur-Tet	1700		2000	2000	2200
Mont Louis				650	225
Perpignan				1800	9250
Prades			1625	1500	1700
Prats-de-Mollo	1000	1900		1450	1050
Pÿ		475		550	300
Rivesaltes				1000	1250
Thuir	500			1125	1350
Villefranche-de-Conflent				650	700

Note: Most sources provide data in number of hearths. Population figures were derived by multiplying the number of hearths by five persons.

Sources: Georges Frêche, "Denombrement de Feux et d'Habitants de 2973 Communatutés de la Région Toulousaine," *Annales du Démographie Historique* (1968-1969): 471; J. Nadal and E. Giralt, *La Population Catalane de 1553 à 1717* (n.p.: 1960), pp. 185-186; Jean-Pierre Pelissier, *Paroisses et Communes de France*, vol. *Pyrénées-Orientales* (Paris: 1986), *passim.*; *Archives Départementales des Pyrénées-Orientales*, 1C 1395, 7 October 1670; *ADPO*, 1C 1691; *ADPO*, 1C 1721; *ADPO*, 1C 1974; *Service Historique du Armée de Terre*, A[1] 300, March 1672; *Bibliothèque Nationale*, Fonds Français, 11801, f° 152-202.

Appendix B
Biographical Sketches

ALBARET, Antoine-Marie de Ponte, Comte d'. The son of Étienne de Ponte d'Albaret, he served in many positions in the provincial government of Roussillon. In the reign of Louis XIV, he served as an *avocat général* (1711–1722) of the Sovereign Council. He also later held the offices of president of the Sovereign Council (1718–1750) and intendant of Roussillon (1740–1750).

ALBARET, Félix Marie Étienne de Ponte d'. (b. 13 November 1652 at Pignerol; d. 14 July 1727 at Perpignan). Before becoming intendant of Roussillon (4 May 1698–1709), he was president at Pignerol and Rouen. He also served as president of the Sovereign Council of Roussillon (1698–1727), army intendant of Roussillon (1698–1709), first president of the Sovereign Council of Roussillon (1698–1727), and *garde des sceaux* (1701–1727). During his tenure as intendant, he organized a choir of the cathedral school (15 March 1699) and a tax-free fair in several rural areas (20 December 1708). (m. Marguerite Birague de Wisque)

ALIZON DE LA ROCHE, Charles. He was a native of Languedoc and son of Jean Alizon de la Roche. Like his father, he served on the Sovereign Council (1702–1712).

ALIZON DE LA ROCHE, Jean. A native of Languedoc, he served as a councillor on the Sovereign Council (1695–1702).

ANGLADA I CODOLOSA, Fausto Joan Baptista Miguel Simo d'. (b. 20 April 1653 in Mataró; d. 9 October 1711 in Perpignan) He joined the French army and was captured in 1674. After his release, he served as an aide-de-camp to the Duke of Noailles. He inherited the arms, name, and estate of his uncle Raymond de Trobat i Vinyes upon the death without heirs of the latter. (m. Francesca de Rocaburna i de Copons)

ANTIGO, Anne-Marie. (b. 19 January 1602 in Perpignan; d. 28 September 1676). She entered the convent of Sainte-Claire de Perpignan at age nineteen, becoming vicar in 1639 and abbess in 1645. She was exiled to Barcelona by Sagarra in 1652 for anti-French sentiments. Anne of Austria allowed her to return to Perpignan on 25 May 1660.

ARDENA I ÇABASTIDA, Comte d'Ille, Don Josep d'. (b. 18 October 1611 in Darnius, Girona; d. 20 November 1677 in Perpignan). He was one of the prime movers in the War of the Reapers, and served as a lieutenant-general in the armies of Louis XIII and Louis XIV. He served as Catalan ambassador to Paris and moved to Roussillon after the fall of Barcelona. For his services to the crown, he was awarded the Vicomté d'Ille in 1642, which was elevated to a comté in 1661. (m. Lluisa de Aragó i de Aibar)

BANYULS I DE COMPTE, Carles de. (b. 4 March 1647; d. 27 July 1687 in Barcelona). His father was Don Tomàs de Banyuls, who fled the province in 1652. Carles remained in Roussillon after his father's flight. He was accused of aiding the Angelets, and was arrested and questioned but released. In 1674, he became implicated as a leader in the Villefranche conspiracy and fled to Barcelona. He was condemned and executed in effigy, and all his goods were seized. (m. Dona Thomasina d'Ardena i d'Aragó)

BANYULS I DE COMPTE, Francesc de. (d. 20 July 1695 in Nyer). Another son of Tomàs de Banyuls, Francesc was a captain in Calvo's regiment and in the Regiment du Dauphin-Étranger, serving faithfully his entire life. He was awarded his father's title of Baron de Nyer and his sister-in-law's Marquisate de Montferrer. (m. Anne-Françoise de Martin)

BANYULS I D'ORIS, Tomàs de. (d. 5 May 1659 in Barcelona). He joined the revolt against Philip IV in 1640 and received command of a regiment. In 1642, Louis XIII made him Procurator Royal of Fiefs and Master of Waters, Ports, and Forests of the Counties of Roussillon and Cerdanya, and commander of the citadel and *ville* of Perpignan. In 1649, he was given the *seigneurie* of Montferrer. In 1652, he turned against Louis XIV and fled to Spain. He served in the Spanish army and was wounded defending Puigcerda from Conti. (m. Francesca Comte i de Llupia)

BARILLON D'AMONCOURT, Marquis de Branges, Antoine de. (b. 6 December 1671; d. 28 June 1741). The son of a French ambassador to England, he was named a councillor of *Parlement* of Paris on 12 January 1692 and Master of Requests in 1700. He became the intendant of Roussillon and intendant of the army in Catalonia in 1710, but was dismissed from both intendancies in February 1711 for incompetence and re-assigned to the intendancy of Pau. (m. Anne Doublet)

BEAULIEU, Germain Michel Camus de. He served as both intendant and *procureur général* of Roussillon (1676–1681).

BOIXÓ, Emanuel. (d. 1674 in Perpignan). He was a priest at Forques and often provided the Spanish with information on French troop movements. He became involved in the Villefranche-de-Conflent conspiracy of 1674. Denied clerical immunity for his crimes, he was executed in Perpignan.

BOIXÓ, Joan. He was a student in Barcelona with relatives in Roussillon, including his brother Emanuel. Under the pretext of visiting those relatives, he served as the courier to the Spanish for the conspirators of 1674.

BONET I ROMANYA, Josep. (b. 2 May 1672 in Perpignan; d. 17 July 1734 in Perpignan). He was created a *Burgès Honrat* of Perpignan in 1689. He served as an *avocat général* of the Sovereign Council (1708–1711) and as a councillor from 22 July 1711 until 1735.

BONEU I PI, Josep de, Comte de Coromina. He was the leading tactician of the Angelet rebellion, planning raids and battles. After the end of the rebellion, he moved to Barcelona, where he became a general in the Spanish armies and led the resistance to Philip V's siege of Barcelona. For his services to the Hapsburg cause, he was created Conde de Coromina. After the Bourbons captured the city in 1715, he fled and died in exile in Italy.

BORDES, Josep. He was a theology student resident in Villefranche-de-Conflent. When the Sovereign Council began investigating the conspiracy of 1674, he agreed to testify in return for immunity.

BRODEAU. A native of Lorraine, he was a councillor on the Sovereign Council (1708–1736).

BRUEIL, Jean-Louis de. (d. 7 January 1675). A native of Quercy, he was appointed Inquisitor of Roussillon in 1662. He was named bishop of Perpignan (1673–1675), but never received papal recognition.

BRUSI, Josep. He was condemned by the Sovereign Council and fined 1,650 livres, the most severe financial penalty levied in connection with the Angelet rebellion.

ÇA CIRERA, Francesc. A leading citizen of Perpignan, he was deeply involved in the conspiracies of 1674.

ÇAGARRIGA I DE LAPUENTE, Don Marcelino de. (b. 1656; d. 5 February 1710 in Perpignan). His father had been an important nobleman in Roussillon, but left at the Peace of the Pyrenees. Marcelino later returned to Roussillon and reclaimed his title as Seigneur d'Alenya. (m. Dona Galderiga de Vilanova i de Oluja, and later Ana Bou i Compter)

CALVO, Francesc de. A native of Barcelona, he served as a councillor on the Sovereign Council (1682–1708) and as an *avocat général* (1688–1708).

CAMPRODON I D'ARMENGOL, Dona Teresa de - (b. 4 November 1637 in Perpignan; d. 13 May 1662 in Perpignan). She was descended from a noble family of Roussillon, and was the wife of Francesc de Foix-Bearn, a respected nobleman. She was executed in May 1662 for the murder of Don Emanuel de Sant-Dionís, and was widely believed to be acting to protect an anti-French conspiracy.

CAMPRODON I D'ARMENGOL, Don Josep de. (d. 23 May 1710 in Perpignan). He moved from Perpignan to Girona in Spain during the trial of his sister, Teresa. He remained there until sometime after 1667. He eventually returned to Roussillon, becoming captain of Chevau-Légers in the Regiment of Roussillon. (m. Dona Narcissa de Sant-Dionís i Pol)

CAMPRODON I DE FOIX-BEARN, Bonaventura de. (b. 9 November 1618 in Perpignan). A *Burgès Honrat de Perpignan*, he was ennobled by Philip IV on 15 February 1635 for service to the crown. In 1640, he joined the Catalan army fighting for independence. His daughter, Teresa de Camprodon, was executed by the French. (m. Dona Maria de Armengol i Serra)

CAMPRODON I SANT-DIONÍS, Don Aleix Josep de. (b. 19 February 1671 in Perpignan). He was the nephew of Dona Teresa de Camprodon. He joined the Archduke Charles during the War of the Spanish Succession, who created him Marquis de Sant-Dionís on 28 August 1709.

CARLIER, Vicomte d'Ully et de Pargnan, Étienne. A native of Picardy, he served as both intendant and *procureur général* of Roussillon (1670–1676). (m. Marguerite de la Porte)

CARRERA, Felip. He served as a councillor on the Sovereign Council (1689–1694). (m. Bonaventura Calva, and later Maria Armengau i Folcra)

CARRERA, Francesc. (b. 11 March 1622 in Perpignan; d. 1 May 1695 in Barcelona). He moved to Barcelona to earn his medical degree and returned to Perpignan to practice medicine. He was elected rector of the University of Perpignan in 1666, but the French refused to allow him the post because he was considered to be pro-Spanish, and he left for Spain. He took up service with the kings of Spain, rising to become the chief medical officer of the Spanish armies.

CARRERA, Josep. (b. 8 December 1680 in Perpignan; d. 1737). He received his medical degree from Montpellier in 1704 and then returned to Perpignan. He was elected rector of the University of Perpignan in 1716, 1723, and 1737, and, unlike his uncle Francesc, was permitted to serve.

CHÂTILLON, Jacques de Souillac, Marquis de. He served as lieutenant-general of Roussillon (1677–1681).

CHAZERON, François de Monnestay de. He served as lieutenant-general of Roussillon (1685–1697).

CHOUPPES, Aimard, Marquis de. He served as lieutenant-general of Roussillon (1660–1677).

COLLARÈS E IZERN, Pere Martir de. (b. 2 July 1659 in Vinça; d. 14 November 1708 in Vinça). He earned a doctorate in canon and civil law. He served as *assesseur de la Capitainerie Générale* and as a councillor on the Sovereign Council (1695–1705). In addition, he was the professor of French law in Perpignan from 1702 until 1708. (m. Maria Bonet, and later Maria Hugo i Font)

COLLARÈS I BONET, Albert de. (b. 6 September 1683 in Vinça; d. 26 October 1753 in Perpignan). He served as *Commissaire Générale des Domaines* and as a councillor on the Sovereign Council (1705–1733).

COPONS I D'AYGUAVIVA-TAMARIT, Don Felip de. (b. 20 January 1614 in Barcelona; d. 5 September 1684 in Perpignan). He was a member of the *Reial Audiència* of Barcelona in 1641 and a councillor of state in 1646, siding with the French during the rebellion against Philip IV. He was then appointed to the Royal Council of Roussillon in 1653. When that body was suppressed in 1660, he was appointed as one of the six original councillors of the Sovereign Council and served in that capacity until 1684. (m. Francesca de Cordelles, and later Dona Eularia de Tamarit i Amat)

COPONS I DE TAMARIT, Don Miquel-Felip de. (b. 18 June 1661 in Perpignan; d. 5 July 1732 in Perpignan). He succeeded his father as a councillor on the Sovereign Council (1684–1695) and also served as a *president à mortier* from 1695. (m. Maria-Theresa de Reart i Batlle)

CORBIÈRE, Jacques. The leader of a group of Huguenots from Languedoc. His group was captured in Banyuls while attempting to flee to England via Spain in 1686. He was sentenced to the galleys for life, but released after one year.

DESCALLAR I DE SOLER, Emanuel. (b. 1648 in Villefranche-de-Conflent; d. 20 Apr 1674 in Perpignan). He was the son of Pere Àngel Descallar i de Llar. His family was exiled by French authorities to Barcelona in 1654, but returned in 1659 as part of the amnesties accompanying the peace. He was again condemned to exile in 1670 for fomenting the Angelet revolts, but his sentence was commuted to 300 livres and one year of exile in Serdinya. After his second return to Villefranche, he became a principal conspirator in the 1674 conspiracy and was executed for his role. His head was hung outside Villefranche for many years as a warning against treason.

ESTAMPES, Jean-Baptiste d'. He was named both Inquisitor and bishop of Perpignan in 1675, but never went to Roussillon to take possession of his diocese.

FIMARCON, Jacques de Cassanet, Marquis de. (b. 15 March 1659; d. 15 March 1730 in Paris). He served as lieutenant-general of Roussillon (1713-1730). (m. Madeleine de Baschi)

FLAMENVILLE, Jean Hervé Basan de. (b. 16 February 1660 at Flamenville; d. 1721). Son of the Marquis de Flamenville of Normandy, he entered the seminary of Saint-Sulpice in 1682. After his studies, he was named *chapelain* of Saint-Saveur d'Octeville (1687) and then served as vicar-general for the bishop of Angers, Michel Le Peletier. He was named bishop of Elne on 8 September 1695, and consecrated by the Archbishop Louis-Antoine de Noailles.

FOIX-BEARN I DESCAMPS, Don Francesc de. (b. 25 May 1640 in Perpignan; d. 27 October 1702). He was Seigneur de Santa-Eugenia, Sureda, Bompàs, Oltrera, Sant Joan de Pladecorts, and Las Fonts, and his family was one of the oldest and most respected among the Roussillonnais nobility. (m. Dona Theresa de Camprodon i de Armengol, and Dona Joana de Vilaplana i Descamps, and Dona Hipolita de Taqui i Fabra)

FONTANELLA I GARRAVER, Don Josep de. (b. at Barcelona; d. 1680 at Perpignan). He was the son of Joan-Pere de Fontanella, a noted Barcelonan jurist, and earned a degree in canon law. His brother Francesc is considered one of the foremost Catalan writers of the seventeenth century. As a member of the *Consell de Cent*, Josep actively promoted the Catalan revolt in 1640. He served as a representative of Catalonia at the negotiations of Münster in 1644. He spent the years 1650 and 1651 in Paris and became an ally of Colbert. He was created Count of Peralada and Viscount of Canet and given the position of regent of the Royal Audiencia of Barcelona. After the annexation, he was appointed *president à mortier* of the Sovereign Council. Near the end of his life he was created Viscount of Fontanella. He and Francesc de Sagarra were bitter rivals throughout their lives, even though both were faithful servants of France. (m. Dona Maria de Palmarola i Vaquer)

FORNIER, Jean-Jacques de. (b. in Languedoc). He became the first professor of French law in Perpignan (1683). In addition, he served as both a councillor (1688–1697) and *president à mortier* (1701–1708) on the Sovereign Council.

FORNIER, Louis. The son of Jean-Jacques de Fornier, he also served as a professor of French law in Perpignan (1708–1752) and as a councillor on the Sovereign Council (1697–1701).

GELCEN, Josep. A lawyer in Perpignan, he became involved in the conspiracies of 1674.

GISPERT I COMA, Anton. (b. 25 October 1675 in Perpignan; d. 25 March 1738 in Perpignan). He was an *avocat général* of the Sovereign Council (1708–1712) and a councillor (1712–1743). He was created a *Burgès Honrat* of Perpignan in 1707. (m. Catherine Bou i Guitart)

GUITART, Marie. A resident of Arles, she had a son serving as a *Miquelet* in the Spanish army. To aid her son, she attempted to subvert the garrison of Fort des Bains in 1674 and was condemned.

LA NEUVILLE, Charles Deschiens de. (b. 28 Sep 1667; d. 7 Mar 1737). Served as Master of Requests (1707), intendant at Béarn (1710), intendant of Roussillon (1711), and intendant of Franche-Comté (1718–1734). (m. Jeanne Desbordes)

LLAR, Francesc de. (b. 1642 at Villefranche; d. 1708). He was a native of Villefranche-de-Conflent and the cousin of Emanuel Descallar. Together with several other leading citizens, they developed the 1674 conspiracy in that town.

LLAR I DE PASQUAL-CADELL, Agnès de. The daughter of Carles de Llar, she is believed to have exposed the 1674 conspiracy to the French in order to win the affections of Parlan de Saignes, an officer in the French army. Despite a pardon from Louvois for any associations she had with the conspirators of 1674, she was unpopular in Villefranch-de-Conflent and became a nun. Her story was novelized in *L'infante* by Louis Bertrand (1920).

LLAR I DE TEIXIDOR, Carles de. (d. 4 May 1674 in Perpignan). He was a native of Roussillon and resident of Villefranche-de-Conflent. He was *seigneur* of Llar, Toès, Flaçà, La Guardia, and Marinyans. In 1671 he was created a noble of Catalonia by Charles II of Spain. He was implicated in the conspiracy of 1674 and, although some historians believe him to have been innocent, he was executed. His head was hung in an iron cage outside the gates of Villefranche as a warning to rebels. (m. Anna de Pasqual-Cadell)

LLÉOPART, Jeroni. (d. 1671 a Elne). He was the son of a Barcelona nobleman and immigrated to Roussillon at the conclusion of the War of the Reapers. He possessed powerful friends at the court in Paris and thereby gained important clerical positions in Roussillon. He served as *vicaire capitulaire* of the Diocese of Elne. He became embroiled in several disputes, in which he triumphed due to his connections in Paris.

LLUPIÀ I BALLARÓ, Emanuel de. (b. 1626 at Perpignan; d. 1708 at Barcelona). He was the son of Gabriel de Llupià i de Pagès-Vallgornera and a leader of the Angelet rebellion. In addition, he was selected to lead 500 troops into Roussillon in conjunction with the conspiracies of 1674. After these failures in Roussillon, he joined the Spanish army. He became a knight of the Order of Alcantara, an officer of artillery, and a vice governor of Catalonia.

MACQUERON, Charles. He served as a secretary to Le Tellier before becoming intendant (1660–1669) and *procureur général* (1663–1669) of Roussillon. The Angelet rebellion began during his tenure, and he was opposed to all negotiations with the rebels.

MANALT I TALLALOQUES, Nicolau de. (b. 6 April 1603 in Perpignan; d. 28 April 1688 in Perpignan). A native and *Burgès Honrat* of Perpignan, he was appointed a member of the Sovereign Council on 7 June 1660, and served until his death. He was the only original member of that body who was a native of the province of Roussillon. (m. Maria Tuixa i Bonet)

MANERA, Lambert. (d. 1675 in Girona). An active leader of the Angelet rebellion, he was killed in combat with the French during a campaign in Catalonia.

MARGARIT I DE BIURE, Marquis d'Aguilar, Don Josep de. (b. 10 February 1602 in Castell-de-Empordà; d. 23 July 1685 in Durban, Aude). He was the son of Felip de Mararit i Sunyer. He was jailed for leading his vassals into skirmishes with neighbors around 1632, and was accused of murder in 1638. He became a leader of the pro-French faction during the revolt of 1640 and was created Baron de Brens and Marquis d'Aguilar by Louis XIV. (m. Dona Maria de Biure i de Cardona)

MARGARIT I DE BIURE, Don Josep de. (d. 1701 in Narbonne). He was a son of the Marquis d'Aguilar. He served as abbot at Saint Martin du Canigou from 1692 to 1698, then held ecclesiastical office in Narbonne until his death.

MARGARIT I DE BIURE, Don Vincenç de. (d. 21 December 1672 in Perpignan). He was the son of Felip de Margarit i Sunyer. A member of the Dominican order, he was appointed bishop of Lleida (1642), Solsona (1646), Barcelona (1651), and Perpignan (1658) by Louis XIV. He was, however, only recognized by the pope at Perpignan, and that only on 17 April 1669. He was also a *conseiller d'honneur* of the Sovereign Council.

MARTÍ I DE VILADOMAR, Don Francesc de. (b. 30 August 1616 in Puigcerda; d. 21 December 1687 in Perpignan). He earned a doctorate in law and served in the *Reial Audiència* of Barcelona. In 1644, he replaced Fontanella as the Catalan representative at Münster, earning the latter's hatred. He was appointed councillor and *avocat général* of the Sovereign Council on 7 June 1660. He retained the latter charge until 1683, and the former until his death. He was a prolific author, and his writings include: *Noticia Universal de Cataluña* (1640), *Avisos del castellano fingido* (1641), *Delirios de la pasión en la muerte de la envida* (1641), *Cataluña en Francia, Castilla sin Cataluña y Francia contra Castilla* (1641), *Manifesto de la fidelidad catalana* (1646), and *Temas de la locura y embustes de la malícia* (1648). (m. Eularia Prexens i Elias)

MARTÍ I PREXENS, Josep de. (b. 1661; d. 10 July 1689 in Perpignan). He succeeded his father as a councillor on the Sovereign Council in 1687, and served until 1689. He also served as an *avocat général* of the Sovereign Council (1683–1689). (m. Dona Maria de Palmarola i Vaquer)

MIQUEL MESTRE, Joan. One of the leaders of the Angelet Rebellion, he was known as "l'hereu Just de Ballestaví." He was primarily responsible for spreading the Angelet rebellion into the Conflent, although he was active in the Vallespir as well.

MONTAGNE. A native of Languedoc, he served as a councillor on the Sovereign Council (1690–1695).

MONTMOR, Louis Habert de. (b. 1644 at Paris; d. 23 Jan 1695 at Montpellier). The son of a Parisian noble family, he was ordained in 1671 and served as doctor of theology at Notre-Dame de La Roche. He became bishop of Perpignan on 6 July 1682, wrote a church manual in 1689, and opened a seminary in Perpignan in 1690. He also served as a *conseiller d'honneur* of the Sovereign Council.

NOAILLES, Adrien Maurice, Comte d'Ayen, Duc de. (b. 29 September 1678 at Paris; d. 24 June 1766 at Paris). The son of Anne Jules, Duc de Noailles, he became the governor of Roussillon on 6 March 1698 after the resignation of his father. He later rose in the service of France, serving on the Council of Regency (1718), being awarded the baton of a marshal of France (1734), and ambassador to Spain (1746). (m. Françoise Charlotte Amable d'Aubigné)

NOAILLES, Anne Jules, Duc de. (b. 1650; d. 1708). His military achievements included being *capitaine des gardes du corps* (1661), *maréchal de camp* (1676), *lieutenant-général* (1682), and a marshal of France (1693). He served as governor of Roussillon from 1678 until he resigned in favor of his son Adrien in 1698. (m. Marie Françoise de Bournonville)

NOELL, Damià. One of the most important leaders of the Angelet rebellion.

OLIVARES, Gaspar de Guzmán, Count-Duke of. He was *valido* (first minister) to King Philip IV of Spain. His attempts to unify the territories of Philip into a single political unit alienated many people within the Spanish empire, and ultimately drove both the Catalans and the Portuguese to revolt in 1640.

OMS I DE VILANOVA, Don Emanuel d'. (d. 1670). He was a native of Roussillon and served in the Catalan army during the War of the Reapers. He came to oppose the French presence in the province, and was convicted of lèse-majesté in 1666. (m. Dona Maria d'Oms i d'Oms)

ORTEGA I CLOSELLS, Rafel de. (b. 8 April 1650 at Perpignan; d. 4 April 1728 at Perpignan). He was honored as a *Burgès Honrat* of Perpignan. He earned a doctorate in canon and civil law and served both as professor of French law (1691) and as a councillor on the Sovereign Council (1708–1724). (m. Maria Piquer i Carles)

PAGÈS, Joan. (d. 7 June 1672). He was a priest at Saint-Laurent de Cerdans in the Vallespir and a leader of the Angelet rebellion. He fled to Spain, and received a parish in Massanet de Cabrenys. He continued to encourage the Angelets from this border town, and the French sent a raiding party to seize him. In retaliation, the Spanish seized Fontanella's grandson and Francesc de Martí's son. The two Spanish hostages were released, but Pagès was put to death for his complicity with the rebels.

PONT, Pere. A native of Barcelona, he left the Principat when the Peace of the Pyrenees was signed. As abbot of Nôtre Dame de Arles-sur-Tech from 1661 to 1684, he served as a *conseiller d'honneur* of the Sovereign Council from 1676. He was strongly pro-French, and aided the Sovereign Council in re-establishing the *gabelle* in the Vallespir.

PRAT I SENJULIA, Isidore de. He was appointed one of the original six councillors of the Sovereign Council on 7 June 1660. On 7 January 1681, he became an *avocat général.* On 7 December 1688, he gave up both of his other positions to become *president à mortier* of the Sovereign Council, which he retained until 1695. Two years after the latter appointment, he was named *garde des sceaux* (1690–1695).

PRATS, Jeroni. A resident of Villefranche-de-Conflent, he kept a record of the 1674 conspiracy. This record was discovered by Fructus de Queralt and was used to implicate many of the conspirators.

PUIG, Francesc. Doctor and a leader of the pro-French faction during the revolt of 1640.

PUIG I TERRATS, Francesc. (d. 19 May 1674 in Perpignan). A Perpignannais lawyer, he played an active role in the conspiracies of 1674. He was arrested, tortured extensively, confessed everything he knew, and was then executed.

QUÉRALT I DE SALVADOR, Josep de. A member of the *Reial Audiència* of Barcelona in 1641, he fled to Roussillon. He was appointed one of the original six councillors on the Sovereign Council. He died in 1661 and was succeeded by his son, Fructus de Queralt i de Sant Andreu. (m. Francesca de Sant-Andreu)

QUÉRALT I DE SANT-ANDREU, Francesc de. (d. 1681). The brother of Fructus, he held a doctorate in canon law. He served as a canon of the Cathedral Chapter of Elne, *vicaire-capitulaire* of the diocese, and *vicaire-général* for Bishop Don Vincenç de Margarit.

QUÉRALT I DE SANT-ANDREU, Fructus de. (d. 1682). He obtained his father's position as councillor of the Sovereign Council upon the latter's death in 1661 and served until 1682. Among his responsibilities was the investigation of the Villefranche-de-Conflent conspiracy of 1674. (m. Theresa Lassus i Pi)

QUINSON, Jean Raymond de Villardis, Comte de. He served as acting lieutenant-general of Roussillon (1698–1713).

REA, Maur de la. He was the abbot of Saint Génis des Fontaines, and was convicted of lèse-majesté in 1666. He had developed a plot, with Emanuel d'Oms, to throw open Collioure to the Spanish.

RIBET, Antoni. He was a consul of Perpignan and became involved in the conspiracy of 1674.

RICQUET, Pierre-Paul. (b. in 1604 at Bézier; d. 1 October 1680 at Toulouse). He served as director of the *gabelle* farm in Languedoc and Roussillon.

RIGAU-ROS I SERRA, Jacint. (b. 20 July 1659 in Perpignan; d. 27 December 1759). Descended from a family of Catalan artists, he went to Montpellier to study art. He reached Paris in 1681, where he gained favor at court and won the Grand Prix de Rome. He was admitted to the French academy in 1700.

SAGARRA, Francesc de. (b. at Lleida; d. 1688). A member of the *Reial Audiència* of Barcelona, he favored the French and moved to Roussillon after the annexation. He was appointed *president à mortier* of the Sovereign Council in 1660, and was a lifelong rival of Josep de Fontanella. He also served as *garde des sceaux* (1660–1688). He was very active in leading the military repression of the Angelets, and was nearly killed in a 1668 raid.

SAGNES, Parlan de. A Catalan officer in the French army, he was the commander of Villefranche-de-Conflent during the conspiracy of 1674. It seems probable that he received information concerning the plot from Ines de Llar.

SALELLES, Guillaume de. (b. at Languedoc). He was both the *garde des sceaux* (1695–1701) and *president à mortier* (1693–1701) of the Sovereign Council.

SALELLES, Guillaume de. The son of the preceding, he served as a councillor of the Sovereign Council (1701–1717).

SANT-DIONÍS I POL, Don Emanuel de. He was a native of Catalonia and an officer in the French army. He developed a relationship with Dona Teresa de Camprodon, some believe to spy on a rebel plot. This view is supported by the fact that he was murdered by a group of men who stabbed him fifty-two times, a murder for which Camprodon was executed.

SICRE, Jacques. A jurist from Montpellier, he taught French law in Perpignan from 1692 until 1694.

SOLER, Joan. (d. 1674 at Perpignan). He was the second consul of Villefranche-de-Conflent, was executed for complicity in the conspiracy of 1674, and his head displayed on the walls of that city.

TALON DE LA MAISON-BLANCHE, Pierre. He was appointed intendant of the army of Catalonia in 1654, and later served as the judge of the *gabelle* in Roussillon (1662–1673). He also served as intendant of the army in Roussillon from 1677 to 1680 and again in 1686. (m. Elisabeth du Lac)

TAMARIT I DE RIFÀ, Francesc de. (d. 1653). A leader of the pro-French faction during the revolt of 1640.

TIXEDAS, Josep. (d. 16 May 1674 in Perpignan). A member of the Duke of Noailles' personal guard, he maintained contact between the conspirators in Villefranche-de-Conflent and Perpignan during the events of 1674. He was arrested and garroted in Perpignan.

TIXEDAS, Macià. He was the brother of Josep Tixedas and an officer in the French cavalry. He was involved in the Perpignan conspiracy of 1674 and was executed in front of the cathedral in Perpignan. His head was displayed for some years in Perpignan as a warning to potential traitors.

TRILLACH, Anton de. He served as a councillor on the Sovereign Council (1694–1711). (m. Geltrudis Esprer)

TRINXERIA, Josep de la. (d. 1689). Born in Prats-de-Mollo, he became the leader of the Angelet rebellion in 1666. In 1673, when it had become apparent that the *Angelets* were losing support, he accepted a commission in the Spanish army, leading its forces into Roussillon on several occasions. For his leading role in the insurrection, he was condemned to death in abstentia by the Sovereign Council.

TROBAT I DE VINYES, Josep de. (d. 1701). A native of Barcelona and brother of Ramon de Trobat, he became a cleric in his native city. At the Peace of the Pyrenees, he immigrated to Roussillon where he served as abbot of Cuxa and as a *conseiller d'honneur* on the Sovereign Council.

TROBAT I DE VINYES, Ramon de. (d. 1698). He was the son of Josep de Trobat i Tria and a native of Barcelona. He trained in the law in that city. During the Catalan revolt of 1640, he sided with the rebels and served in the army. He came to the notice of the French, and served as an adviser to Mazarin at the negotiations for the Peace of the Pyrenees. A prominent member of the French government in Roussillon, he was named one of the original six councillors of the Sovereign Council on 7 June 1660, promoted to *president à mortier* on 24 November 1680, and named its first president 18 April 1691. In addition, he was an *avocat général* of the Sovereign Council from 1660 until 1681, when he was named intendant of Roussillon, a position he retained until his death in 1698. (m. Catherine Codolosa)

TRULL, Joan del. (d. 9 April 1671). He was the second consul of Prats-de-Mollo. He decided to collaborate with the French against the Angelets, and was killed by the rebels in retaliation.

UBERT, Jaume. He was a priest in the Vallespir and was convicted of aiding the Angelet rebels.

VILAFORMU, Diègue. He served as a councillor-clerk (1660–1688), councillor (1688–1690), and *garde des sceaux* (1688–1690) of the Sovereign Council.

VILANOVA, Don Jacint. A leader of the pro-French faction during the revolt of 1640.

VILAPLANA I D'AGULLÓ, Francesc de. (b. 1597 at Copons; d. 1649 in Perpignan). He murdered a *batlle* in 1620 and was condemned to perpetual exile at Peñón in North Africa. His sentence was commuted to military service in Flanders in the 1630s, but he deserted near Perpignan. He later became a leader of the pro-French faction during the revolt of 1640.

VILAR I REYNALT, Miquel de. (b. at Perpignan; d. 9 April 1728 in Perpignan). He earned doctorates in both philosophy (1666) and law (1668) from the University of Perpignan and was honored as a *Burgès Honrat* of Perpignan (1678). He also served as an *avocat général* (1689–1708), a councillor (1681–1708), and *president à mortier* (from 1708) on the Sovereign Council. As reward for his service, he was created Seigneur du Vilar d'Ovança and de Planes (1700) and given a patent of nobility (1702). (m. Joana Coll i Naubiola)

VILAROJA, Josep. He was a notary in Perpignan and became involved in the conspiracies of 1674. He became frightened and confessed in return for immunity.

Appendix C
Public Officials and Clergy

GOVERNORS OF ROUSSILLON

Anne, Duc de Noailles	1660–1678
Anne-Jules, Duc de Noailles	1678–1698
Adrien-Maurice, Duc de Noailles	1698–1718

INTENDANTS

Charles Macqueron	1660–1669
Étienne Carlier	1670–1676
Germain Michel Camus de Beaulieu	1676–1681
Ramon de Trobat i de Vinyes	1681–1698
Félix Marie Étienne de Ponte d'Albaret	1698–1709
Antoine de Barillon d'Amoncourt	1710–1711
Charles Deschiens de La Neuville	1711–1715

LIEUTENANTS GENERAL

Aimard, Marquis de Chouppes	1660–1677
Jacques de Souillac, Marquis de Châtillon	?–1681
François de Monnestay de Chazeron	1685–1697
Jean Raymond de Villardis, Comte de Quinson	1698–1713
Jacques de Cassanet, Marquis de Fimarcon	1713–1730

BISHOPS OF PERPIGNAN

François Perez Roy	1638–1641
Don Vincenç de Margarit i de Biure	1669–1672
Jean-Louis de Brueil	1673–1675
Jean-Baptiste d'Estampes	(never took possession)
Louis Habert de Montmor	1680–1695
Jean Hervé Basan de Flamenville	1695–1721

PRESIDENTS À MORTIER OF THE SOVEREIGN COUNCIL

I.	Josep de Fontanella	7 June 1660
	Ramon de Trobat	24 December 1680
	Massia de Salelles	10 January 1693
	Jean-Jacques de Fornier	26 April 1701
	Miquel de Vilar	25 October 1708

II.	Francesc de Sagarra	7 June 1660
	Isidore de Prat	7 December 1688
	Miquel-Felip de Copons	12 July 1695

MEMBERS OF THE SOVEREIGN COUNCIL   APPOINTED

I.	Felip de Copons	1660
	Miquel-Felip de Copons	1684
	Pere Martir de Collarès e Izern	1695
	Albert de Collarès i Bonet	1705

II.	Francesc de Martí	1660
	Josep de Martí i Prexens	1687
	Philippe Carrera	1689
	Anton de Trillach	1694
	Josep Bonet i Romanya	1711

III.	Nicolau de Manalt i Tallaloques	1660
	Jean-Jacques de Fornier	1688
	Louis Fornier	1697
	Guillaume IV de Salelles	1701

IV.	Isidore de Prat i Senjulia	1660
	Diègue Vilaformu	1688
	De Montagne	1690
	Jean Alizon de La Roche	1695
	Charles Alizon de La Roche	1702
	Anton Gispert i Coma	1712

V.	Ramon de Trobat i de Vinyes	1660
	Miquel de Vilar i Reynalt	1681
	Rafel de Ortega i Closells	1708

VI.	Josep de Quéralt i de Salvador	1660
	Fructus de Quéralt	1661
	Francesc de Calvo	1682
	Brodeau	1708

SECRETARIES OF STATE FOR WAR

Le Tellier, Marquis de Louvois	1662–16 July 1691
Le Tellier, Marquis de Barbezieux	16 July 1691–5 January 1701
Michel de Chamillart	January 1701–9 June 1709
Daniel-François Voysin	17 June 1709–15 September 1715

POPES

Alexander VII Chigi	7 April 1655–22 May 1667
Clement IX Rospigliosi	20 June 1667–9 December 1669
Clement X Altieri	29 April 1670–22 July 1676
Innocent XI Odescalchi	21 September 1676–12 August 1689
Alexander VIII Ottoboni	6 October 1689–1 February 1691
Innocent XII Pignatelli	12 July 1691–27 September 1700
Clement XI Albani	23 November 1700–19 March 1721

Appendix D
Glossary of Foreign Terms

alguazil: Policeman.

Amirauté de Collioure: French admiralty court given competence over all maritime disputes in the province.

arrêt: Judgement.

avocat général: attorney-general.

batlle: Bailiff or mayor of a village.

bayle: French rendering of *batlle*.

bourse: French institution that regulated commerical matters.

burgès honrats: Individuals granted special patents of nobility by the city of Perpignan.

Cahiers de Doléances: Lists of grievances presented to the government during the French Revolution.

canon bénéficier: Beneficed canon.

Capitainerie Générale: Decided cases involving persons whom the governor had granted special exemptions.

capitation: Personal tax, nominally payable by all the king's subjects.

Chambre du Domaine: An alternate name for the *Consistoire du Domaine*.

chancellerie-garde des sceaux: Keeper of the seals.

chancellerie-secrétaire et garde-minutes: Recorder and keeper of the minutes.

clavaire: French rendering of *clavari*.

clavari: Locally appointed arbiter of disputes; the first person to hear most grievances.

clerc de procureur: Prosecutor's clerk.

commis: clerk.

commis adjoint: Assistant clerk.

commis de la foraine: Clerk of the Aliens; official responsible for registering foreigners.

Comtat de Cerdanya: Prior to 1659, a Spanish territory of northern Catalonia including all of the Cerdaña valley.

Comtat de Conflans: A small region along the Franco-Spanish border, it was incorporated into French Roussillon in 1659.

Comtat de Rosselló: Prior to 1659, a Spanish territory of northern Catalonia which included the plain of Roussillon, the Vallespir, and the Conflent.

conseillers d'honneur: Those who, based on birth or benefice, hold salaried positions on the Sovereign Council.

conseillers honoraires: Individuals permitted to attend meetings of the Sovereign Council without salary or right to vote.

Consell de Cent: Council of 100; Catalan governing body.

Consistoire du Domaine: Court supervising water rights, questions of nobility, and the regalian rights in Roussillon.

Consulat de la Llotja de Mar de Perpinyà: Catalan court responsible for disputes arising from all mercantile activity in the province.

corps de ville: Body of village residents who possessed the right of political participation.

Corts: Catalan representative body.

Councillor Commissaire: Judge of the *Consistoire du Domaine*.

cours des bayles royaux: Courts of the first instance for the eleven royal *baillages*.

cours des tiers: Courts to which disputants could elect to submit their grievances arising from certain contracts.

curé: Beneficed clergyman.

Diputació: A governing body of Catalonia.

docteur en droit: One who holds an advanced degree in canon or civil law.

don gratuit: A financial donation from the clergy to the king.

douanes: Customs duties.

droit d'empereage: French rendering of *pariatge*.

droits de rente. Right to collect rents.

fermìer: One who purchased the right to collect taxes.

fusiliers de montagne: An alternate French phrase for *Miquelets*; often distinguished by long-term service.

gabelle: tax on salt.

gavatxos: Catalan term to describe contemptuous foreigners, particularly the French.

généralité: Administrative unit for the collection of taxes.

Gent: Residents.

grand-archidiacre d'Elne: Archdeacon of Elne; the most important deacon in Roussillon.

grande sacristain: Chief Sexton.

greffier en chef: Chief clerk of the Sovereign Council.

hussier à verge: Bearer of the emblems of the Sovereign Council.

hussier audiencier: Usher or crier of the Sovereign Council's court.

intendant: Chief official of French Roussillon; responsible for the administration of justice, the collection of taxes, and the supervision of the army.

Juge des Gabelles: Judged cases involving officials of the gabelle.

Juge des Tabacs: Judged grievances arising from the royal tobacco monopoly.

Juge des Traites: Judged disputes about extra-provincial commerce.

Juridiction des Four Banaux de Perpignan: Court that decided cases involving the Knights of Malta, usually involving disputes over ovens.

justice seigneuriale: Justice administered by a nobleman in his lands, superseding some royal courts.

mà major: Class of citizens possessing patents of urban nobility; the *burgès honrats*.

minot: French measure of approximately 39 liters.

Miquelet: Catalans who fought in an unconventional syle as part of a regular army for short periods; both the French and Spanish armies raised units of *Miquelets*.

monnaie: mint.

ordinaire: An ecclesiastical judge.

pariatge: Catalan *ad valorum* tax of approximately 0.2% levied on all goods in transit through the province.

president à mortier: Presiding president of a court.

procureur général: Attorney general of the Sovereign Council.

réaux d'argent: A silver coin.

regnicole: Subject of the king of France.

segadors: day-laborers; reapers.

Sobreposats de la Horta: Local bodies which heard cases arising from animal damage to property and estimated the damage done.

somatens: Catalan militia that could only be legally employed in defensive operations.

sous-viguier: Assistant to a *viguier*.

syndic majeur: Chief syndic.

Table de Marbre: Ultimate court of appeals for maritime disputes; located in Paris.

Tribunal de la Monnaie de Perpignan: Court of the Perpignan mint.

Tribunal de la Pieuse Aumône: Institution responsible for administering poor relief.

Usatges: Compilation of Catalan judicial precedents which served as the cornerstone of the Constitutions of Catalonia.

valido: Favorite minister of the Spanish king.

vegueria: Catalan judicial district; there were three in Roussillon.

vicaire capitulaire: Vicar of a religious chapter.

vicaire général: Vicar-general.

vicaire général apostolique: Vicar-general appointed by the pope.

viguerie: French term for *vegueria*.

Notes

1. John C. Rule, "The Aesthetic Impulse: Colbert de Torcy's Education in the Fine Arts," in *The Ascendancy of French Culture During the Reign of Louis XIV*, ed. by David L. Rubin (Washington, D.C.: 1992), p. 1881.

2. Quoted in *The Journal of Peasant Studies* 20 (October 1992), 195.

3. *Archives Départementales des Pyrénées-Orientales* [Hereafter cited as *ADPO*], 1C 1291, 12 January 1682.

4. *ADPO*, 12J 30, 26 September 1691, f° 264.

5. A. Morel-Fatio, ed. *Recueil des instructions*, vol. 11 *Espagne I* (Paris: 1894), p. 129.

6. *ADPO*, 1C 1407, 23 November 1676.

7. *Extrait de la Generalité de Perpignan ou Province de Roussillon*, 1710. *Archives Nationales* [hereafter cited as *AN*], MM 972.

8. *ADPO*, 1C 1241, 18 September 1685.

9. The intendant of Roussillon in 1778, a century after annexation, estimated the population at 108,000. *ADPO*, 1C 1308.

10. *ADPO*, 1C 1408, 1 March 1682; B. Alart, ed., *Documents sur la langue catalane des anciens Comtés de Roussillon et de Cerdagne* (Paris: 1881), p. 6.

11. *ADPO*, 1C 1278; *Bibliothèque Nationale* [hereafter cited as *BN*], Fonds Français, 11308; *Service Historique du Armée de Terre* [hereafter cited as *SHAT*], A^1 1466, 8 December 1700; Joëlle Iema, "L'Evêche d'Elne de 1659 à 1721. Actions politiques et pastorales" (Mémoire de Maîtrise, Université de Toulouse, 1979), pp. 13-14.

12. *SHAT*, A^1 1289, 20 July 1693.

13. Jordi Carbonell, ed., *Gran Enciclopèdic Catalana*, 15 vols. (Barcelona: 1970-1980), 15:126-127.

14. Quoted in Arthur Terry, *Catalan Literature* (New York: 1972), pp. 64-65.

15. Joseph Calmette and Pierre Vidal, *Histoire de Roussillon* (Paris: 1931), pp. 172-173.

16. Don Juan de Garay, 11 October 1640, Quoted in John Elliott, *The Revolt of the Catalans* (Cambridge: 1963), p. 487.

17. *Arxiu de la Corona d'Aragó* [hereafter cited as *ACA*], Generalitat de Catalunya, Vol. 84; Elliott, pp. 473-477.

18. Peter Sahlins, *Boundaries: The Making of France and Spain in the Pyrenees* (Berkeley: 1989), pp. 34-35.

19. *ACA*, Consell d'Aragó, Legajo 313; Fernando Sanchez Marcos, *Cataluña y el Gobierno Central tras la Guerra de los Segadores, 1652–1679* (Barcelona: 1983), p. 142; Geneviève Gavignaud, "La frontière pyrénéene et la partie française de la Catalogne depuis 1659," *Frontières et limites de 1610 à nos jours. Actes du 101ᵉ congrès national des sociétés savantes* (Lille: 1978), p. 156.

20. *SHAT*, A4S1§6/C1, No. 27.

21. *SHAT*, A¹1106, 1 March 1691; *SHAT*, A4S1§6/C1, No. 27.

22. *BN*, Fonds Français, 11308.

23. *SHAT*, A4S1§6/C1, No. 27.

24. Morel-Fatio, *Recueil des Instructions*, Vol. 11 *Espagne* I, 129.

25. *ADPO*, 1E 887, 5 April 1698; Sharon Kettering, *Patrons, Brokers, and Clients in Seventeenth-Century France* (Oxford: 1986), pp. 134, 203.

26. *BN*, Fonds Français 4195, f° 163-169v°.

27. *ADPO*, 2B 25, f° 5 - 6v°; Jean de Boislisle, ed. *Mémoriaux du conseil de 1661*, 3 vols. (Paris: 1905 - 1907), 1:255.

28. *ADPO*, 2B 38, f° 59, 18 April 1691; *SHAT*, A¹ 300, 12 December 1671; *SHAT*, A¹1106, 4 March 1691; Guy Clerc, *Recherches sur le Conseil Souverain de Roussillon (1660–1790)*, 2 vols. (Paris: 1974), 1:22.

29. *ADPO*, 2B 25, f° 59 - 59 v°, 78; Clerc, 1:19; Philippe Wolff, ed., *Histoire de Perpignan* (Toulouse: 1985), p. 84.

30. Clerc, 1:27-30.

31. Louis Assier-Andrieu, *Le peuple et la loi. Anthropologie historique des droits paysans en catalogne française* (Paris: 1987), p. 73.

32. *ADPO*, 1C 1278.

33. *ADPO*, 1B 402, 7 December 1688; *ADPO*, 1C 1278.

34. *BN*, Fonds Français, 11308; *ADPO*, 1C 1256; *ADPO*, 1C 1278.

35. *BN*, Fonds Français, 11308; *ADPO*, 1C 1278.

36. *ADPO*, 1C 1278; Jean-Jacques Larrère and Christiane Villain-Gandossi, "Le *Llibre del Consolat de Mar*: les gens de mer, leurs droits et leurs obligations," *Actes du 106ᵉ congrès national des sociétés savantes* (Perpignan: 1981), pp. 160-167; Guy Romestan, "Le *Consulat de Mer* de Perpignan dans la première moitié du XVᵉ siècle," in *Actes du XXXVIIᵉ et XXXVIIIᵉ Congrès de fédération historique du Languedoc méditerranéen et du Roussillon.* (Montpellier: 1964-1965), pp. 157-159.

37. *SHAT*, A¹ 1289, 20 July 1693.

38. *ADPO*, 1C 1278.

39. Clerc, 1:19-185.

40. Feuillet de Conches, ed., *Journal du Marquis de Dangeau*, 19 vols., (Paris: 1854-1859), 6:340.

41. Marcel Marion, *Dictionnaire des institutions de la France aux XVIIᵉ et XVIIIᵉ siècles* (New York: 1968), pp. 293-299.

42. *SHAT*, A¹ 1106.

43. *SHAT*, A¹ 2330, 8 March 1711.

44. *ADPO*, 1E 887; *SHAT*, A¹ 2328; *SHAT*, A¹ 2330; *SHAT*, YA 35, d'Albaret file, 17 August 1750; *Journal du Marquis de Dangeau*, 13:80; Michel Antoine, *Le gouvernement et l'administration sous Louis XV: dictionnaire biographique*, (Paris: 1973), pp. 50, 209.

45. *BN*, Fonds Français, 11308; *BN*, Fonds Français, 21542, f° 424-429; Marcel Langlois, ed., *Mme de Maintenon. Lettres*. 5 vols. (Paris: 1939), 5:330-331; Marion, pp. 259-261; Geneviève Maze-Sencier, ed., *Dictionnaire des maréchaux de France du moyen age à nos jours*, (Geneva: 1988), pp. 336-339.

46. *ADPO*, 3B 1, April 1691; *ADPO*, 3B 1, 20 December 1718; Joachim Darsel, "L'amirauté en Languedoc et Roussillon," *Actes du 96ᵉ congrès national des sociétés savantes* (Paris: 1976), 2:20-23; Jean-Gabriel Gigot, "Notes sur l'Amirauté de Collioure," *Bulletin du société agricole, scientifique et littéraire des Pyrénées-Orientales* 73 (1958): 77-79; F. Olivier-Martin. *Histoire du droit français des origines à la révolution* (Paris: 1951), pp. 556-557; Roland E. Mousnier, *The Institutions of France under the Absolute Monarchy 1598-1789*, trans. Arthur Goldhammer, 2 vols. (Chicago: 1979-1980), 2:296-299.

47. Yves Malartic, "Le sel in Catalogne (XIIIᵉ - XVᵉ siècles)," *Actes du 106ᵉ congrès national des sociétés savantes* (Perpignan: 1981), pp. 184, 190-192.

48. *ADPO* 2B 63, 21 February 1670.

49. Sahlins, pp. 81-83.

50. *ADPO*, 1C 1011, 23 January 1683.

51. *ADPO* A9, 1 Dec 1702; *ADPO*, 2B 27, f° 150-151; *ADPO*, 2B 91, 28 January 1792; *ADPO*, 1J 28; *BN*, Fonds Français, 11308; Clerc, p. 53; Wolff, pp. 100-108; P.L. Jacob, *Curiosités de l'histoire de France* (Paris: 1858), pp. 184, 209-215; Louis Moréri, *Le grand dictionnaire historique*, 10 vols. (Paris: 1759), 8:207.

52. *ADPO*, 1C 1565, 9 June 1681.

53. *ADPO*, H 220, 29 June 1696; Auguste d'Oriola de Pallares, *Les consuls de Perpignan* (Perpignan: 1912), p. 132.

54. *ADPO*, 1C 1520, 30 October 1662.

55. *BN*, Fonds Français, 4195, f° 163-169v°; *SHAT*, A¹ 899, 12 July 1689.

56. Boislisle, *Mémoriaux du conseil de 1661*, 1:81, 2:163-164.

57. *ADPO*, 2B 86; *ADPO*, 2B 25, f° 10v° - 12 v°, July 1664; *ADPO*, 2B 61, 8 February 1668; *ADPO*, G 380, 18 August 1680; *SHAT*, A¹ 300, 8 August 1671.

58. *ADPO*, 1B 401, January 1677; *ADPO*, 2B 86; *ADPO*, 1C 157; *ADPO*, 1C 719; *ADPO*, 1C 1238; *ADPO*, 1C 1395; *ADPO*, 1C 1406; *ADPO*, 1C 1738, 19 October 1684; *ADPO*, H 264, 13 May 1696; *ADPO*, H 274, 3 August 1661; *SHAT*, A¹ 300, 27 August 1671; Philippe Lazerme de Regnes, *Noblesa Catalana. Cavaliers y Burgesos Honrats de Rosselló y Cerdanya*. 3 vols. (La-Roche-sur-Yon: 1975), 1:80, 137, 148, 208, 230, 3:377.

59. *ADPO*, 1C 1359, 12 August 1664.

60. *ADPO*, 1C 12; *ADPO*, 1C 14; *ADPO*, 1C 158, 9 May 1691; *ADPO*, 1C 162; *ADPO*, 1C 165; *ADPO*, 1C 165, May 1693; *ADPO*, 1C 232; *ADPO*, 1C 301, 7 November 1694; *ADPO*, 1C 302; *ADPO*, 1C 303; *ADPO*, 1C 559, 26 April 1692; *SHAT*, A¹ 901, 22 August 1689.

61. G. Armadel, "La fin de la Monnaie de Narbonne," *Bulletin de la Commission Archéologique de Narbonne* (1892): 131-132; Colson, "Recherches sur les monnaies qui ont eu cours en Roussillon," *Bulletin du société agricole, scientifique*

et littéraire des Pyrénées-Orientales 9 (1854): 213-214; Morer, "Notice historique sur le rétablissement de l'Université de Perpignan sous la domination française," *Bulletin du société agricole, scientifique et littéraire des Pyrénées-Orientales* 8 (1851): 263.

62. *ADPO*, 1C 1051, 23 March 1686.

63. *ADPO*, 1C 1155; *ADPO*, 1C 1241, 18 September 1685.

64. *ADPO*, 1C 1429, 20 December 1700; *SHAT*, A¹ 1466, 1 February 1690.

65. *ADPO*, 1C 165, July 1694; *ADPO*, 1C 1232; *ADPO*, 1C 1241; *ADPO*, 1C 1615, 13 January 1709; Georges Hachon, *Vauban et le Roussillon* (Saint-Léger-Vauban: 1991), p. 34.

66. *ADPO*, 1C 251; *ADPO*, 1C 267; *ADPO*, 1C 268.

67. *ADPO*, 1C 1, January 1672; *ADPO*, 1C 1400, 22 January 1674; *SHAT*, A¹ 300, March 1672.

68. *ADPO*, 8 AC 1, f° 171.

69. Quoted in Jean Capeille, *Dictionnaire de Biographies Roussillonnaises* (Marseille: 1914), p. 97.

70. *ADPO*, 1C 127, 5 February 1664; Capeille, *Biographies roussillonnaises*, p. 97; Lazerme, *passim.*; Ministère de la Guerre, *Historiques des corps de troupe de l'armée française (1569-1900)* (Paris: 1900), pp. 112-113, 472-473, 512-513; Pinard, *Chronologie historique-militaire*, 8 vols. (Paris: 1761), 4:104-105, 363-364; Susane, *Histoire de l'infanterie française*, 5 vols. (Paris: 1876), 1:216-220.

71. In Maurice Sautai, *Les milices provinciales sous Louvois et Barbezieux (1688-1697)* (Paris: 1909), p. 109.

72. *ADPO*, 1C 737, 25 May 1691; *ADPO*, 1C 1397; *SHAT*, A¹ 1015, 10 May 1690.

73. Sautai, p. 299.

74. *ADPO*, 1C 1407, 23 November 1676.

75. *ADPO*, 1C 127; *ADPO*, 1C 135; *ADPO*, 1C 159; *ADPO*, 1C 170; *ADPO*, 1C 171; *ADPO*, 1C 180; *ADPO*, 1C 737.

76. *ADPO*, 2B 25, f° 16 - 20v°, 26 July 1664; *ADPO*, 1C 721; *ADPO*, 1C 1359, 14 December 1663; *ADPO*, 1C 1362; *SHAT*, A¹ 2181, 27 January 1709.

77. *ADPO*, 2B 72, 24 December 1660.

78. *ADPO*, 1C 1327, 16 January 1681; *ADPO*, 1C 1327; *ADPO*, 1C 1335; *ADPO*, 1C 1354; *ADPO*, 1C 1362.

79. *BN*, Fonds Français, 20148, f° 118.

80. *BN*, Fonds Français, 4195, f° 222v° - 223v°, 6 October 1660.

81. *ADPO*, 1C 1363, 21 May 1666.

82. *ADPO*, 1B 401, March 1661; *ADPO*, 2B 59, 20 April 1661; *ADPO*, 2B 25, f° 16 - 20v°, 26 July 1664; *ADPO*, 1C 721; *ADPO*, 1C 1362, 14 July 1662; *ADPO*, 1C 1362, 9 June 1663; *ADPO*, 1C 1409, 23 May 1685.

83. *ADPO*, 2B 26, f° 186-189, July 1690.

84. *ADPO*, 1C 1291; *ADPO*, G 167, 5 April 1688.

85. *ADPO*, 2B 25, f° 16 - 20v°, 26 July 1664; *ADPO*, 2B 26, f° 1-2v°, 27 May 1678; *ADPO*, 2B 72, 14 January 1704; *ADPO*, 1C 1366; *SHAT*, A¹ 672, 23 June 1678.

86. Gabriel Hanotaux, ed., *Recueil des instructions,* vol. 6 *Rome I,* p. 201; Boislisle, 2:64; Marquis de Roux, *Louis XIV et les provinces conquises* (Paris: 1938), p. 240.

87. Louis Habert de Montmor, *Avis pour les curés, vicaires, confesseurs, et autres ecclésiastiques du Diocèse d'Elne* (Perpignan: 1689), pp. 23, 187.

88. Jean Capeille, "Jean Hervé Basan de Flamenville, Evêque d'Elne (1695-1721)," *Bulletin du société agricole, scientifique et littéraire des Pyrénées-Orientales* 59 (1936):119.

89. *ADPO,* 1C 1363, 24 August 1666.

90. *ADPO,* 1C 1329, 28 Aug 1684; Gabriel-Jules, Comte de Cosnac, and Édouard Pontal, eds., *Mémoires du Marquis de Sources sur le règne de Louis XIV,* 13 vols. (Paris: 1882-1893), 7:153; Capeille, *Dictionnaire de biographie roussillonnaises,* pp. 16-18; Iemma, p. 48.

91. *ADPO,* H 153, 29 March 1698; Iemma, pp. 32-36; Paul Taverner, "Le clergé séculier en Vallespir de 1640 à 1700. Rôle social et politique" (Mémoire de Maîtrise, Université de Provence, 1977), pp. 19-20.

92. *ADPO,* 1C 1340, 14 January 1673; *ADPO,* H 49, 8 January 1676.

93. *ADPO,* 2B 72, 14 January 1704; *ADPO,* 2B 91, 26 July 1664; *ADPO,* G 18, 4 February 1702; *ADPO,* G 260, 26 May 1683; *ADPO,* G 380, 18 August 1680; *SHAT,* A^1 1289, 24 January 1693; Taverner, pp. 28-29, 32.

94. Philippe Torreilles, "Le collège de Perpignan depuis ses origines jusqu'à nos jours," *Bulletin du société agricole, scientifique et littéraire des Pyrénées-Orientales* 34 (1893): 380-381.

95. *ADPO,* 1C 718, 21 April 1662.

96. *ADPO,* 1C 1292, 8 November 1662; *ADPO,* 1C 1358, 21 April 1662; Morer, "Rétablissement de l'Université de Perpignan," p. 261; Joseph-Sébastien Pons, *La littérature catalane en Roussillon au XVIIe et au XVIIe siècle* (Paris: 1929), p. 328; Torreilles, "Le collège de Perpignan," pp. 434-435; Wolff, p. 109.

97. *ADPO,* 1C 1339, September 1663.

98. *ADPO,* 1C 1359, 26 September 1664; *ADPO,* 1C 1362.

99. *ADPO,* 1C 720, 9 January 1672.

100. *ADPO,* 1C 1339; *ADPO,* 1C 1397, 9 January 1672; Roux, p. 263.

101. *ADPO,* 1C 1291.

102. *ADPO,* 1C 1291, 12 January 1682.

103. *ADPO,* 1C 1291, 22 March 1683; *SHAT,* A^1 657, 6 August 1681; Jean Guibeaud, "Notes statistiques sur l'instruction publique à Perpignan," *Bulletin du société agricole, scientifique et littéraire des Pyrénées-Orientales* 34 (1893): 524-525; Philippe Torreilles and Émile Desplanque, "L'enseignement élémentaire en Roussillon," *Bulletin du société agricole, scientifique et littéraire des Pyrénées-Orientales* 36 (1895): 247.

104. *ADPO,* 2B 25, f° 52-73v°; *ADPO,* 2B 26, f° 69-69v°, 21 July 1683; *ADPO,* 2B 26, f° 335v°-336, 22 April 1698; *ADPO,* 2B 28, f° 115-155v°, 26 May 1702; *ADPO,* 1C 1008; *ADPO,* 1C 1291; *ADPO,* 1C 2018; Jean-Marie Carbasse, "L'enseignement du droit français à l'Université de Perpignan (1683-1791)," *Bulletin du société agricole, scientifique et littéraire des Pyrénées-Orientales* 96 (1988):133-138.

105. *ADPO,* 2B 26, f° 107, 13 July 1685; *ADPO,* 1C 179.

106. *ADPO*, 112 AC 1, 8 September 1676.

107. *ADPO*, series D 11.

108. *ADPO*, 1C 1291.

109. *ADPO*, G 124, 18 October 1692.

110. *ADPO*, 1C 179; *ADPO*, 1C 1315.

111. *ADPO*, A 7, February 1700.

112. *ADPO*, A 7, February 1700.

113. *ADPO*, 2B 72, 14 January 1704; *ADPO*, 1C 179, 15 April 1700; *ADPO*, 1C 1407, 23 November 1676; Assier-Andrieu, p. 76.

114. *SHAT*, A^1 899, 12 July 1689.

115. *ADPO*, 1C 719, 25 March 1667; *ADPO*, 1C 1364; *SHAT*, A^1 300, 2 March 1672; *SHAT*, A^1 1106, 9 January 1691; Jean Guibeaud, *Étude sur les noms de baptême à Perpignan de 1516 à 1738* (Perpignan: 1898), p. 136; Wolff, p. 86.

116. *ADPO*, 2B 25, f° 13-14v^o, 3 May 1662; *ADPO*, 2B 91, 1 May 1662; *SHAT*, A^1 657, 6 August 1681.

117. *ADPO*, 2B 85, 7 November 1659.

118. *ADPO*, 2B 25, f° 25-25v^o, 14 July 1662.

119. *ADPO*, 2B 25, f° 16-20v^o, 26 July 1664.

120. *ADPO*, 2B 25, f° 13-14v^o, 3 May 1662.

121. *ADPO*, 2B 25, f° 5-6v^o, June 1660; *ADPO*, 2B 26, f° 130, 24 February 1687; *ADPO*, 2B 72; *ADPO*, 2B 90, 3 May 1662; *ADPO*, 2B 91, 26 July 1664; *ADPO*, 2B 91, 23 February 1684; *ADPO*, 1C 166; *ADPO*, H 232, 15 March 1673; *ADPO*, 12J 31, f° 35-37, *circa* May 1700.

122. A few Catalan laws survived even into the Fifth Republic in Roussillon. See, for example, J. M^a. Font Rius, "Els Costums de Catalunya al Rossello i Cerdanya," *Revista Jurídica de Cataluña* 66 (January-March 1967): 643-646.

123. *ADPO*, 2B 26, f° 144-159, April 1686; *ADPO*, 2B 71, 26 July 1686; *ADPO*, 1C 1134; *ADPO*, 1C 1137; *ADPO*, 1C 1316.

124. *ADPO*, 2B 27, f° 33-34v^o, February 1663; *ADPO*, 2B 27, f° 151, 22 November 1671; *ADPO*, 2B 91, 28 January 1702; *ADPO*, 1C 1862, 13 March 1682.

125. *Constitutions y Altres Drets de Cathalunya...* (Barcelona: 1704), p. 299.

126. Albert de Rochas d'Aiglun, ed., *Vauban: Sa famille et ses écrits. Analyse et extraits*, 2 vols. (Paris: 1910), 2:26.

127. *Constitutions y Altres Drets*, pp. 16, 158.

128. Boislisle, *Mémoriaux du conseil de 1661*, 1:258; Roux, p. 167; Assier-Andrieu, p. 71.

129. Basil Collier, *Catalan France* (London: 1939), pp. 33-51; Sahlins, p. 32.

130. *ADPO*, 2B 85, 7 November 1659.

131. *ADPO*, 12 J 31, f° 35 - 39v^o.

132. *ADPO*, H 220, 29 June 1696; *ADPO*, 1J 390, 2 February 1662.

133. *ADPO*, 1C 1292, 5 November 1662; Morer, p. 263.

134. *SHAT*, A^1 1106, 9 January 1691.

135. *Constitutions y Altres Drets*, p. 7.

136. *ADPO*, 1C 301, 8 June 1692.

137. *ADPO*, 12J 30, 26 September 1691, f° 264.

138. *SHAT*, A^1 300, 25 August 1671.

139. *SHAT* A¹ 1706, 11 February 1703.

140. *ADPO*, 1C 28; *ADPO*, 1C 147; *ADPO*, 1C 149, 7 October 1688; *ADPO*, 1C 150; *ADPO*, 1C 296; *ADPO*, H 274, 11 September 1665; *ADPO*, G 17; *SHAT*, A¹ 1289, 17 May 1694.

141. Quoted in Philippe Torreilles, "Les testaments des consuls de Perpignan au XVIIᵉ siècle," *Bulletin du société agricole, scientifique et littéraire des Pyrenées-Orientales* 44 (1903): 293.

142. *ADPO*, 2B 1649, November 1669; Charles Delormeau, "Instruction par un conseiller au Conseil Souverain de Roussillon d'un procès contre des fugitifs de Labastide-Rouairoux arrêtés à Banyuls (Mai 1686)," in *XLIIᵉ congrès du fédération historique du Languedoc méditerranéen et du Roussillon* (Montpellier: 1970), pp. 61-63; Paul de La Fabrègue-Pallarès, "L'affaire de l'échange des Pays-Bas catholiques et l'offre de rétrocession du Roussillon à l'Espagne, 1668-1677,"*Bulletin du société agricole, scientifique et littéraire des Pyrenées-Orientales* 69 (1954):50.

143. *ADPO*, 1C 405; *ADPO*, 1C 718; *ADPO*, 1C 1008; *ADPO*, 1C 1155; *ADPO*, 1C 1365; *ADPO*, 1C 2043, 22 February 1683; *ADPO*, 1C 2043, 9 May 1689; *ADPO*, 1C 2043, 12 August 1702.

144. *ADPO*, 1C 270; *ADPO*, 1C 274; *ADPO*, 1C 325; *ADPO*, 1C 329; *ADPO*, 1C 1249; *ADPO*, 1C 1359, 26 September 1664; *ADPO*, 1C 1430; *SHAT*, A¹ 241, 22 March 1669; *ACA*, Consell d'Aragó, Legajo 315, 10 November 1662; *ACA*, Consell d'Aragó, Legajo 325, 22 November 1675.

145. *SHAT*, A¹ 300, 6 April 1672; *SHAT*, A¹ 300, 16 April 1672; *SHAT*, A¹ 300, 1 February 1673; *SHAT*, A¹ 465, 17 July 1675; *SHAT*, A¹ 563, 9 December 1677; *SHAT*, A¹ 1015, 5 June 1690; *SHAT*, A¹ 1016, 10 July 1690; *SHAT*, A¹ 1108, 27 January 1691; *SHAT*, A¹ 1106, 3 February 1691; *SHAT*, A¹ 1891, 12 August 1705; *ACA*, Consell d'Aragó, Legajo 325, 4 July 1668; *AHCG*, XIII.1.3.

146. *SHAT*, A¹ 1602, 6 September 1702.

147. *ADPO*, 1C 718, 26 September 1666; *ADPO*, 1C 1292; *ADPO*, 1C 1316, 9 August 1713; *SHAT*, A¹ 356, 1 April 1673.

148. *ADPO*, 1C 1409, 17 September 1685.

149. *ADPO*, 1C 1531.

150. *ADPO*, 2B 26, fᵒ 4 -5, January 1681; *ADPO*, 2B 1621; *ADPO*, 2B 1624; *ADPO*, 2B 1626; *ADPO*, 2B 1627; *ADPO*, 2B 1629; *ADPO*, 2B 1630; *ADPO*, 2B 1631; *ADPO*, 2B 1632; *ADPO*, 2B 1637; *ADPO*, 2B 1640; *ADPO*, 2B 1644; *ADPO*, 2B 1647; *ADPO*, 2B 1649; *ADPO*, 2B 1653; *ADPO*, 2B 1654; *ADPO*, 2B 1664; *ADPO*, 2B 1665; *ADPO*, 2B 1669; *ADPO*, 2B 1691; *ADPO*, 2B 1717; *ADPO*, 2B 1746; *ADPO* 1C 251; *ADPO*, 1C 737, 3 September 1694; *ADPO*, 1C 1232, 19 September 1690; *ADPO*, 1C 1838; *ADPO*, 1J 390, *passim*.

151. *ADPO*, 2B 1635.

152. Capeille, *Biographies roussillonnaises*, pp. 101, 559; Lazerme, 1:263, 2:121.

153. Capeille, *Biographies roussillonnaises*, pp. 101, 559.

154. Jean Sagnes, ed., *Le pays Catalan*, 2 vols. (Pau: 1983), 1:521; Aymeric de Descallar, "Révoltes et complots Catalans au XVIIᵉ siècle (1654–1674)," *Centre d'études et recherches catalanes* 6 (1959): 371.

155. Lazerme, 1:263-267.

156. *ADPO*, 2B 1635; *ADPO*, 1C 1359; *ACA*, Consell d'Aragó, Legajo 325, 17 May 1666; Sagnes, 1:521.

157. Sagnes, 2:520; Alícia Marcet i Juncosa, *Abrégé d'histoire des terres catalanes du nord* (Perpignan: 1991), p. 133.

158. Sagnes, 1:523.

159. *ADPO*, 1J 390, 2 February 1662; *ADPO*, 1J 390, 16 February 1662; Collier, p. 55.

160. Pierre Clément, *Lettres, instructions et mémoires de Colbert*, 8 vols. (Paris: 1861), 2:337-338.

161. *ADPO*, 2B 1624.

162. *ADPO*, 2B 960.

163. In G.B. Depping, ed., *Correspondance administrative sous le règne de Louis XIV*, 4 vols. (Paris: 1850-1855), 3:179.

164. *SHAT*, A¹ 300, 6 April 1672.

165. *SHAT*, A¹ 300, 16 April 1672; *SHAT*, A¹ 356, 1 February 1673; *SHAT*, A¹ 1015, 16 June 1690; *SHAT*, A4S1§6/C1, No. 16.

166. *ADPO*, 1E 472, 12 April 1640; *SHAT*, A¹ 356, 1 February 1673; Descallar, p. 372.

167. See, for example, Jean Sagnes and Alícia Marcet i Juncosa.

168. *SHAT*, A¹ 300. 16 April 1672; Albertí, ed. *Diccionari Biogràfic*, 4 vols. (Barcelona: 1970), 1:324-235, 2:549, 3:31, 168, 345, 4:388-389; Marcet, "Le Roussillon," p. 110;Carbonell, *Gran Enciclopèdic Catlana*, 2:125.

169. Marcet i Juncosa, p. 140.

170. *SHAT*, A¹ 300, 16 April 1672; Taverner, p. 28.

171. Quoted in F. Pasquier, *Famille Catalane ralliée à la France* (Perpignan: 1923), p. 38.

172. *ADPO*, 1C 1395.

173. Sagnes, 1:523; Roux, p. 86.

174. Clément, *Lettres de Colbert*, 4:318; Depping, *Correspondance administrative*, 3:176-177, 180.

175. Depping, *Correspondance administrative*, 3:179; Descallar, p. 373; Roux, p. 87.

176. *SHAT*, A¹ 240, 10 February 1669; Marcet, "Les roussillonnais," p. 67; Sagnes, 1:524.

177. *ADPO*, 2B 64, 16 November 1668.

178. *ADPO*, 1C 1366, 1 January 1669.

179. *SHAT*, A¹ 241, 10 April 1669.

180. *ADPO*, 1C 719, 20 February 1669, f° 23.

181. *ADPO*, 2B 27, f° 108.

182. *ADPO*, 1J 227, 8 April 1669.

183. *ADPO*, 1C 720, 27 August 1669, f° 1 - 1v°.

184. Clément, *Lettres de Colbert*, 2:337-338.

185. Charles Godard, *Les pouvoirs des intendants sous Louis XIV. Particulièrement dans les pays d'élections de 1661 à 1715* (Paris: 1901, reprint Geneva: 1974), p. 64.

186. *ADPO*, 2B 63.

187. *ADPO*, 1C 1366, 7 November 1669.

188. *ADPO*, 2B 1660; Sagnes, 1:524; Descallar, p. 373; Marcet i Juncosa, p. 136; Roux, p. 87.

189. Clément, *Lettres de Colbert*, 2:343.

190. *ADPO*, 2B 63, 21 February 1670.

191. *ADPO*, 1C 1395, 4 September 1670.

192. *ADPO*, 2B 99, 30 May 1670.

193. *ADPO*, 2B 27, f° 124-124v°, 11 January 1671; *ADPO*, 2B 1659; *ADPO*, 1C 1395, 7 October 1670; *ADPO* 124 AC 25, 31 July 1670.

194. *ADPO*, 2B 27, f° 121-121v°, August 1670; *ADPO*, 1C 1395; *ADPO*, 1C 1397.

195. Descallar, p. 374; Carbonell, *Gran Enciclopèdic Catalana*, 6:151.

196. *ADPO*, 2B 1664; Sagnes, 1:525.

197. *ADPO*, 1C 1637, 7 March 1672.

198. *ADPO*, 1C 720, 5 February 1672; *ADPO*, 1C 720, 8 March 1672, f° 8v°.

199. *ADPO*, 1C 720, 6 May 1672, f° 13; *SHAT*, A¹ 300, 16 April 1672.

200. *ADPO*, 2B 67, f° 148v°-149, March 1672; Sagnes, 1:525.

201. Albertí, 2:549; Descallar, p. 374.

202. Carbonell,*Gran Enciclopèdic Catalana*, 2:125.

203. *SHAT*, A¹ 356, 1 February 1673; *SHAT*, A¹ 1015, 16 June 1690; Marcet, "Les roussillonnais," p. 67; Sagnes, 1:526; Carbonell, *Gran Enciclopèdic Catalana*, 2:125.

204. *AN*, G⁷ 506, 19 May 1685.

205. *ADPO*, G 18, 4 February 1702.

206. J.H.M. Salmon, "The Audijos Revolt: Provincial Liberties and Institutional Rivalries under Louis XIV," *European History Quarterly* 14 (1984): 119-140.

207. *SHAT*, A¹ 415, 24 April 1674.

208. *SHAT*, A¹ 415, March 1674.

209. See, for example, Descallar, pp. 376-377; Sagnes, 1:530.

210. *SHAT*, A¹ 415, March 1674; *SHAT*, A¹ 415, 30 May 1674.

211. *ADPO*, 1C 1402; *SHAT*, A¹ 415.

212. *ADPO*, 1C 1401; *ADPO*, 1C 1402.

213. *SHAT*, A¹ 415, 25 October 1674; Capeille, *Biographies roussillonnaises*, p. 319.

214. *ACA*, Consell d'Aragó, Legajo 325, *passim*.

215. *ADPO*, 1C 1402; *SHAT*, A¹ 672, 18 February 1679.

216. *SHAT*, A¹ 563, 9 December 1677.

217. *SHAT*, A¹ 1015, 5 June 1690.

218. *SHAT*, A¹ 1015, 5 June 1690; *SHAT*, A¹ 1016, 10 July 1690.

219. *ADPO*, 2B 1754, 30 July 1692; *ADPO*, 2B 1802, 19 April 1707.

220. Quoted in Susane, 1:209.

221. *ADPO*, 2B 1676; *ADPO*, 1C 1409, 17 September 1685; *ADPO*, 1C 1409, 25 November 1685; *ADPO*, 1C 1691, 30 April 1694.

222. *ADPO*, 2B 1675.

223. Marcet, "La résistance," p. 138; Sagnes, 1:535.

224. *ADPO*, 1C 1111, 15 September 1713; *SHAT*, A¹ 465, 17 July 1675; *SHAT*, A¹ 1289, 4 February 1694; Lazerme, I:104, 227; J. Nadal and E. Giralt, *La*

population catalane de 1553 à 1717 (Paris: 1960), pp. 185-187; Sanabre, pp. 600-602.

225. Iemma, pp. 32-33; Wolff, p. 86.

226. *ADPO*, G 160.

227. *ADPO*, 1C 719, 6 March 1669.

228. *ADPO*, G 160, 3 November 1663; *ADPO*, G 160, January 1671; *ADPO*, G 161.

229. *ADPO*, 2B 1640; *ADPO*, G 124; *ADPO*, H 274, 5 July 1670; Philippe Torreilles, "L'annexion du Roussillon à la France – la vacance du siège d'Elne (1643-1669)," *Bulletin du société agricole, scientifique et littéraire des Pyrénées-Orientales* 41 (1900): 193-200, 206-208.

230. *ADPO*, 2B 1674; *ADPO*, 1C 720, 8 March 1672; *ADPO*, 1C 720, 29 September 1672; *ADPO*, 1C 1340; *ADPO*, 1C 1397, 8 March 1672; *SHAT*, A^1 356, 1 April 1673.

231. *ADPO*, H 8, 29 October 1660.

232. *ADPO*, 2B 1638; *ADPO*, 1C 1363; *ADPO*, 1C 1364; Wolff, pp. 87-89.

233. *AN*, MM 972, f° 6.

234. *ADPO*, 2B 72; *ADPO*, 1C 1327.

235. *ADPO*, 1C 1316, 9 August 1713; Feuillet de Conches, ed., *Journal du Marquis de Dangeau*. 19 vols. (Paris: 1854-1859), 1:90-91.

236. *ADPO*, 1C 1363, 24 August 1666.

237. *ADPO*, 2B 1659.

238. Iemma, p. 45; Taverner, p. 29.

239. Taverner, p. 56.

240. *ADPO*, 1C 718, 12 March 1666.

241. *ADPO*, 1C 718; *ADPO*, 1C 1394; *ADPO*, 1C 1397, 7 February 1672; *SHAT*, A^1 300, 12 December 1671.

242. *ADPO*, 1C 1051.

243. *ADPO*, 1C 1363; *ADPO*, 1C 1862, 13 March 1862; *SHAT*, A^1 300, 8 August 1671.

244. *SHAT*, A^1 356, 22 February 1673.

245. *ADPO*, 1C 1366, 23 August 1669.

246. *SHAT*, A^1 300, 25 August 1671.

247. *ADPO*, 1C 793, 30 March 1701.

248. *SHAT*, A^1 2405, 27 May 1712.

249. *ADPO*, G 2, 6 February 1699; *SHAT*, A^1 300, 2 March 1672.

250. *ADPO*, 1B 401; *ADPO*, 1C 1868, 20 April 1669.

251. *ADPO*, 1C 1633; *ADPO*, 1C 1697; *ADPO*, 1J 390, 2 February 1662; *SHAT*, A^1 300; Roux, p. 256.

252. *ADPO*, 2B 72, 24 January 1661; *ADPO*, 1C 1397, 29 September 1672.

253. *ADPO*, 2B 26, f° 130, 24 February 1687.

254. *ADPO*, 2B 25, f° 16 - 20v°, 26 July 1664.

255. *ADPO*, G 2, 6 February 1699.

256. *SHAT*, A^1 899, 12 July 1689.

257. *ADPO*, 2B 99, 18 June 1694; *ADPO*, 1C 166; *ADPO*, 1C 1407, 23 November 1676.

258. *ADPO*, 2B 26, f° 14-15, 3 May 1681.

259. Clerc, p. 136; Roux, p. 168; Sagnes, p. 520: Archives départmentales des Pyrénées-Orientales, *Sous-série 2B. Fonds du conseil souverain.* 2 vols. (Perpignan: 1990), 1:7.

260. *ADPO,* 1C 1292, 5 November 1662; *ADPO,* 2B 26, f° 186-189, July 1690; *ADPO,* D 9, f° 17, 17 December 1663; *ADPO,* D 10, f° 13; *ADPO,* G 124, 18 October 1692.

261. *ADPO,* 1C 1363.

262. *ADPO,* 2B 1640, October 1666; *ADPO,* 1C 718, 26 September 1666; *ADPO,* 1C 719, 28 January 1667; *ADPO,* 1C 1363, 15 January 1666; Torreilles, "L'annexion du Roussillon," pp. 204-208.

263. *SHAT,* A[1] 465, 17 July 1675.

264. Albert Cazes, *Armorial du Roussillon,* 3 vols. (Perpignan: 1982-1985), 1:13, 25-26, 28-29, 35, 36; Colson, pp. 29-260.

265. *SHAT,* A[1] 1015, 10 May 1690; Victor Belhomme, *L'armée française en 1690* (Paris: 1895), pp. 59, 71, 94-95, 116; André Corvisier, *L'Armée Française de la fin du XVIIe siècle au ministère de Choiseul,* 2 vols. (Paris: 1964), 1:401.

266. *SHAT,* A[1] 1015, 5 June 1690.

267. *SHAT,* A[1] 1289, 4 February 1694.

268. *SHAT,* A[1] 1602, 30 August 1702; *SHAT,* A[1] 1602, 6 September 1702; *SHAT,* A[1] 1602, 13 December 1702; *SHAT,* A[1] 1891, 12 August 1705; *SHAT,* A[1] 1891, 22 August 1705; *SHAT,* A[1] 1891, 1 September 1705; *SHAT,* A[1] 1989, 24 March 1706; *SHAT,* A[1] 2181, 27 January 1709; *SHAT,* A[1] 2257, 28 July 1710.

269. *ADPO,* 1C 1407, 23 November 1676.

270. Archibald Lewis, "The Catalan Failure in Acculturation in Frankish Greece and the Islamic World during the Fourteenth Century," in *Medieval Society in Southern France and Catalonia,* ed. Archibald Lewis (London: 1984).

271. *ADPO,* H 352, 2 May 1675.

272. *ADPO,* 1C 1111, 15 September 1713.

273. *ADPO,* 1C 718; *SHAT,* A[1] 1989; Lazerme, 1:227-230, 263-267, 304, 2:148.

274. Quoted in Roux, p. 168.

275. *SHAT,* A[1] 1891, 22 August 1705.

276. Lewis, "The Catalan Failure."

277. *ADPO,* 2B 1624.

278. Sahlins, pp. 110-113.

279. *ADPO,* 1E 366; *ADPO,* 1E 783; *ADPO,* 1E 887; *SHAT,* A[1] 300, 2 April 1672; Henry Aragon, *Les monuments et les rues de Perpignan* (Perpignan: 1928), *passim;* Christian Camps, "Les noms des rues de Perpignan." (Mémoire de Maîtrise, Université de Montpellier, 1974), *passim;* Guibeaud, *Noms de baptême, passim;* Lazerme, *passim.*

280. *ADPO,* 1T 41.

281. *AN,* F[17] 10782, 31 January 1861.

282. Quoted by E. Frénay, *L'école primaire dans les Pyrénées-Orientales (1833-1914)* (Perpignan: 1983), p. 31B.

283. Georges Livet, "Royal Administration in a Frontier Province: The Intendancy of Alsace under Louis XIV," in *Louis XIV and Absolutism,* ed. Ragnhild Hatton (Columbus, Ohio: 1976), pp. 186-187.

284. *Ibid.*, p. 187.

285. *Ibid.*, pp. 177-196; Georges Livet, "Louis XIV et les provinces conquises," *XVII*ᵉ *Siècle* (1952): 481-507; Livet, *L'intendance d'Alsace sous Louis XIV, 1648-1715*, (Paris: 1956); Dion, R. *Les frontières de la France*, (Paris: 1947).

Bibliography

ARCHIVAL MATERIALS
Archives Départementales des Pyrénées-Orientales, Perpignan
Series A (Acts of Sovereign Power):
  1, 3, 7, 9.

Sub-Series 1B (Courts and Jurisdictions):
  400, 401, 402.

Sub-Series 2B (Records of the Sovereign Council):
  25, 26, 27, 28, 57, 58, 59, 61, 63, 64, 67, 68, 70, 71, 72, 85, 86, 87, 88, 90,
  91, 92, 99, 105, 401, 960, 1621-1624, 1626, 1628-1633, 1635, 1637, 1638,
  1640, 1642, 1643, 1646, 1648, 1649, 1651, 1653, 1654-1661, 1663-1665,
  1667-1670, 1672-1678, 1681, 1683, 1691-1697, 1700, 1703, 1704, 1708,
  1715, 1717, 1737, 1740, 1750, 1752, 1754, 1756, 1757, 1762, 1771, 1773,
  1802, 1808, 1822.

Sub-Series 3B (*Amirauté de Collioure*):
  1.

Sub-Series 1C (Provincial Administration):
  1, 12, 14, 28, 127, 147, 149, 150, 155, 158, 159, 165, 166, 171, 173, 179,
  180, 251, 253, 274, 287, 296, 301, 325, 329, 338, 405, 559, 718-721, 737,
  793, 1008, 1011, 1039, 1047, 1051, 1102, 1111, 1134, 1155, 1232, 1241,
  1249, 1256, 1278, 1291, 1292, 1308, 1315, 1316, 1327, 1329, 1335, 1339,
  1340, 1343, 1354, 1358, 1359, 1362-1366, 1394, 1395, 1397, 1398, 1400-
  1409, 1429, 1430, 1520, 1531, 1565, 1615, 1632, 1633, 1637, 1646, 1677,
  1678, 1686, 1687, 1691, 1697, 1705, 1721, 1727, 1738, 1750, 1757, 1759,
  1779, 1825, 1838, 1862, 1868, 1912, 2018, 2042, 2043, 2065.

Series D (The University):
  9, 10, 11, 22.

Sub-Series 1E (Family Papers):
  132, 171, 209, 245, 262, 366, 369, 417, 472, 516, 534, 632, 699, 713, 783,
  799, 887, 911, 926.

Series G (Secular Clergy):
  2, 17, 18, 53, 99, 124, 155, 160, 161, 167, 260, 261, 380, 446.

Series H (Regular Clergy):
  8, 18, 44, 49, 55, 56, 68, 153, 174, 219, 220, 232, 257, 264, 274, 290, 352.

Series J:
  1J 28, 1J 204, 1J 227, 1J 390, 1J 515, 12J 28, 12J 30, 12J 31.

Communal Archives:
  8 AC 1, 8 AC 2, 112 AC 1, 112 AC 4, 124 AC 25.

Sub-Series 1T (Education):
  41.

Service Historique du Armée de Terre, **Vincennes**
A4S1§6/C1.

Series A^1:
  240, 241, 300, 356, 415, 456, 465, 563, 657, 672, 795, 899, 901, 1015,
  1016, 1106, 1108, 1234, 1289, 1338, 1466, 1602, 1706, 1800, 1887, 1891,
  1977, 1989, 2181, 2257, 2328, 2330, 2331, 2405, 2560, 2563, 2564, 2886-
  2890.

YA 35.

Arxiu de la Corona d'Aragó, **Barcelona**
Consell d'Aragó:
  Legajos 217, 240-242, 312-315, 317, 325, 519-521, 547.

Arxiu Històric de la Ciutat de Girona, **Girona**
I.1.1; I.1.2.7; VII.2.6.1; XIII.1.3; XXII.1.2.3; XXII.1.2.4; XXII.1.5.11; XIX.1.2.

Archives Nationales, **Paris**
F^{17} 10782; G^7 506; MM 972.

Bibliothèque National, **Paris**
Fonds Français: 4195, 11308, 11801, 20148, 21542.

OTHER SOURCES

Constitutions y Altres Drets de Cathalunya, Compilats en Virtut del Capitol de Cort LXXXII de las Corts per la S.C.Y.R. Majestat del Rey Don Philip IV, Nostre Senyor Celebradas en la ciutat de Barcelona any MDCCII. Barcelona: 1704, 1973.

Manual de Novells Ardits vulgarment apellat Dietari del Antich Consell Barceloní. Volum Dotzé, Anys 1636 (Agost)–1641 (Juliol). Barcelona: 1910.

Aiglun, Albert de Rochas d'. *Vauban. Sa famille et ses écrits. Ses oisivetés et sa correspondance. Analyse et extraits.* 2 vols. Paris: 1910, 1972.

Alart, B.-J., ed. *Documents sur la Langue Catalane des Anciens Comtés de Roussillon et de Cerdagne.* Paris: 1881.

Albertí, ed. *Diccionari Biogràfic.* 4 vols. Barcelona: 1970.

Antoine, Michel. *Le Gouvernement et l'Administration sous Louis XV. Dictionnaire Biographique.* Paris: 1973.

Aragon, Henry. *Les Monuments et les Rues de Perpignan.* Perpignan: 1928.

Armadel, G. "La fin de la Monnaie de Narbonne." *Bulletin de la Commission Archéologique de Narbonne* (1892): 120-134.

Assier-Andrieu, Louis. *Le Peuple et la Loi. Anthropologie Historique des Droits Paysans en Catalogne Française.* Paris: 1987.

Ayats, Alain. "Louis XIV et le Roussillon." *Bulletin du Société Agricole, Scientifique et Littéraire des Pyrénées-Orientales* 100 (1992): 85-102.

Badia i Margarit, Antoni M. *La Formació de la Llengua Catalana.* Barcelona: 1987.

Belhomme, Victor. *L'armée française en 1690.* Paris: 1895.

Blanc, François-Paul. "La Noblesse Municipal de Perpignan. Essai de Définition Juridique." *Bulletin du Société Agricole, Scientifique et Littéraire des Pyrénées-Orientales* 100 (1992): 63-84.

Blanchon, Jean-Louis. "Le Cerdagne devant la Rivalité Franco-Espagnole au XVIᵉ Siècle." *Conflent* 29 (1965): 212-215.

Boislisle, Jean de, ed. *Mémoriaux du conseil de 1661*, 3 vols. Paris: 1905–1907.

Bouille, Michel, and Brousse, Jean-François. *Chemins du Roussillon.* Ille-sur-Tet: 1969.

Calmette, Joseph, and Vidal, Pierre. *Histoire de Roussillon*. Paris: 1931.

Camps, Christian. *Les Noms des Rues de Perpignan*. Montpellier: 1974.

———. *Perpignan Pas à Pas*. Le Coteau: 1983.

Capeille, Jean. "Jean Hervé Basan de Flamenville, Evêque d'Elne (1695–1721)." *Bulletin du Société Agricole, Scientifique et Littéraire des Pyrénées-Orientales* 59 (1936): 117-138.

———. *Dictionnaire de biographies roussillonnaises*. Marseille: 1978.

Carbasse, Jean-Marie. "L'Enseignement du Droit Français à l'Université de Perpignan (1683-1791)." *Bulletin du Société Agricole, Scientifique et Littéraire des Pyrénées-Orientales* 96 (1988): 131-142.

Carbonell, Jordi, ed. *Gran Enciclopèdic Catalana*. 15 vols. Barcelona: 1970-1980.

Cazes, Albert. *Villefranche de Conflent*. 2nd edn. Perpignan: 1966.

———. *Le Roussillon sacré*. Prades: 1977.

———. *Armorial du Roussillon*. 3 vols. Perpignan: 1982–1985.

Clément, Pierre, ed. *Lettres, instructions et mémoires de Colbert*. 8 vols. Paris: 1861.

Clerc, Guy. *Recherches sur le Conseil Souverain de Roussillon (1660–1790)*. 2 vols. Paris: 1974.

Collier, Basil. *Catalan France*. London: 1939.

Colson. "Recherches sur les Monnaies qui ont eu en Cours en Roussillon." *Bulletin du Société Agricole, Scientifique et Littéraire des Pyrénées-Orientales* 9 (1854): 29-260.

Comet. "L'Imprimerie à Perpignan depuis les Origines jusqu'à nos Jours." *Bulletin du Société Agricole, Scientifique et Littéraire des Pyrénées-Orientales* 48 (1907): 239-368.

de Conches, Feuillet, ed. *Journal du Marquis de Dangeau*. 19 vols. Paris: 1854–1859.

Corvisier, André. *L'Armée Française de la fin du XVIIe siècle au ministère de Choiseul*, 2 vols. Paris: 1964.

Cosnac, Gabriel-Jules, Comte de, and Pontal, Édouard, eds. *Mémoires du Marquis de Sourches sur le règne de Louis XIV*. 13 vols. Paris:1882–1893.

Darsel, Joachim. "L'Amirauté en Languedoc et Roussillon." In *Actes du 96ᵉ Congrès National des Sociétés Savantes*. 2 vols. Paris: 1976, 2:9-27.

Delormeau, Charles. "Instruction par un Conseiller au Conseil Souverain de Roussillon d'un Procès contre des Fugitifs de Labastide-Rouairoux Arrêtés à Banyuls (Mai 1686)." *Actes du XLIIᵉ Congrès du Fédération Historique du Languedoc Méditerranéen et du Roussillon*. Montpellier: 1970, 61-71.

Depping, G.B., ed. *Correspondance administrative sous le règne de Louis XIV*. 4 vols. Paris: 1850–1855.

Descallar, Aymeric de. "Révoltes et Complots Catalans au XVIIᵉ siècle, (1654–1674)." *Centre d'Études et Recherches Catalanes* 6 (1959): 369-382.

Desplanque, M.E. "Les Infames dans l'Ancien Droit Roussillonnais." *Bulletin du Société Agricole, Scientifique et Littéraire des Pyrénées-Orientales* 34 (1893): 437-521.

Dion, R. *Les Frontières de la France*. Paris: 1947.

Elliott, John Huxtable. *The Revolt of the Catalans*. Cambridge: 1963.

Font Rius, J. M. "Els Costums de Catalunya al Rossello i Cerdanya." *Revista Jurídica de Cataluña* 66 (January-March 1967): 643-646.

Frénay, E. *L'École Primaire dans les Pyrénées-Orientales (1833–1914)*. Perpignan: 1983.

Gadoury, Victor, and Droulers, Frédéric. *Les Monnaies Royales Françaises de Louis XIII à Louis XVI, 1610–1792*. Monte Carlo: 1978.

Gavignaud, Geneviève. "La Frontière Pyrénéene et la Partie Française de la Catalogne depuis 1659." *Actes du 101ᵉ Congrès National des Sociétes Savantes*. 2 vols. Lille: 1976, 1:155-170.

Gigot, Jean-Gabriel. "Notes sur l'Amirauté de Collioure." *Bulletin du Société Agricole, Scientifique et Littéraire des Pyrénées-Orientales* 73 (1958): 75-94.

Giralt. "Notice Historique des Communes de Aiguatèbia, Railleu, Caudiès, Sansa et Oreilla." *Bulletin du Société Agricole, Scientifique et Littéraire des Pyrénées-Orientales* 41 (1900): 269-312.

Godard, Charles. *Les Pouvoirs des Intendants sous Louix XIV. Particulièrement dans les Pays d'Elections de 1661 à 1715*. Paris: 1901; reprint Geneva: 1974.

Guibeaud, Jean. "Notes Statistiques sur l'Instruction Publique à Perpignan." *Bulletin du Société Agricole, Scientifique et Littéraire des Pyrénées-Orientales* 34 (1893): 522-527.

———. *Étude sur les Noms de Baptême à Perpignan de 1516 à 1738.* Perpignan: 1898.

Hachon, Georges. *Vauban et le Roussillon.* Saint-Léger-Vauban: 1991.

Hanotaux, Gabriel, ed. *Recueil des instructions données aux ambassadeurs et ministres de France.* VI *Rome (1648–1687) I.* Paris: 1888.

Henry, D.M.J. *Histoire de Roussillon Comprenant l'Histoire du Royaume de Majorque.* 2 vols. Marseille: 1974.

Iemma, Joëlle. "L'Evêche d'Elne de 1659 à 1721. Actions Politiques et Pastorales." Mémoire de Maîtrise, Université de Toulouse, 1979.

Jacob, P.L. *Curiosités de l'histoire de France.* Paris: 1858.

Kettering, Sharon. *Patrons, Brokers, and Clients in Seventeenth-Century France.* Oxford: 1986.

La Fabrègue-Pallares, Paul de. "L'Affaire de l'Échange des Pays-Bays Catholiques et l'Offre de Rétrocession du Roussillon à l'Espagne, 1668–1677." *Bulletin du Société Agricole, Scientifique et Littéraire des Pyrénées-Orientales* 69 (1954): 47-63; 70 (1955): 115-134.

Langlois, Marcel, ed. *Mme de Maintenon. Lettres.* 5 vols. Paris: 1935–1939.

Larrère, Jean-Jacques, and Villain-Gandossi, Christiane. "Le *Llibre del Consolat de Mar*: Les Gens de Mer, leurs Droits et leurs Obligations." *Actes du 106ᵉ Congrès National des Sociétés Savantes.* Perpignan: 1981, pp. 153-167.

Lazerme de Regnes, Philippe. *Noblesa Catalana. Cavaliers y Burgesos Honrats de Rosselló y Cerdanya.* 3 vols. La Roche-sur-Yon: 1975.

Lewis, Archibald R. "The Catalan Failure in Acculturation in Frankish Greece and the Islamic World during the Fourteenth Century." In *Medieval Society in Southern France and Catalonia*, Article no. XIV, ed. Archibald R. Lewis. London: 1984.

Livet, Georges. "Louis XIV et les Provinces Conquises. Etat des Questions et Remarques de Méthode," *XVIIᵉ Siècle* (1952): 481-507.

———. *L'intendance d'Alsace sous Louis XIV, 1648–1715.* Paris: 1956.

———. "Royal Administration in a Frontier Province: The Intendancy of Alsace under Louis XIV." In *Louis XIV and Absolutism*, ed. Ragnhild Hatton. Columbus, Ohio: 1976, 177-196.

Lloansi, Bernard. "La Fausse Monnaie devant le Conseil Souverain de Roussillon (XVII᷄ - XVIII᷄ siècle)." *Bulletin du Société Agricole, Scientifique et Littéraire des Pyrénées-Orientales* 100 (1992): 135-188.

Malartic, Yves. "Le Sel en Catalogne (XIIIᵉ–XVᵉ siècles)." *Actes du 106ᵉ Congrès National des Sociétés Savantes*. Perpignan: 1981, 181-200.

Marcet, Alice. "Les Roussillonnais Face au Centralisme Louis-Quatorzien." *Marseille* 101 (1975): 65-68.

———. "Le Roussillon, une Province à la Fin de l'Ancien Régime." In *Régions et Régionalisme en France du XVIIIᵉ Siècle à nos Jours*, ed. Christian Gras and Georges Livet. n.p.: 1977, 103-116.

———. "La Résistance à la Francisation dans les Montagnes Catalanes au XVIIᵉ Siècle." *Actes du Lᵉ Congrès de la Fédération Historique du Languedoc Méditerranéen et du Roussillon*. Montpellier: 1980, 129-140.

Marcet i Juncosa, Alícia. *Abrégé d'Histoire des Terres Catalanes du Nord*. Perpignan: 1991.

Marion, Marcel. *Dictionnaire des Institutions de la France aux XVIIᵉ et XVIIIᵉ Siècles*. New York: 1968.

Martí Viladamor, Francesc. *Temas de la locura o embustes de la malicia impugnada por la verdad autenticada*. Paris: 1648.

Maze-Sencier, Genevieve, ed. *Dictionnaire des maréchaux de France du moyen age à nos jours*. Geneva: 1988.

de Montmor, Louis Habert. *Avis pour les curés, vicaires, confesseurs, et autres ecclésiastiques du Diocèse d'Elne*. Perpignan: 1689.

Morel-Fatio, A., ed. *Recueil des instructions données aux ambassadeurs et ministres de France. XI Espagne (1649–1700) I*. Paris: 1894.

Morer. "Notice Historique sur le Rétablissement de l'Université de Perpignan sous la Domination Française." *Bulletin du Société Agricole, Scientifique et Littéraire des Pyrénées-Orientales* 8 (1851): 261-266.

————. "Note Historique sur les Prisonnières d'État du Chateau de Villefranche." *Bulletin du Société Agricole, Scientifique et Littéraire des Pyrénées-Orientales* 9 (1854): 372-375.

Moréri, Louis. *Le grand dictionnaire historique.* 10 vols. Paris: 1759.

Mousnier, Roland E. *The Institutions of France under the Absolute Monarchy 1598-1789,* trans. Arthur Goldhammer, 2 vols. Chicago: 1979–1980.

Nadal, J. and Giralt, E. *La Population Catalane de 1553 à 1717.* n.p.: 1960.

Olivier-Martin, Fr. *Histoire du Droit Français des Origines à la Révolution.* Paris: 1951.

Padilla, Amado M. "The Role of Cultural Awareness and Ethnic Loyalty in Acculturation." In *Acculturation. Theory, Models and Some New Findings,* ed. Amado M. Padilla. Washington: 1980, 47-84.

de Pallares, Auguste d'Oriola. *Les Consuls de Perpignan.* Perpignan: 1912.

Pasquier, F. *Famille Catalane Ralliée à la France.* Perpignan: 1923.

Pasquier, J. *L'Impôt des Gabelles en France aux XVIIe et XVIIIe Siècles.* Geneva: 1978.

Pinard, *Chronologie historique-militaire,* 8 vols. Paris: 1761.

Pla Cargol, Joaquín. *Biografias de Gerundenses.* Girona: 1948.

Pons, Joseph-Sébastien. *La Littérature Catalane en Roussillon au XVIIe et au XVIIIe Siècle.* Paris: 1929.

Romestan, Guy. "Le *Consulat de Mer* de Perpignan dans la Première Moitié du XVe Siècle." *Actes du XXXVIIe et XXXVIIIe Congrès du Fédération Historique du Languedoc Méditerranéen et du Roussillon.* Montpellier: 1964–1965, 155-168.

Roque, Louis, ed. *Documents sur l'Histoire de Saint Laurent de Cerdans à Travers les Âges.* 2 vols. Arles-sur-Tech: 1987.

Rouffiandis. "Les Prisons du Castillet de Perpignan." *Bulletin du Société Agricole, Scientifique et Littéraire des Pyrénées-Orientales* 61 (1943): 5-16.

de Roux, Antoine. *Perpignan à la Fin du XVIIe Siècle. Le Plan en Relief de 1686.* Paris: 1990.

de Roux, Marquis. *Louis XIV et les Provinces Conquises.* Paris: 1938.

Sagnes, Jean, ed. *Le pays Catalan*. 2 vols. Pau: 1983.

Sahlins, Peter. *Boundaries: The Making of France and Spain in the Pyrenees*. Berkeley: 1989.

Sales, Núria. *Senyors Bandolers, Miquelets i Botiflers*. Barcelona: 1984.

Salmon, J. H. M., "The Audijos Revolt: Provincial Liberties and Institutional Rivalries under Louis XIV." *European History Quarterly* 14 (1984): 119-149.

Sanabre, José. *La Acción de Francia en Cataluña en la Pugna por la Hegemonía de Europa (1640 – 1659)*. Barcelona: 1956.

Sanabre, Josep. *El Tractact dels Pirineus i la Mutilació de Catalunya*. Barcelona: 1959.

———. *El Tractat dels Pirineus i els seus Antecendents*. Barcelona: 1961.

———. *La Resistència del Rosselló a Incorporar-se a França*. Perpignan: 1985.

Sanchez Marcos, Fernando. *Cataluña y el Gobierno Central tras la Guerra de los Segadores, 1652 - 1679*. Barcelona: 1983.

Sautai, Maurice. *Les Milices Provinciales sous Louvois et Barbezieux (1688–1697)*. Paris: 1909.

Serra Puig, Eva. *La Guerra dels Segadors*. Barcelona: 1966.

Susane, *Histoire de l'infanterie française*, 5 vols. Paris: 1876.

Taverner, Paul. "Le Clergé Séculier en Vallespir de 1640 à 1700. Rôle Social et Politique." Mémoire de Maîtrise, Université de Provence, 1977.

Terry, Arthur. *Catalan Literature*. New York: 1972.

Torreilles, Philippe. "Le Collège de Perpignan depuis ses Origines jusqu'à nos Jours." *Bulletin du Société Agricole, Scientifique et Littéraire des Pyrénées-Orientales* 34 (1893): 345-436.

———, ed. *Mémoires de M. Jaume*. Perpignan: 1894.

———. "L'Annexion du Roussillon à la France - la Vacance du Siège d'Elne (1643–1669)." *Bulletin du Société Agricole, Scientifique et Littéraire des Pyrénées-Orientales* 41 (1900): 165-220.

————. "Les Testaments des Consuls de Perpignan au XVIIe Siècle." *Bulletin du Société Agricole, Scientifique et Littéraire des Pyrénées-Orientales* 44 (1903): 249-298.

Torreilles, Philippe, and Desplanque, Émile. "L'Enseignement Élémentaire en Roussillon." *Bulletin du Société Agricole, Scientifique et Littéraire des Pyrénées-Orientales* 36 (1895): 145-398.

Valls Taberner, Ferran, ed. *Privilegis i Ordinacions de les Valls Pirenenques.* 3 vols. Barcelona: 1915-1920.

Vidal, Pierre. *Histoire de Perpignan des Origines au XIXe Siècle.* Paris: 1897.

de Warren, Raoul. *Grand Armorial de France.* 2nd edn. 6 vols. Paris: 1949.

Wolff, Philippe, ed. *Histoire de Perpignan.* Toulouse: 1985.

Index

About the Author

DAVID STEWART is Assistant Professor of History at Hillsdale College.

ISBN 0-313-30045-3

EAN

9 780313 300455

90000>

HARDCOVER BAR CODE